FOR RICHER, FOR POORER

Paul Smith has been working as a journalist in the Scottish national, regional and local press for more than 15 years, covering news and sport. As an author, he has penned a series of football titles, including *To Barcelona and Beyond: The Men Who Lived Rangers' European Dream*, *Shooting Star: The Colin Stein Story* and *Rangers' Cult Heroes*. He lives in Kintore, Aberdeenshire, and is the son of former Rangers and Scotland player David Smith.

FOR RICHER FOR POORER

Rangers: The Fight for Survival

PAUL SMITH

MAINSTREAM
PUBLISHING

EDINBURGH AND LONDON

First published in Great Britain in 2012 by
MAINSTREAM PUBLISHING COMPANY
(EDINBURGH) LTD
7 Albany Street
Edinburgh EH1 3UG

ISBN 9781845967369

A catalogue record for this book is available
from the British Library

Printed and bound by
CPI Group (UK) Ltd, Croydon, CR0 4YY

1 3 5 7 9 10 8 6 4 2

To Coral, Finlay, Mia and Zara

ACKNOWLEDGEMENTS

WHAT WAS ALREADY a complex subject became far more complicated along the way as events at Ibrox snowballed and the process of administration began. The final chapter in this story has certainly not been written, but the tale up to this point could not have been told without the help of many people. My thanks go to Bill Campbell, Graeme Blaikie, Claire Rose and the rest of the team at Mainstream for their patience, support and incredible attention to detail in an ever-changing project that must surely be unlike any other. Colin MacLeod too provided his valued input, not to mention encouragement, along the way, while Eric McCowat's imagery fits the story perfectly. I also owe a debt of gratitude to a long list of people who spared their time to contribute, both on and off the record, and offer valuable insights into the workings of Rangers Football Club and the men at the top. Those include Gordon Smith, Lorenzo Amoruso, Mel Stein, Mark Dingwall, George Adams, Mike Wilson, Freddie Fletcher, Ian Broadley and, in the calm before the storm of administration and the revelations it brought, Craig Whyte himself. Many others, who preferred not to be named, also lent their support and expertise to give a flavour of life at the club. Closer to home, as ever my eternal thanks go to Team Smith – Coral, Finlay, Mia and Zara – for the love and laughter that's behind everything I do.

INTRODUCTION

'We don't do walking away.'

Ally McCoist, 2012

FOR RICHER, FOR poorer, for better, for worse. Three men had served as owner of Rangers prior to the dramatic events of February 2012, and that trio share one common bond – none was chosen by the supporters who are the lifeblood of the football club. In almost every other way, Lawrence Marlborough, David Murray and Craig Whyte are very different men, and each of their tenures has been marked by very different decisions.

Marlborough can be remembered as a revolutionary. He was the man who took Rangers into single ownership for the first time in the club's history and recruited Graeme Souness to lay the foundations for the success that followed. Then, in the blink of an eye, he was gone, set sail for foreign shores, never to reappear in the limelight and never to show any tangible interest in the club again.

Murray will always be revered as the chairman who delivered nine in a row, who broke down barriers and who dared to dream. His was ambition with a capital 'A'. Realistically, he will also be remembered for allowing debt to spiral and for the painful end to his reign, with the decision to hand over to a man subsequently deemed 'not fit and proper'. His stay in the chairman's seat was far longer than those of his predecessor and his successor – but his departure was protracted too.

Whyte will forever be known as the man who was in charge when one of the world's great sporting institutions was brought to its knees, the individual who had to pick up the phone and call in the administrators. It was on Whyte's watch that liquidation first became a real and terrifying prospect, an option that at one stage appeared unthinkable and then became seemingly inevitable.

Whyte had arrived as the master of his own destiny, or so it appeared.

He talked the talk and had the opportunity to walk the walk – to learn from the experiences of his predecessors and go his own way as he negotiated the winding path of football-club ownership. But it would transpire that the taxman, among others, would have a major say in the outcome of his dalliance with football.

A few whispered their concerns and doubts from the outset, but none could have predicted the next dramatic chapter in the enthralling and captivating story of Rangers following Whyte's arrival. The only safe assumption was that the choppy waters of football-club ownership would not allow for plain sailing. One minute, you are riding high on the crest of a wave, the next bailing out water as the swell threatens to swamp you.

Marlborough and Murray went through it, to varying degrees, while Whyte, early in his spell of service, quickly developed a sense of what lay in store as the scrutiny of him and his businesses reached fever pitch – even before his fledgling sporting empire crumbled beneath him.

It is like no other role in business and arguably like no other in football: as custodian of the proud history and heritage of Rangers Football Club, there is a burden to be carried. Many men have carried it with pride; in recent years, others have failed to shoulder it at all.

It takes a certain type of personality to cope with the peculiar demands of the job, particularly over a long-term tenure. When the 2012–13 season kicked off, it would be the 25th campaign since David Murray first took control in 1988–89. It was an incredible landmark, and although he never quite made it to a quarter of a century not out, there could be no mistaking the momentous changes that took place on Murray's watch.

Think back to 1988, when the deeds were first signed over from Marlborough. Sky Television was just a glint in Rupert Murdoch's eye, two years from its launch. Predators were something you found in the jungles of the Amazon, not in the catalogues of Adidas. It was a time when defenders could knock the ball back to their goalkeeper without fear of retribution, with the pass-back law still four years away, and when the Bosman ruling sounded more like a John Grisham thriller than a piece of football legislation.

Away from sport, Labour was still very much 'Old' and Margaret Thatcher showed no sign of losing her grip on the nation. Glasgow was basking in the glory of the city's gala Garden Festival, and Britain was digging deep to support a new charity appeal by the name of Comic Relief. Surely it would never catch on.

Rangers, too, has changed since then. In 1988, Graeme Souness was still a snarling presence at the heart of the team, his team. It was a time when the manager could travel south to sign the biggest and best names in the English game without batting an eyelid, long before the talent drain was reversed. There was no Murray Park and no third tier on the iconic Main Stand. Standing was still permitted; Catholic players were not. All of those things and many more besides changed during the Murray years.

As much as anything, the sea change in almost every aspect of life at the club during Murray's tenure is an illustration of the chairman and owner's longevity. He remained at the helm longer than any chairman in the top flight of Scottish football during his era and was on hand to push home his side's dominance. Rangers have not remained at the top of their game for as long as they have, albeit with sporadic dips in form, by accident. The right people have been chosen and left to manage as they see fit, knowing there was a plentiful supply of advice and guidance as and when required. That was Murray's way. His successor's was very different – with dramatic consequences.

In 1988, there was optimism and there was a sense that anything was possible. Flip forward to the tail end of Murray's nearly 25-year spell in charge and you find a club facing a battle on all fronts. The taxman, creditors, former directors, law firms – at times a queue has been forming in a not so orderly manner outside Ibrox, everyone looking for a pound of flesh.

Where did it all go wrong?

The chapters that follow aim to examine that question in detail, from the boom years when Champions League cash first began to roll in to the gluttonous Dick Advocaat era when Rangers gorged on expensive foreign fodder. Any account of the financial excess of that time can be summed up in three words: Tore André Flo. The £12-million splurge on the Chelsea frontman in 2000 represented the peak of the transfer activity, a shining example of how the borrowing stacked up as huge sums were splurged with boundless optimism. When the good times were rolling and the banks were on side, it was all good fun, no cause for alarm. Then the world turned upside down, the financial markets collapsed and new borrowing disappeared in an instant. The banks got twitchy, the taxman became inquisitive and the owner grew tired. Throw that all together and out of the blender comes an unhealthy mix.

Delve into the detail and you soon come to realise that the club's affairs have been far from straightforward. Like the other companies under the Murray umbrella, Rangers was just one piece in a very large jigsaw. Unlike the other companies, it took up a disproportionate amount of the owner's time as he became embroiled, heart and soul, in Ibrox affairs.

The reward was success, and plenty of it. For years, Murray and his Rangers team were the benchmark for achievement in Scottish football. For the bulk of his time as chairman and custodian, trophies flowed thick and fast – almost as fast as the star signings flooded in.

However, Murray, quite understandably, faced the ire of supporters as the full extent of the debts facing the club became apparent. The irony was that few had voiced concerns years earlier, when the expensive new faces had begun to sap resources and – admittedly unbeknown to most – the deficit crept up to record levels. While the silverware stacked up and the star players rolled in, there was no reason to question the running of the club. What fan would?

When Whyte arrived with grand promises and ambitious plans, there was caution but also a willingness to suck it and see. After all, Murray had been unknown when he'd arrived, and, on the park at least, the results had been favourable. It could have been the start of a bold new era; instead, it was the dawn of dark, dark days.

Ambitions change with time. The dream was now simply to keep the Rangers name alive, to live to fight another day on the football pitch. The hunger to feast on a lavish banquet of success was replaced with a humble thirst for survival, in whatever form.

The only guarantee is that the marriage between the club and its supporters will never be broken, no matter who occupies the chairman's seat or whatever shape the club may take. For richer, for poorer. In a time of crisis, it was left to Ally McCoist to take on the role of spokesman for the Rangers staff, players and supporters, with the most succinct of observations: 'We don't do walking away.'

CHAPTER 1

'The bond between players, staff and supporters now is probably as great as it's ever been in the football club, which is a very, very positive thing.'

Ally McCoist, May 2012

WHAT BEGAN WITH a 1–1 draw with Hearts at Ibrox ended with a 4–0 canter against St Johnstone in Perth. Football. Remember that? The 2011–12 season will not be consigned to the memory bank because of Steven Naismith's equaliser against the Jambos or Sone Aluko's hat-trick against the Saints. The biggest battle was not on the pitch; it was in the boardroom.

The final day of the most eventful campaign in what had, up to that nightmarish year, been a proud history was a compact version of the craziness that had enveloped Rangers for months up that point.

While Aluko should have been hogging the limelight with his sparkling treble, all attention was focused not on the pitch but on the directors' box at McDiarmid Park. Sitting within easy reach of the forest of camera lenses was Charles Green – the new chief in waiting. The sound of clicking shutters was something Green was rapidly becoming accustomed to, having faced the nation's press just hours earlier at a Murray Park media conference called to unveil him as the man chosen by administrators to end the agony at Rangers and replace the beleaguered Craig Whyte in the seat of power.

What somehow felt like the end of the story was really only the beginning, with a long road ahead of both Green and the administrators as they attempted to bring the sorry saga to an end. At least the season had drawn to a close with some form of conclusion, even if it had been left, typically, until the last minute.

Duff & Phelps, the administrators who had been appointed in February 2012 as the creditors closed in and Whyte fought to cling on

13

to power, had taken three months to find their chosen solution. That solution involved Green and a consortium of 20 backers from Britain and as far afield as Singapore.

After the false dawn of the offer by US tycoon Bill Miller, the preferred bidder until his decision to withdraw from the race, and the very public courtship by the Blue Knights consortium, spearheaded by former Ibrox director Paul Murray and Scottish businessman Brian Kennedy, it was the Green camp that had come to the fore.

Green and Whyte. There was a certain irony in the colour scheme that held the key to saving Glasgow's boys in blue from disappearing into football's financial abyss. It came to pass that Whyte agreed to sell his 85 per cent shareholding in Rangers to Green for a token fee to allow his global consortium to attempt to clear up the mess that the club was mired in.

Green joked he had paid £2 for the majority stake and given Whyte a 100 per cent profit. In truth, though, the time for jokes had long since passed as the severity of the situation weighed down on a loyal Rangers support.

It was left to joint administrator David Whitehouse to restore optimism to the battered fans, stating:

> The structure and quantum of the offer from Mr Green is such that it is acceptable to us as administrators and, having been in discussions with major creditors throughout the process, we believe this presents the best prospect of financial recovery for creditors.
>
> Mr Green, through a corporate vehicle, has entered into a binding commitment to inject funds into the Rangers Football Club plc so that the administrators can propose a Company Voluntary Arrangement which, if approved by creditors, will result in their claims being compromised for specific amounts and the company exiting administration free of the historic debt and with new owners. Work on issuing a CVA proposal has already started and will proceed with utmost urgency.

Even if creditors rejected proposals for a CVA, which would give them a fraction of the money they were owed, Green had made a commitment to Duff & Phelps to go ahead with the takeover using the newco business model that supporters had been dead against when it had been proposed by Miller and his American advisors. The newco route – leading to the liquidation of the club in its traditional guise and reformation as a new company free of debt – was viewed as a last resort for Green and his group, whereas for Miller it was the first and only option considered.

So the season ended with Green as the heir to the throne, the potential saviour after a torrid year in which Rangers had been dragged to the brink and which had ended with manager Ally McCoist and his playing staff heading off on their summer holidays not knowing whether they would be playing in the SPL, the Third Division or not at all when the action resumed for 2012–13.

It put the pressure squarely on Green's shoulders, but the Englishman was confident he could deliver on behalf of the mystery men and women he represented. As a former chief executive of Sheffield United, he knew the game he was getting himself into. His motivation for targeting Rangers appeared to be as much about business as sport, though.

Speaking for the first time about his attempt to rescue the club from its perilous situation, Green said:

> Rangers has a fantastic history and we want to retain and preserve that history. That's why our offer will try to preserve it through the CVA route and that has always been at the forefront of our plans. We want to build on that history to make sure that Rangers has a future.
>
> I have been looking at the club on behalf of the consortium since the administrator was appointed. We haven't conducted our business in public and you haven't seen any names until my name came out on Thursday. We have been working behind the scenes and haven't built around rhetoric – it's been on fact – and now we want this club to go forward.
>
> The interest of the investor pool is not to walk around and have photo shoots to develop images. They want to do it for the right reasons. We have got a great set of names. There are 20 individuals and families who have pledged support. It was not just my role to acquire the club on behalf of these individuals but to make sure the structure going forward is the best for its fans.

What Green was proposing was to take Rangers full circle. Until Lawrence Marlborough had gained overall control in the early 1980s, the club had never had an outright owner. Marlborough had been followed by David Murray and Craig Whyte in the seat of power. Debt had spiralled during Murray's tenure; financial collapse had ensued on Whyte's watch. Green, a complete outsider, pointed to the structure as one of the reasons for the problems the club found itself shrouded in. He said:

I can assure you that there will not be any investor who owns more than 15 per cent. I don't believe that any one person should own a football club. I think when we look round at certain clubs where one individual is in control there is no contingency and things are driven by their ability to sign a cheque. If Abramovich leaves Chelsea tomorrow, tell me Chelsea's future. How does it run? I want to build a model here so that when I leave after all this is stabilised there is a board of directors as a plc company and a football-club board, with people who understand this club far better than I do. We have a whole plan to take this club forward.

There are some investors from the UK, there are some investors from the Middle East and there are some investors from Asia and from the Far East. The reason I have selected some of these people is that in those areas they have fantastic connections and my vision for Rangers is to develop the brand in those areas. In Indonesia, Hong Kong, China the demand for football is insatiable and I believe this product, one of the world's leading football names, would benefit from exposure out there.

The press call at Murray Park, hastily convened just two hours before the last game of the term kicked off in Perth, put Green on the stage to answer questions for the first time since his name had risen to prominence in the week leading up to that point. The quirks of Miller's interest from his home in Tennessee and the aggressive pursuit by the Blue Knights had been played out in the media, but Green appeared proud to have flown under the radar. He revealed:

I was invited to a meeting, immediately after the administrator was appointed, by a stockbroker who was a representative of a Singaporean family that were interested in looking at Rangers and wanted to know if I would get involved. I said no, I'm retired and I don't want to get involved. A week later, they came back again and said they'd really like me to get involved, and I had started to look at things. Football is addictive and I started to look at it after 15 years away from the game. But I only like to do things if I can win. I knew the strength and the value of the brand and the product, and I started to think that it was worthwhile and something I ought to get involved in.

We started to put together who would invest. That was the first thing. I spoke to people in the Middle East who said they would definitely be interested. We then knew we had the financial resource so I contacted the administrator around four or five weeks ago. I have met with someone from Duff & Phelps regularly and they couldn't believe nothing had leaked to the press. We weren't in a position to make a bid at the point that Bill Miller was named preferred bidder. We came in later, with others ahead of us in the process, but they weren't ahead of us in terms of being able to put cash on the table.

Green promised to be open and honest with supporters, although he stressed he was not able to name the individuals involved in his group at that stage. What he did say was that there were some Rangers supporters among them – people he said he had to 'worry about', since fans don't always make good business decisions. Under his guidance, he stressed, financial governance would be king.

With the historical debt wiped out by a CVA or liquidation, he was aiming for a return to European football and, eventually, a club making profit rather than losing millions each year as it had been. He had taken advice from Graeme Souness, as other bidders had done, and had held talks with Craig Whyte to smooth the process. He was at pains to point out that he had no previous link to the most recent owner and added:

> I met Craig Whyte for the very first time a week last Tuesday in London, having arranged that meeting through our broker advisors. I explained to Mr Whyte what the intention is for Rangers from the consortium I was leading and asked him if he'd transfer his shares.
>
> I'm sure everyone knows a CVA can only happen with the consent of Mr Whyte handing over his shares. Mr Whyte listened to my plans, didn't commit but said he would think about it. I met him a week later with the broker again. By this time, the administrator of course had given preferred status to Bill Miller and I think that did help our case because it really focused everyone's attention. I then met Mr Whyte for a final time with the lawyers where he signed the legal documentation exclusively with my group to pledge his shares and his debenture to this bid on the basis the CVA would proceed.
>
> Have I ever met him before? Never. There was a comment in the press that I had a business relationship with him through a financial services company I was chairman of in 2000. Well, that's as serious as you've all got relationships with him because you shop at Tesco, he shops at Tesco, so therefore you've got a business relationship with him. Its complete and utter rubbish.
>
> I was asked have I paid him money for the shares. The answer is yes, I paid him £1 because legally I had to. He paid £1 to David

Murray for the shares and I gave him his £1 back. Actually, I paid him £1 out of my own pocket too, so he made 100 per cent profit. The only thing that Craig Whyte has asked is that, with the information I've got, that if I know something is a falsehood then I will correct it. I won't lie to anyone, I won't make up things that aren't true, but if I know something is false or is not how it's been presented, then I'll correct it.

The consortium would pay £8.5 million into the pot to be shared by creditors, with that figure to be topped up with any money clawed back through litigation instigated by the administrators against Craig Whyte's legal representatives and with money still to be paid by Everton for the purchase of Nikica Jelavic. According to Duff & Phelps, it was by a 'considerable margin' the best offer on the table.

Having had discussions with creditors – including HMRC, due to the overdue tax bills, and Ticketus, the company who had bought the rights to future season-ticket sales from Whyte – they were confident that a compromise could be reached through a CVA. That would have to be rubber-stamped by creditors, but the alternative of liquidation would leave them empty-handed. Something, after all, is better than nothing.

Green issued an open invitation for additional investment, saying that if he could raise a billion, he'd raise a billion – but that he was happy with the consortium he already had in place.

So who is Charles Green? A Yorkshireman, he has extensive experience of engineering takeovers. He made his money through a management buyout of a company he worked for in Manchester and has since established a reputation as a venture capitalist and executive with several organisations and has held office as a director or secretary of at least 39 businesses.

His involvement in football stems from his posting as chief executive at Sheffield United. He was appointed in 1996 by the Conrad Group following their purchase of the club. He spent around two years with the Blades, boasting success in floating the club on the stock exchange, as well as boosting attendances and revenue from merchandise sales, but making unpopular decisions along the way as star players, including Brian Deane, were sold. He stepped down after being confronted by demonstrating fans and stressed that he had left United with no debts and cash in the bank.

He had worked in a variety of sectors, such as property and agriculture, and in various countries, including in the medical sector in Dubai. That global reach helped attract the finance required to progress with his vision for a Rangers takeover, and he intended to use his vast experience, as his 60th birthday loomed, to put the Ibrox affairs back in order. Doing that would take time and patience.

SFA documents released in the days leading up to Green stepping forward had revealed the extent of flux within Rangers during the Whyte tenure. The association, in what is described as 'findings in fact', painted a picture of a club where the board was not presented with accounts and where financial controller Ken Olverman had his authorisation limit for signing checks slashed from £10,000 under the previous regime to £100 under Whyte. Olverman was told to ditch the previous practice of settling bills within 30 days and extend that to 60 days. He was ordered to withhold payments to HMRC and had no knowledge of the multimillion invoice issued to Ticketus for the deal Whyte had brokered. According to the SFA, the invoice to the firm did not follow standard Rangers format and looked as though it had been generated using computer clip art.

Even before Whyte had assumed control, splits were apparent in the club. The directors tasked with vetting prospective owners had been given sight of an investigation into Whyte's business background, commissioned by an unnamed third party, and were concerned. They showed the report to Murray and attempted to persuade him not to go through with the deal, but the owner said he was under pressure from his group's bankers to proceed. The relationship between Murray and the club's chief executive Martin Bain was 'damaged' by the process, according to the SFA's findings.

From the point of Whyte's takeover, a timetable of the gradual erosion of the previous regime's control and structures – with directors departing one by one and the new owner demanding control of areas that previously would have been the concern of the board as a whole – was set out as part of the SFA investigation. The timetable ended with the appointment of the administrators – an undignified halt.

Whyte had strolled into Ibrox at the end of the 2010–11 season with grand plans and bright ambitions for the future. At the end of 2011–12, it was the turn of Charles Green to outline his intentions for a club in turmoil and his desire to clear up the debris the administrators had found in their path. For manager Ally McCoist, the players and the rest of the Rangers staff, judgement would be reserved.

McCoist had met with Green on the eve of the final day of the season and was pleased to have given the new man a display to be proud of with the 4–0 demolition of St Johnstone in Perth. The manager was cautiously optimistic, commenting after the match:

It's certainly a good game for any new owner to come and watch when your team wins 4–0 away from home, so I would think there's a big smile on Charles's face.

The passion was flowing out the stands from the support and I thought the players did them proud. I'm really pleased for another thank you for the fans and the support that the players gave them, because the players really, really appreciate the rallying. The bond between players, staff and supporters now is probably as great as it's ever been in the football club, which is a very, very positive thing.

He added: 'We're all very well aware and very appreciative of the fact that there's an awful lot of hard work still to be done.'

CHAPTER 2

'What is of paramount importance is the long-term security, survival and prosperity of this great football club.'

Craig Whyte, 2012

THE HISTORY OF Rangers Football Club is etched with a succession of dates memorable for many reasons, good and bad. The 24th of May, for example, represents the ecstasy of the 1972 success in Barcelona. The 2nd of January will for all time be a day for remembering the 66 killed in the Ibrox disaster the previous year. The 7th of May was a time for celebration in 1997 as nine in a row was clinched. The 14th of February? Well, that will forever be recalled as a dark moment.

St Valentine's Day 2012 was when the romance was taken out of Rangers, when supporters came to realise that their love for the club was not enough to keep it alive – the day the administrators arrived to start their work.

In an instant, the enormity of the financial woes that had beset Ibrox for years had crystallised. No longer was the fiscal furore one that could be swept under the carpet, left for another day far in the future. The appointment of the administrators blew away the lingering optimism that the storm could be weathered and left Rangers supporters in the midst of a swirling tornado, not quite sure who or what would be left standing when calm was restored. It was the only show in town, with the media blizzard accompanying the announcement not always helping to give clear vision of the road ahead.

Until that week, the spectre of administration had been conveniently shut in the Ibrox closet. It was Craig Whyte himself, on 13 February, who delivered the news that that particular door was being thrown wide open. In a long statement, Whyte said:

The club announces today it has served notice of Intention to the Court of Session to appoint administrators.

Since I took over the majority shareholding of the club in May last year, it was clear to me the club was facing massive financial challenges both in terms of its ongoing financial structure and performance and the potential consequences of the HMRC first tier tax tribunal.

I have taken the decision that the most practical way to safeguard the long-term future of the club is to go through a formal restructuring process. It may still be possible to avert this but that is not the most likely way forward.

What is of paramount importance is the long-term security, survival and prosperity of this great football club. That is the job I knew I was taking on when I became majority shareholder in the club and it is in the best interests of Rangers that it is completed before the end of this season.

It has meant turbulent times. We have gone from a club mired in excess of £20 million bank debt to a club which is trying to stand on its own feet, earning more than it spends.

From my early days as chairman I saw that administration was a very real option to enable the club to address these challenges and make a fresh start. Frankly, the case for administration in pure financial terms was compelling but I was acutely aware that such a great institution as Rangers could not be viewed exclusively in financial and business terms . . .

The new owner had a track record of taking on ailing companies and extensive experience of the administration and liquidation processes. Indeed, his first-ever business venture, Whyte Hire in Glasgow in the 1990s, ended up in voluntary liquidation. Outside observers had suggested from the outset that his intention for Rangers might be similar. Why it took nine months to go through with it, only Whyte can say.

Perhaps he had been expecting a swifter resolution to the 'big tax case', as the tribunal over the employee benefit trust issue will forever be known. A hangover from the David Murray years, the potential liability ran into tens of millions, and delay after delay in finding a resolution to the dispute between the club and Her Majesty's Revenue and Customs (HMRC) only served to heighten the state of flux surrounding the already perilous economic balancing act at Ibrox.

Whyte's statement continued:

The fact is that Rangers [*sic*] ongoing financial position and the HMRC first tier tribunal are inextricably linked. As I have said before, Rangers costs approximately £45 million per year to operate and commands around £35 million in revenue. From the outset I have made it clear that I do not think it is in the best interests of Rangers to throw good money after bad. Against a backdrop of falling revenues, costs have to be cut significantly. Painful as though that may be [*sic*], it is the future of clubs such as ours.

There is no realistic or practical alternative to our approach because HMRC has made it plain to the club that should we be successful in the forthcoming tax tribunal decision they will appeal the decision. This would leave the club facing years of uncertainty and also having to pay immediately a range of liabilities to HMRC which will be due whatever the overall result of the tax tribunal. In blunt terms, if we waited until the outcome of the tax tribunal, the risk of Rangers being faced with an unacceptable financial burden and years of uncertainty is too great.

We should not forget the tribunal relates to a claim by HMRC for unpaid taxes over a period of several years dating back to 2001 which, if decided in favour of HMRC, the club would be unable to pay.

If HMRC were to agree, even at this late stage, a manageable agreement with the club, then a formal insolvency procedure could yet be averted. It goes without saying that would be our preferred outcome.

If not, further investment in the club would be impossible as the threat of winding up by HMRC cannot be removed. The Rangers FC Group, the majority shareholder in the club, is prepared to provide further funding for the club on the basis the funding is ring-fenced from the legacy HMRC issue.

In short, this was the final throw of the dice. The threat of administration was an attempt to put pressure on the tax authorities to concede in their pursuit of the full amount and come to a compromise arrangement. With HMRC getting tough on football clubs that at times appeared to feel as though they operated outside of the normal business realm, it looked to be a desperate tactic with little chance of success. With that in mind, the administrators had been enlisted – even if the final decision to enter administration had not yet been taken.

Whyte added:

The club has engaged Duff & Phelps, a specialist restructuring practice, to assist in finding a solution to the present position. As a result of that advice, it has been decided to seek the protection of a moratorium from HMRC action whilst a Company Voluntary Arrangement (CVA) proposal is made to creditors.

This, if approved by creditors within a month, would minimise any points deduction and allow the club to participate in European football. In short, if the club proceeds into administration then it will have to emerge from that process, with the agreement of creditors, within a month or so in order to be able to play in Europe next season.

The choice of company to help with the process should have come as no surprise. It was effectively the same firm – with offices in London, Manchester and Birmingham – that had advised Whyte during his takeover in the first place. Partner David Grier was there with Whyte when he arrived at Ibrox for his first game as owner, amid trumpets and fanfare. Grier had at that time been a leading player with financial consultancy firm MCR, who were subsequently taken over by Duff & Phelps.

The firm, when pressed on Grier's link to Whyte and the initial deal, insisted it was not an unusual situation and that they were comfortable handling the administration. Presumably they were equally comfortable profiting from the administration process in the way MCR had from the advice handed out at the time of the takeover.

Joint administrator Paul Clark told reporters:

> We act as officers of the Court and we are accountable to the Court. We have a statutory duty to act in the best interests of creditors and stakeholders and that is what we will do. This administration will be carried out under the most rigorous public scrutiny and will be conducted to the highest professional standards.

Duff & Phelps' website claims they are 'renowned for saving businesses, reputations and livelihoods, even in the most difficult of situations'; even so, they would have their work cut out at Ibrox. The company boasts of rescuing a number of businesses with household names – but surely none as big or recognisable as Rangers. However, among the many services offered are 'tax arrears solutions', skills well suited to the unfolding situation on the South Side of Glasgow.

Clark and David Whitehouse were the men spearheading the Duff & Phelps team parachuted into Glasgow on their rescue mission. Manchester-based Whitehouse, with more than 20 years' experience in corporate restructuring, is managing director of the company's Northwest operation and has worked across several continents.

Clark was a founding partner of MCR. Prior to his involvement in restructuring work, his background was in accountancy. According to Duff & Phelps, Clark brings with him a 'reputation for pragmatism', and the company also claims that Clark's 'comprehensive knowledge of the law and best practice is fundamental to his success in developing creative solutions to financial problems'. Again, all would be tested to the limit at Ibrox.

Travelscope, the tour operator that fell into difficulties in 2007 despite an £80-million turnover, is listed among his previous administration projects. In employment terms, Travelscope was a bigger operation than Rangers, with 250 employees at its Gloucester base when Clark was appointed administrator, compared with the 177 on the payroll at Rangers. At the travel firm, he slashed 182 posts through redundancy within weeks of entering the building.

It had been envisaged that a similar course of action might be taken at Ibrox, and even Whyte pointed to that possibility when he first announced that the move into administration was on the cards. In his statement, the owner said:

> An administration process will, regrettably, lead to a cost-cutting programme and the potential loss of jobs across the business. It gives no one any pleasure to consider that possibility, but it is one that is facing businesses in any walk of life.
>
> There will, no doubt, be people – some of them who presided over the club in past years – who will contend that the steps we are announcing today are unnecessary. All I would say to these people is that if they want to step up to the plate and invest money in Rangers to avoid a restructuring of the business, then I would be most willing to talk to them. In the past unfortunately, there were people who not only failed to prevent Rangers being engulfed by our current problems but chose not to invest their money to help put it right.
>
> As I said recently, these are tough times but I can reassure Rangers supporters that the club will continue and can emerge as a stronger and financially fitter organisation that will compete at the levels of competition our fans have come to expect.
>
> As chairman of the club, every action I take will be in the interests of Rangers and there are many people working at the club who are dedicated to making Rangers a success.
>
> I would like to thank supporters for their great commitment to

Rangers. This great football club can recover from the situation in which it now finds itself and be the force in football that the fans deserve.

It was anticipated that it would be the following week before the formal move into administration took place, with a ten-day grace period between the notice of intention and the deadline for following through on it.

Instead, it was just a day later, at 2.50 p.m. on 14 February 2012, that Duff & Phelps confirmed the bleak news that the process was complete – with the bombshell news that it was an unpaid tax bill of £9 million, for PAYE and VAT due in the time between Whyte's acquisition of the club and the announcement, that had forced the issue. HMRC made a legal bid to appoint its own administrator, forcing a rapid change of pace by Whyte – who continued to put a brave face on the situation, claiming: 'Rangers will always be here, as I've said before. We will come out stronger and come out a better business and most importantly in a position to put as good a team as we can on the pitch and to win trophies, which is what we all want as Rangers fans.'

Clark, who revealed that HMRC had been working with the club over the course of a number of months in an attempt to sort out their problems, said: 'Rangers has a long and proud sporting tradition – one we all wish to see continue. All stakeholders involved with Rangers are working hard to ensure the long-term future of this national institution.'

Reassuring words, but they would be hollow unless the administrators could quickly deliver a plan to extract the proud institution from the financial mire. The world and his wife lined up to pass comment, up to and including Prime Minister David Cameron. While the Tory leader said he wanted the club to 'survive and to thrive', former owner David Murray said he was 'hugely disappointed' by the decision and its timing.

More disappointed still was manager Ally McCoist, who saw his side's title hopes, which were very much still burning at that time, extinguished by an immediate ten-point penalty deduction by the SPL.

The sorry saga reopened the takeover can of worms that had been capped when Whyte had taken control. For years up that point, a long line of runners and riders had jockeyed for position at the head of the queue, and some familiar names again began to emerge from the pack. Director Dave King, former director Paul Murray and many others besides were touted as heirs to the Ibrox throne. Murray was most vocal and the administrators admitted there had been 'several expressions of interest from parties not connected to the club' within two days of their arrival.

Ally McCoist and his playing staff had been assembled at Murray Park as Duff & Phelps got to grips with the rapidly evolving situation. A subdued meeting allowed the administrators to lay their cards on the table and confirm their plans for a review of the staff, including players, at the club. On the flip-side, unlike their Hearts counterparts, there was no question of wages being withheld. The Tynecastle side had themselves been embroiled in a wrangle with HMRC at around the same time and had, as part of their own financial manoeuvring, delayed paying wages on several occasions.

At a press conference on 16 February, Clark said: 'As a result of our preliminary assessment, we are wholly confident that Rangers will continue as a football club. We do not think that liquidation and the closure of the club is a likely outcome at all. We need to stabilise the financial position and ensure from now on income exceeds expenditure. We fully understand the 140 years' history of Rangers Football Club and are taking steps to ensure this history will endure.'

While the hysteria surrounding the potential threat to Rangers the institution was understandable, beneath the surface there was a more human side to the situation. Almost two hundred permanent staff who relied on the club to put food on the table and clothes on their backs were left in limbo while the administrators picked the bones of the Ibrox ledgers and attempted to come up with a way of saving money and getting back on an even keel.

The wage bill was an obvious place to start, and a wealth of departments within the club were left on tenterhooks as the process began. The playing staff understandably received the most attention, but the reality was that players made up a minority of the head count. With a first-team squad of 32 and with 35 Under-19 players on the books, as well as 18 coaching and support staff between the top team and the academy system, there were more non-playing employees. Posts at risk included 13 in the media and PR operation, the squad of 22 detailed with handling marketing and hospitality and 20 in the ticket office. There were also 16 on the ground and maintenance staff, 10 spearheading community projects and 11 in executive and clerical roles.

Given that the permanent staff of 177 did not include Under-17 players, scouts or any of the match-day staff or contract staff in the areas of security, stewarding and catering, it was clear that job losses could have ramifications for hundreds of families with Rangers connections.

At Motherwell, when the Fir Park club found itself in administration, there were savage cuts to the playing staff to help balance the books. Nineteen players were made redundant within a week. A similar course of action was expected when Duff & Phelps moved in at Ibrox, but instead a new strategy began to emerge. The opportunity for players to agree to take a fraction of their wage materialised. The money saved, particularly from the big earners, would be used to keep other members of staff in a job. The now-familiar sliding scale was proposed – with the top-paid stars asked to forfeit 75 per cent of their pay packet, middle earners 50 per cent and the lower-paid members of staff 25 per cent.

On paper, it sounded feasible; in practice, it proved more difficult. David Whitehouse described talks with players and their representatives as 'very frustrating', with a clutch of stars unable to commit to the deal on the table. The issue appeared to be with clarifying what they would get in return; requests for contracts to be altered to allow players to move on for reduced transfer fees were believed to be at the heart of the protracted negotiations.

Some decided they wanted no part in it at all. The emerging talents of Gregg Wylde and Swedish Under-21 international Mervan Çelik, who had only joined in the previous month's transfer window, made history when they became the first Rangers players to be made redundant – albeit at their own request. They left without a pay-off, free to find another club and with a unique place in Ibrox folklore that neither would have expected, or wanted, when he first pledged his future to the cause. Wylde was subsequently signed by Bolton Wanderers.

Those who remained took a hit in the pocket for the good of the club, something lost on those who argued the well-heeled footballing fraternity could easily afford to make the sacrifice. Whether you're earning £100 per week or £100,000 per week, if you have commitments to match your income then a 75 per cent pay cut is going to hurt.

Clark was in no doubt about that. In a statement, he commented:

> The agreement on very substantial wage reductions and voluntary departures from the club represents a major sacrifice by the Rangers players.
>
> The discussions have been lengthy and by no means easy for anyone involved but the most important objective in all of this process has been to achieve an outcome that will help save the club.
>
> The players deserve great credit and we are in no doubt that this agreement is the best way to achieve the necessary cost savings to

ensure the continuing operations of the club while preserving the fabric of the playing squad. The agreement has also directly prevented substantial job losses among non-playing staff both at Ibrox and Murray Park.

In addition to the players taking a cut, so too did Ally McCoist and the rest of the senior football management team. It meant that the only jobs lost during the first, minor round of redundancies were one at the London office of the club that had been set up after Whyte's takeover – Misha Ser had been appointed just a month earlier to head the London operation as global partnerships director – and one other post behind the scenes at Ibrox.

Clark's statement continued:

> Everyone involved in the process, the Duff & Phelps team, the manager, the PFA Scotland and, most importantly, the players themselves, made every effort possible to reach a consensual position where job losses among the playing staff were either prevented or kept to the minimum. This required a commitment to very substantial temporary wage cuts and we're very pleased to say that after all our discussions this has been achieved.
>
> The considerable sacrifice the players at Rangers have made has saved the jobs of other people at the club and we fully recognise the football staff are paying a very heavy price for the greater good. It is to their eternal credit the players and the management have sought to find a solution that helps protect the fabric of the club.
>
> We are especially grateful to the manager, Ally McCoist, who has put the interests of the club, his players and the staff first and foremost at all times. Senior first-team players have also been very helpful in trying to secure a successful outcome.
>
> We should be absolutely clear that this club is in a perilous financial situation and there are no easy options. If substantial cost reduction could not be achieved then the club would not survive until the end of the season. Administration is never a painless process and it is imperative if the club is to survive that the business trades viably through the period of administration. We still hold to our view that the future of Rangers can be secured and the measures announced today will be an important part of the recovery process.

The administrators were stung by criticism of their handling of the situation, with some commenting that, instead of stalling long enough to conclude the agreement, they ought to have made swift and deep incisions into the playing squad, making redundancies on the scale previously seen at Motherwell and Dundee. Duff & Phelps argued that this would have been 'folly' and would have stripped away value from a club they still hoped to sell on as a viable going concern.

Just days earlier, the administrators had been talking about the very real possibility of Rangers not being able to see out the season. It was an unthinkable situation but one they floated as likely unless a cash injection could be made or significant costs stripped from the business. The decision by the players to accept the pay-cut proposal provided the solution, although it could not prevent all of the pain.

By safeguarding the immediate future of the club and agreeing to stay and fight for the cause, the same players were also committing to a club that would be absent from Europe the following season.

A 31 March deadline for satisfying UEFA criteria was impossible to meet. The club would have had to have emerged from administration by that date to be eligible and the company accounts would have needed to be signed off by auditors before then. All outstanding tax bills would also have had to have been cleared, while European rules stipulated that all football creditors would have to be paid. Rangers were not in a position to qualify on any of those four counts.

It was just another kick in the teeth for a set of supporters who had grown used to regular Continental competition and who not so long ago had been travelling south for the UEFA Cup final in Manchester. Those heady days seemed like a distant memory as the reverberations of the most turbulent period in the history of the Ibrox boardroom continued to be felt far and wide.

CHAPTER 3

'I will admit there have been times when I have wished that I had never entertained the idea of taking over Rangers.'

Craig Whyte, 2012

IT COST CRAIG Whyte the princely sum of one pound to buy David Murray's controlling interest in Rangers. Of course, there's no such thing as a free lunch, or a free football club, and the deal came with conditions. The prime one was that the new man would take care of the not-inconsequential matter of an £18-million bank debt.

No problem, said Whyte. Great, said Murray. Job done. Or at least that was the edited version available for public broadcast and consumption. There was a less clean-cut take on the whole takeover tale, a financially explicit one that remained hidden until the administration process delved deep into the mechanics of the Ibrox accounts.

It transpired that the pound coin in David Murray's pocket was the extent of the cash injection Whyte had made. The remainder, the millions rather than pence, had come not from his own funds, as had been suggested, but from the club itself, in a roundabout way.

It transpired that Whyte had struck a deal with Ticketus, a company familiar in football boardrooms up and down the country as a friend of chairmen everywhere.

The Ticketus business model is simple. It buys, in advance, bulk blocks of tickets at a discounted rate from a club or event organiser. Then, when the event or season draws nearer, it profits by recouping the full face value of the tickets when they are sold to the public.

Everyone is a winner. The club or organisation benefits by getting money in advance for an event that has yet to take place, helping with the tricky issue of cash flow, while Ticketus cashes in, in time, by making a profit on its initial investment.

The firm is best known for its deals on football season tickets but also operates in other sporting spheres, as well as the world of entertainment. In times when bank lending is fallow, an alternative line of credit can be a major boon. As Ticketus's website explains:

> Many businesses at the moment have been struggling to get normal bank finance due to the wider state of the economy. Football is in a similar situation and, for reasons such as already having a mortgage on the stadium, banks are often not interested in providing additional finance.
>
> Ticketus offers a solution since it does not lend money, but instead provides working capital in exchange for tickets – an asset that banks rarely will lend against.
>
> Many clubs see advanced ticket sales as a preferential solution to bank loans as it provides access to finance without taking on debt . . .
>
> . . . In the case of football, there is often a difference between when a club receives money from activities such as media rights revenue, competition prize money, player transfers and of course ticket income, compared to their expenses on player wages, utilities and rent. This often means football clubs can have cash rich periods and leaner periods each year, so the operators of the club might choose to bring forward some of these revenue streams and so smooth out cash flow.
>
> Ticketus is a flexible partner for football clubs and has helped provide club cash flow, stadium improvement funding and buying players in the past by buying tickets from a club in advance.

Whether the firm knew it had also helped purchase a football club, as was the case with the money advanced to Whyte and Rangers, is for them alone to know. The company says it does not comment on individual cases, although it did break from that self-imposed rule to make several statements in the wake of Rangers going into administration.

It was left to the club's administrators, Duff & Phelps, to provide public confirmation of a story that Whyte had been at pains to deny up to that point. The *Daily Record* had been shot down by the club owner when they had earlier reported the nuts and bolts of the purchase scheme. Eventually, the paper was vindicated when David Whitehouse said:

> There has been widespread concern raised with us, not least by Rangers supporters and season-ticket holders, about the agreement between the club and Ticketus.

32

Following information received, it is now apparent that the proceeds from the Ticketus arrangements amounted initially to a sum in the region of £20 million plus VAT. Subsequently, £18 million was transferred to the Lloyds Banking Group.

The application of the remainder of these proceeds is subject to further examination.

We are now investigating all the circumstances surrounding both the purchase of the majority shareholding in Rangers Football Club plc and the flow of funds which stemmed from the transaction and were intended to fulfil the purchasers' obligations at the time of the sale.

Just weeks earlier, Whyte had written an open letter to supporters in which he admitted a relationship with Ticketus but denied there was anything unusual about it. As he pointed out, Rangers had first entered into an agreement with Ticketus during David Murray's ownership, back in 2009. It should be pointed out that the arrangement at that time was for far less than the £24 million that Whyte was advanced.

When Duff & Phelps laid bare their assessment that the Ticketus money had actually been used to pay the bank debt associated with the conditions of the takeover, Whyte had no option but to lay his cards on the table in a full and frank confession that was tinged with a mixture of regret and defiance. In a statement issued on his behalf, he was quoted as saying:

'The arrangement with Ticketus – which was a three-season deal NOT four, as has been reported – was originally to provide additional working capital as had been the case previously under the old board. My corporate advisors came to me with the proposition that it was entirely possible, as well as highly beneficial, to negotiate a deal with Ticketus that would allow us to complete the takeover and maximise working capital for the club's day-to-day business.

'The Ticketus deal was by far the best way to protect the club given the circumstances in that they have no security over any assets. The only person at risk from the deal is me personally because I gave Ticketus personal and corporate guarantees underwriting their investment; the club and the fans are fully protected. In terms of exposure, I am personally on the line for £27.5 million in guarantees and cash.

'By any stretch of the imagination that is a very substantial commitment to the football club of which I have been a supporter since I was a boy and dearly wish to see through this crisis so that Rangers emerge as a financially fitter and stronger institution. I am the biggest stake-holder in Rangers and I face huge financial losses personally if the restructuring fails or is not allowed to proceed.'

The message Whyte wanted to convey was that he could, had he seen fit, have cleared the £18-million debt to Lloyds from his own personal and business funds. He didn't, he suggested, because he was advised not to by those paid to guide him through the takeover process.

By that stage, his reputation, already tarnished by the club's plunge into administration, was well and truly on the line and he came out fighting, deciding that attack was the best form of defence, to borrow from football parlance.

The statement continued:

'Despite the frenzy of media speculation and misinformation everything I have done has been with the best interest of this football club at heart. Any suggestion that I am trying to make a fast buck or have indulged in illegal manoeuvring is clearly ludicrous.'

. . . As far back as November 2010, at the start of the takeover plans and long before there was any discussion about approaching Ticketus, Sir David Murray and Lloyds Banking Group were provided with – and were satisfied with – proof of funds amounting to £33 million. It was several months later, when negotiations were still on-going that the proposed Ticketus deal – '100 per cent the best deal for Rangers' – was mooted.

'There is nothing irregular or untoward about it, much as certain sections of the press would like everyone to believe,' said Mr Whyte. 'In business terms it makes perfect sense and is the best possible deal for the club.'

What Whyte could not deny was that his failure to acknowledge the Ticketus deal had backfired in a catastrophic manner. Again, he applied corporate reasoning to his tactics in dealing with the issue of the publicity surrounding the funding arrangements. The statement quoted him as saying:

'I regret now not making the arrangements more transparent, but at the time I regarded it as I do with all my other business dealings, as a confidential transaction. In retrospect I should have been completely open about it, but I'm not sure Ticketus would have been very happy about their confidentiality being breached. In any event, the deal was, and still is, fully guaranteed by me so the accusation that I paid the bank debt without any personal financial commitment is just plain wrong and quite ridiculous. This was a way of trying to maximise working capital for the club.

'It also has to be remembered that this was not me working alone and in isolation. I hired top-rate corporate, financial, legal and tax specialists to guide me through this process and when you're paying for that kind of advice, it would be daft not to follow it.'

What Duff & Phelps were left to do was to try to establish where the remaining £6 million from the £24 million advance from Ticketus, the money left over after Lloyds had been squared up, had gone. As they had stated earlier in the process, they 'did not have visibility' of that money – an odd turn of phrase, almost as though it might have dropped down the back of a sofa at Murray Park.

What they also had to get to the bottom of was why HMRC was claiming that £9 million of PAYE and VAT had not been paid during the time of the Whyte-led board's reign. It appeared that the money had been deducted from staff each month as usual when wages were processed but had not been passed on to the authorities.

Whyte, again on the attack, claimed that tax officials had been responsible for that particular problem and that around half of the bill emanated from the so-called 'wee tax case', another of the issues inherited from the previous regime. The statement continued:

> Craig Whyte explains: 'It is simply not true to say that Rangers or I have reneged on paying these liabilities since the takeover. The truth is that around £4.4 million of the £9-million demand is, in fact, the "wee tax case", including penalties, and which is in dispute. We offered to pay £2.5 million of the PAYE and VAT up front with the remainder at £500,000 a month, but HMRC flatly rejected that . . .
>
> '. . . Remember also, that HMRC had frozen some [of] our bank accounts while we were in dispute. On top of that we had other funds frozen because of legal claims by certain former members of the board all of which contributed to why we fell into arrears on our monthly PAYE liabilities.'

Even taking into account the claims that only £4.6 million of the latest tax bill came from Whyte's regime, it was still another chunk of cash that had been used for something other than the stated purpose – although Whyte always staunchly maintained that every penny in and out of the club during his tenure had been accounted for.

It transpired that funds were being held in a client account of legal firm Collyer Bristow, which had acted for Whyte during his takeover in 2011. The administrators went to the High Court in London in an attempt to secure those funds to help with their efforts to keep Rangers afloat, and £3.6 million was subsequently transferred to Duff & Phelps' own lawyers, for safe keeping, while a decision was made whether it was indeed club money. Another strand in the tangled web.

Between the revenue from Ticketus, the unpaid PAYE and VAT, and the sale of Nikica Jelavic to Everton, for a fee believed to be in the region of £5.5 million, there had been several fresh sources of income for Whyte to tap into. Still, he argued in the 21 February statement, it was not enough:

> 'The fact is that Rangers, had they not gone [into] administration now for the reasons I have given, would have done so some time in the future whoever the owner was because they could not go on funding losses of up to £15 million a year. People seem to forget that the previous board under Alastair Johnston were talking seriously about administration two years ago. If things had turned out differently with HMRC, then I seriously believe I had the correct plan that would have avoided administration and put Rangers back on a sound financial footing.
>
> 'Of course, there would have been some pain especially after the spendthrift days when the massive debts were run up in the first place – but that's the hard facts of life.'

While Duff & Phelps pored over the books in an attempt to complete the missing links in an increasingly complex financial chain, it was left to Whyte himself to say what others had already assumed – his short time as chairman was drawing to a close:

> 'If I can succeed in coming through this administration process I am very keen on the idea of gifting the majority of my shares to a supporters' foundation. It makes a lot of sense, but fan ownership would work only after the current process [is] completed because the club has to get into a position where it is running at break-even in order for that prospect to be viable.
>
> 'I am open to all serious offers of outside investment. Indeed, I am currently in active discussion with a number of potential bidders and investors. However, the reality is that everyone needs to have a final settlement of the big tax case one way or another.
>
> 'I remain very confident that Rangers will emerge from this and

move on in a much better position than it found itself in before the takeover. There is a lot of raw emotion at the moment, and that is understandable, but I'm sure people will look back on this and realise that I was absolutely right in what I did.

'. . . I will not continue as Rangers Chairman post-restructuring. Regardless of administration and irrespective of the tax case, the club had serious long-term structural problems financially and they needed to be addressed with some urgency. I knew that when I stepped up to the plate and, despite the accusations and abuse that I have suffered over weeks and months, I was determined to see things through. I will admit there have been times when I have wished that I had never entertained the idea of taking over Rangers.

'But I am a Rangers fan, and, like other Rangers fans I don't do walking away.'

CHAPTER 4

'Rangers are in a better place now than they have been in the last three or four years. That's what's important.'

Craig Whyte, 2011

EVERY RANGERS-SUPPORTING SCHOOLBOY dreams of one day running out of the Ibrox tunnel to a tumultuous reception: scarves waving and chants ringing out around the ground as a sea of red, white and blue shifts in waves under the floodlights.

On an early summer evening in 2011, that moment was recreated. However, it was not a schoolboy emerging from the tunnel but a grown man, the run was replaced by a more businesslike stride and there was no crowd to greet the new recruit.

His name was Craig Whyte and the date was 7 May. Just 24 hours earlier, he had been confirmed as the new owner of Rangers Football Club. In a whirlwind introduction to the role, he bounded into Ibrox the following afternoon ready to take his place in the directors' box for his first match in office. It ended in resounding success; the new regime was off and running. What he could not have predicted was how quickly the novelty would wear off and the runaway train would thunder towards the terminus of administration.

While Whyte's decision-making and motives will always be questioned, it is difficult to suggest he was not enthusiastic when he first checked in at his new place of work. Just months after he took his place in the chairman's seat, Whyte took time out from a schedule that saw him shuttling between London, Monaco, his Highland castle and Govan to answer my questions about his early days in the role. The new owner told me: 'The day after the takeover was announced to the stock exchange, Rangers were at home to Hearts and I walked up Edmiston Drive to the stadium to a great reception from the fans.

39

'After the match, which Rangers won 4–0, there was a moment when everyone had left and I walked back out into the empty stadium. That was really the first time that I had a chance to take in everything and what it meant. I already knew the size of the task facing me, but at that moment I felt elated and excited about meeting the challenge that lay ahead.

'I am proud to be the owner of Rangers. As a young boy, my dad used to take me to Ibrox and I have been a keen Rangers fan ever since. Being the owner of this fantastic football club means a great deal to me personally.'

In the aftermath of the administration announcement and the revelations that brought, Whyte had suggested pangs of regrets about his involvement. Even before the problems began to surface, he told me that the possibility of pulling out of the takeover had crossed his mind. Speaking in 2011, he told me: 'I was first alerted to the idea in the autumn of 2010. I was attracted to the idea both as a businessman who specialises in turning round companies in distress and as a keen Rangers fan since I was a young lad.

'Negotiations with Sir David Murray started in October 2010. Unfortunately, not long afterwards news of the talks was leaked to a journalist and the remainder of the negotiations and due diligence process had to be conducted under the full glare of the media spotlight.

'There were a couple of occasions when I became frustrated by the obstacles that were being put in the way of progress and I could have walked away. But we got there in the end and I am glad I persevered because Rangers is a great football club with a great future as well as an international institution of which I am very proud to be the chairman and majority shareholder.'

It was not in the Blue Room or the Ibrox boardroom that pen was finally put to paper but in the less symbolic surroundings of a lawyer's office in Edinburgh. It was on 6 May 2011 that the deal was concluded.

Whyte admitted: 'My initial feelings were a mixture of relief and excitement. Relief that the deal was finally completed after weeks and months of negotiation, and excitement about taking over one of the world's great football clubs.'

What followed that landmark day was the briefest of honeymoon periods. Within a matter of days, a storm was brewing as the new owner received a rude awakening. If he didn't already know the pressures facing the man at the head of the club, he quickly found out. A tsunami of legal argument arose as claims, counterclaims and general suspicion began to surface.

When Whyte first bounded through the iconic front door, he looked like a man without a care in the world, the proverbial kid in the sweetie shop. The former Glasgow schoolboy had come back home and put himself in a position of power, influence and prestige. Then the cracks began to show and the prophecies of doom proliferated on the back pages and the airwaves. Rangers set to go into administration, or worse, a ten-point deduction, a twenty-five-point deduction – they were all floated as potential outcomes as a media storm was whipped up in the infancy of the new owner's leadership.

The turbulent introduction was not what Whyte would have hoped for. Trophies, the currency of all chairmen, rather than headlines were what he craved, but all eyes were fixed on events off the field of play. It was an early test of character and an opportunity for Whyte to show his mettle. He chose to come out fighting, embracing a siege mentality that pitted him and the club against the world. The BBC were banned, the Herald Group newspapers were banned. The gloves were off.

It would be wrong to suggest it was all a huge surprise. Throughout the takeover process, he has claimed, it became apparent that not everyone was supportive of his decision to press forward with his plans.

Whyte told me: 'There were plenty of people – many of them journalists and, of course, some others who wanted the club for themselves – who tried to dissuade me. But when push came to shove, only I was prepared to step up to the plate at a time when Rangers was under severe pressure from the bank and its entire future was uncertain.

'Only time will tell whether I come to regret my decision to buy Rangers, but at the moment I am relishing the challenge that ownership of the club presents and I am confident that Rangers will continue to be a major force in both domestic and, hopefully, European football.'

As with any deal on the scale of the one he concluded with David Murray, Whyte had done his homework. A long period of due diligence gave him an insight into the workings of the club – although there were still surprises lurking in the Ibrox cupboards.

Even in the years before he thought of buying the club, Whyte claimed, he had taken a keen interest as a supporter. He told me: 'I could see that, like many other big football clubs, it was running up a major debt burden and that sooner or later this would have to be addressed. As I have said many times since taking over Rangers, the club has a great future but it has to start living within its means. That requires a more realistic approach not only by the club but also by the fans and everyone else connected with Scottish football.

'Like many businesses the size of Rangers, it is a complex model and the due diligence itself took a long time to work through. There is a great deal of work to be done to get the business into the kind of shape I would like but I am confident it will be done.

'It would be fair to say that there are always likely to be a few surprises – that's one of the reasons that due diligence has to be so thorough. Rangers was no different to many other businesses in which I have been involved. But the fact that every cough and spit was played out in the full glare of the public spotlight was a new experience for me.

'I knew, of course, that as the owner of an institution such as Rangers there would be a good deal of interest in who I am and my business record. That's fair enough. But I am willing to admit that I was not expecting the scrutiny of my private life and my other businesses to be so intense. I am a naturally private person and, outside of Rangers, I am determined to keep my private life just that.

'I always knew that taking on a business such as Rangers would bring with it pressures that do not necessarily occur with other enterprises because it is not just a business, it is a way of life for thousands of people, not only in Scotland, but also around the world. The time and effort I am having to invest in Rangers is very considerable and, yes, probably rather more than I had anticipated. But I am confident it will all be worth it.'

Or so he thought. In the final analysis, only Whyte will be in a position to assess whether it was indeed worth going through the whole arduous process. Only Whyte can be sure of the motives behind his involvement in the whole sorry episode. What is certain is that his profile has been raised to an incredible level – from relatively unknown businessman to one of Scotland's most talked-about individuals.

Through everything that has emerged, Whyte has displayed a determination, hinted at in his interview with me, to maintain his privacy. The veil of secrecy surrounding his business and private life was infuriatingly frustrating for the media and, in no small measure, a huge concern for the supporters of the club he governed.

So who is he? Why did he decide to saddle himself with what, at face value, looked like a whole lot of debt and a mammoth amount of expectation? And just what was his track record in business before Rangers became the tag he would forever wear around his neck?

Those seeking answers for those questions and others like them were given short shrift. When pressed by one journalist to reveal where he had made his money and how much he has tucked away in the bank, Whyte retorted:

If I asked you how much money you have, you would be within your rights to tell me to get lost, it's none of my business. All that matters is that I'm delivering on what I said I would deliver on. Rangers are in a better place now than they have been in the last three or four years. That's what's important. As long as I deliver on what I said I would deliver on, what difference does it make?

Just like that of his predecessor in the Ibrox seat of power, Whyte's empire is a complex one. The pattern is not so much a mosaic of businesses and enterprises, more a mesmerising tessellation that is near impossible for the untrained eye to decipher. He concedes that he has more than 20 firms operating in the UK but stubbornly refuses to go into detail.

The one that was getting all the attention was among his most recent acquisitions: Rangers. Whyte had to learn fast when it came to dealing with the most unique business he will ever be involved with.

He told me: 'You always have to be prepared to learn from mistakes. I think when we get to the next transfer window, we may do a few things a bit differently. On the field, failing to qualify for European competition was clearly a major frustration and disappointment. Off the field, the uncertainty over the tax case has obviously been quite challenging.

'Generally, I am happy with the way things are going. My ambitions for the team and for the club as a business are exactly the same – to be successful. They go hand in glove.'

He was speaking about his ambitions for the January 2012 transfer window. It is difficult to imagine that the aims tallied with the actual outcome of that period, when the club was roundly criticised for failing to strengthen the side at a time when the battle for the SPL title was very much alive. Mervan Çelik, the young Swede who subsequently volunteered for redundancy, was the only player recruited. It did not appear to fit with the ambitious masterplan that had been spoken about.

Whyte never promised to match Murray for longevity. Even at the start, he put no timescale on his stewardship, but, having found himself fully immersed after taking control, he did admit that there might come a point when he would be prepared to take a step back from the day-to-day running of operations. Just months before administration, he told me: 'I will certainly stay on as chairman until we regain full stability of the club and the business and they are moving forward in the right direction. However, it was never my intention to be so hands-on throughout, since I do have a large number of other business interests which need my attention.'

What exactly those interests are may become clearer in the fullness of time. The international man of mystery, with bases in the Highlands of Scotland and the sun-soaked coastline of Monte Carlo, was determined not to let his guard slip. It was an attitude that won over some in the Rangers fraternity, impressed by his willingness to stand up to the so-called media establishment. For others, it was a worrying sign that perhaps something was awry. The latter camp was right to worry.

Efforts to unravel his track record in commerce have barely scratched the surface, with most observers pointing towards a history in taking on firms in trouble and turning a profit from them in the long run, either by operating them or selling them on.

The truth, and it is a difficult one for any journalist to swallow, is that Whyte has done a very good job of flying under the media radar. Basically, we know as much as the man himself wants us to know. And that, it would seem, is very little.

It has not always been that way, however. As a budding young entrepreneur, Whyte was much happier to talk openly about his achievements in his fledgling years and his great ambitions for the future. He opened his heart to writer Terry Houston, who penned the 1996 book *Great Scots in Business: The Next Generation*, vowing to establish himself as one of the most prominent individuals of his generation.

Whyte told Houston: 'I want to have a substantial and profitable and world-wide business; I want to become a fully listed company on the stock exchange, and I want to have major league personal wealth – which for me is over £100 million.' Why that figure? Whyte responded: 'It's just what you use to measure yourself against the Hansons, the Goldsmiths, and the Bransons of this world.'

Confidence was never in short supply. Whyte was still in his 20s at that stage, and it was clear from early in his career as a multifaceted businessman that he had ideas that he hoped would take him to a lofty station in life.

He came from a family steeped in enterprise. Growing up in Motherwell, he had a comfortable upbringing with the trappings of his parents' success. His father, Tom, had worked to build up a plant hire firm, while his mother, Edna, had her own business interests as the owner of a babywear shop.

Whyte's own early work was alongside his father in the earthy world of construction, working on the desk at the plant hire firm, handling bookings as well as getting his hands dirty cleaning out machinery or helping with repairs in the workshops at weekends while he was still at school.

It was a distinctly working-class pursuit for a boy who had chosen the middle-class surroundings of the fee-paying Kelvinside Academy for his secondary education. His sister had opted for the local comprehensive in Motherwell, Dalziel High School, when the siblings were given the choice by their parents.

Whyte said that the fact that a number of his friends had opted for Kelvinside was a key motivator, although it is hard to imagine the prestige of the grand A-listed building in the heart of the West End was not also appealing to a teenage go-getter with big ideas.

So many luminaries have passed through Kelvinside, from politicians and sportsmen to business heavy-hitters – with Ian Livingston, who rose to become CEO of BT, and Sir Thomas Risk, the former Bank of Scotland governor, among them.

It was while at Kelvinside that Whyte made his first serious money, serious, at least, for a teenager. Fascinated by the stock market, the plucky 15-year-old took his first punt on shares – and he backed winners. Within two years, he had turned his original stake, cash saved from his Saturday job with his dad's firm, into £20,000 and was ready to leave school with some financial clout. His friends were apparently none the wiser, with the hobby remaining firmly private.

It has been reported that Whyte went on to become Scotland's youngest self-made millionaire – although quite how you define that, or confirm it, for that matter, is anyone's guess.

What is known is that the proceeds from his early share-trading exploits were used as capital when Whyte secured backing from the banks – an early lesson for him that to grow fast, you need a reliable line of credit. His came in the shape of an initial £60,000 overdraft, a facility that was joined by £500,000 of backing from finance houses as he embarked on a rapid buying spree to stock a new plant hire business.

It was not designed to rival his father's own enterprise; the family firm had already been sold by that point. Whyte Hire was born of a desire to keep the name involved in an industry that had been kind to the clan. Based at the Gallowgate in Glasgow, the firm recorded a six-figure profit in its first year and looked on a firm footing.

Then came the fall. In its third year of trading, the company faltered as demand for equipment slowed and a major client withheld a £300,000 payment. The business was eventually placed in voluntary liquidation, bogged down by debts of £300,000.

Speaking of its failure, Whyte told Houston: 'It hurt my pride more than anything else. For the first couple of years afterwards, I wouldn't tell anyone about it, I swept it under the carpet. Then I realised there's no point in doing that.'

Rather than being put off by the Whyte Hire experience, the man who put his name to the firm bounced back. He ventured once again into plant hire, with City Plant, and built on a security firm he had already established, the UK Security Group.

Vital Holdings, as the group became known after the acquisition of Vital Security, was soon posting profits in excess of £1 million and employing almost 750 people. A number of security firms were bought over, leading the company into the English market for the first time and also providing a foothold in the retail security sector. Kwik Save, HMV, Superdrug and Asda were among the clients.

Whyte also looked overseas for opportunities in the early and mid-1990s, buying a controlling stake in the Vietnam Trading Company. Closer to home, office cleaning and scaffolding hire were among the other sectors he branched out into as he aggressively positioned himself in a variety of industries.

He regularly appeared on rich lists. He was said to be worth more than the Gallagher brothers as they hit the stratosphere with Oasis, and he had the trappings to go with it: the waterfront penthouse in Glasgow, the Mercedes . . . the executive box at Ibrox, he claims. There is, according to his own accounts, substance to his credentials as a lifelong Rangers fan, and his trips to the ground are said to stem back to his childhood, when his father would take him to watch games from the Copland Road end.

By the dawn of the new millennium, Whyte had relocated to Monaco. BBC Scotland claimed in *Rangers: The Inside Story*, a hotly disputed documentary broadcast in 2011, that it was around this time that Whyte was disqualified from holding UK directorships, the central prong to a litany of claims made by the corporation during an explosive half-hour production.

The programme prompted the Rangers owner to go to war with the BBC, banning its reporters and cameras from Ibrox and Murray Park and threatening to sack any member of staff caught cooperating with them. He vowed to fight the allegations in the courts and claimed the documentary was part of an anti-Rangers agenda.

In fact, the allegations about his disqualification were accurate – as the BBC had always maintained they were. Whyte admitted as much in November 2011, confirming he had been subject to a seven-year barring order passed down in 2000. His failure to notify PLUS Stock Exchange, on which the club's shares were listed, led to a £50,000 fine, meted out after the club had entered administration.

The claims and counterclaims become a maze of mirrors. What is certain is that Whyte, who still had a base in Monaco, returned to Scotland in 2006, when he snapped up the sixteenth-century Castle Grant on the outskirts of the Highland village of Grantown-on-Spey for £720,000, with much more expected to be lavished on restoration. By then, he had established a reputation as a venture capitalist and the fanfare that greeted the news of his interest in Rangers was a far cry from the subsequent allegations by the BBC.

He was described as a 'financial whizz-kid', a 'billionaire' and a 'high-roller' as the press were swept along in the euphoria of finally having an end to the will-he-won't-he saga. Nobody was interested in Whyte's business prowess or the finer details of his activities with Liberty Capital, the British Virgin Islands-registered corporation through which his empire is channelled.

It was no time for minutiae; it was time to hail the new emperor of Ibrox. On 6 May 2011, the announcement was made that Whyte had taken control of the club in exchange for the princely sum of one pound. David Murray, having originally been reported to be holding out for a sum in the region of £4.5 million for his shares, had agreed to cut loose on the cheap – in exchange for unburdening himself of the huge bank debt and the impending bill from the taxman, estimated at £2.8 million for the wee tax case and potentially tens of millions more if the big case did not go the club's way.

Despite the potentially heavy price to pay, Whyte strolled into Ibrox with the air of a man who had just won the lottery, greeted by a scrum of photographers and reporters as well as a clutch of appreciative fans who had turned out for the occasion. Whyte, who was the proud new owner of an 85.3 per cent stake in Rangers, said:

> As a keen Rangers supporter, I now look forward to helping the club secure its future as a leading force in Scottish and European football. I know the club has gone through some difficult spells in recent times, but it is my commitment to the manager, his backroom team, the players and, most importantly, the loyal supporters that I will do all I can to ensure further success in the weeks, months and years to come.

The previous day, he had been on the east coast to meet Murray in Edinburgh and thrash out the finer details of the deal, which saw the shareholding bought by Wavetower – a holding company owned by Liberty Capital, which in turn was owned by Whyte. What would the traditionalist John Lawrence and his peers on the Rangers board have made of it all?

While on the surface all was well in the world, behind the scenes things were not quite so serene. Briefly, a statement from the Independent Board Committee, the group set up to vet potential buyers, flickered up on the club's own website. It appeared on what should have been a day of celebration, as Whyte crossed the threshold. Not surprisingly, the words of warning from the committee, who at that point were also still active directors, was quickly removed from public display. But the sentiments had been clear, for those quick enough to catch them.

Alastair Johnston, Martin Bain, John Greig, John McClelland and Donald McIntyre issued a joint statement in which they made it clear that they took no responsibility for the deal to sell to Whyte: 'The decision on the sale and purchase of the majority shareholding in the club firmly and ultimately rests between Murray MHL Limited and Lloyds Banking Group.' The committee went on to reiterate the fact that it had 'no power to block' the sale of the club to Whyte and referred to 'differing views on the future revenue generation and cash requirements of the club'. The gang of five said they were 'concerned about a lack of clarity on how future cash requirements would be met' and that the outstanding tax case was a particular worry in this respect.

Because of the size of his controlling interest in Rangers, Whyte would normally have been required to make an offer to all remaining shareholders for their stakes. The committee agreed that, because he had not technically paid a penny for a single share transferred from Murray, there would be no benefit in putting a similar offer to the minority shareholders. Instead, they insisted that the new owner compile a detailed explanation of his plans for the future, which could be distributed to the remaining shareholders.

Johnston, Bain, Greig, McClelland and McIntyre said they were 'committed to [ensuring] that the transaction and future investment and funding proposals should be transparent to all the shareholders and supporters of the club'. The group had never come out in support of the Whyte takeover, and this was a defiant final stand.

By October 2011, the five had disappeared one by one from the new-look board. There were, of course, different circumstances in the various cases, but the end result was the same.

The only departure about which Whyte publicly expressed so much as a pang of regret was the resignation of club legend Greig, although the man himself claimed he had been ostracised by the new regime.

Donald Muir and Mike McGill had left the board as soon as the takeover had gone through, as had always been expected to happen. Johnston had initially agreed to stand down from his role as chairman but later changed his mind. Paul Murray, who had been a rival to Whyte in the running to gain control, also refused to step down – and both men were then dismissed. Johnston had urged fans to 'remain vigilant and continue to exert pressure' on the new regime, remarks that only fanned the flames as the row heated up.

Chief executive Martin Bain and finance director Donald McIntyre were suspended, pending an internal inquiry over various aspects of the running of Rangers, and it descended into a high-profile game of tit for tat as the situation was dragged through the courts.

Meanwhile, Whyte laid out his plans for the future in a circular he had issued to shareholders in the aftermath of the takeover – the document the takeover committee had been so keen to see. What his new London-based company The Rangers FC Group Ltd was promising (having been renamed from Wavetower) was relatively straightforward.

They pledged to retain the existing staff, on existing conditions, and set out plans for an immediate injection of £5 million into the playing squad. There was also a promise for £20 million of investment in the squad over a five-year period as well as funds to maintain and repair infrastructure at Ibrox. The circular went into some detail, highlighting the need for £1.7 million to improve kitchen facilities and the public-address system at the ground.

The new parent company was set up with three directors. Whyte was at the helm, with Phil Betts and Andrew Ellis also on the board. Ellis, whose own attempts at a takeover had been batted away after protracted media ping-pong, had joined the party after all.

Whyte told shareholders that his own investments spanned several markets, including technology, and reached as far as the Netherlands, Switzerland and France. Finance, corporate recovery, investment and stockbroking were listed among his business interests.

Betts, 48 when appointed to the Rangers board, was a man with three decades of experience in banking and finance. He had launched his career with the Midland Bank and had also worked for Royscot Trust as well as Fraser Russell chartered accountants as their in-house asset finance specialist, advising clients on fixed asset purchases and suitable funding mechanisms. In 2005, Betts branched out on his own when he formed Primary Asset Finance LLP, specialised in refinancing and restructuring companies. He had, according to the circular, 'helped many businesses to raise funding and worked closely with them to support their turnaround'. It sounded very much as though Whyte was going into the Rangers project with his eyes open; it was an organisation being prepared for major restructuring, one way or another.

Ellis, aged 44 when he was appointed as a director, was said to have 'significant experience at director level at professional football clubs'.

As everyone knew, that equated to unspectacular spells with Queens Park Rangers and Northampton Town. Ellis was described as an expert in residential and commercial property. He was also said to act as a consultant to 'high net worth individuals on domestic and overseas property developments'.

All well and good. A new broom sweeping clean, a new structure with new areas of expertise. Except it could never be simple – not with the tax cases looming. The huge uncertainty created by those potential bills was the elephant in the Blue Room for the new owner, and the potential consequences could not be ignored, not forever.

Pictures of sheriff officers arriving at Ibrox in August 2011 to serve papers on officials over the small case rammed home the message. It was undignified, not what more than a century of tradition demanded of a proud and upstanding organisation.

Then, just a month later, it took a judge to say what everyone feared: Rangers were at real risk of insolvency. That verdict was delivered by Lord Hodge as he heard former chief executive Bain's case for unfair dismissal.

In the process of freezing £480,000 of Rangers assets, to cover the cost of potentially finding in Bain's favour, Lord Hodge said the prospect of a £49-million tax bill was dire for the future of the club and that he felt the fine print of Whyte's takeover showed 'an appreciation by The Rangers FC Group of a risk of insolvency' if the tax case went against the club.

After months of playing down the spectre of serious financial repercussions, there was an almost cathartic process as the admissions flowed thick and fast. The threat was very real and, now, very public.

Whyte, when asked if the club would appeal if the taxman won the case and landed a £49-million bill on the doorstep, told STV News at the time of the court case:

> I think that's a decision we will take at the time. What I will say is that I think it's impossible for any business to operate with this level of public scrutiny, with that tax debt hanging over us for potentially months and years to come. I think it's to the benefit of Rangers and everybody involved with Rangers that a conclusion is reached with this as quickly as possible.

But would a negative result lead inevitably to administration? Whyte replied:

> It's in some ways worrying but in other ways it would draw a line

50

under a sad event and a sad period in history and would be a chance for a fresh start for Rangers. Whatever happens, Rangers are here, Rangers are moving forward and it's maybe one step back to take two steps forward so I would say to Rangers fans that I appreciate their concern but we can sort this out and we will sort this out. My message is, whatever we do, it will be in the best long-term interests of Rangers Football Club. Trust us to sort it out, and whatever happens Rangers will be moving forward and playing at Ibrox.

He was adamant that administration had not been the masterplan all along, as had been suggested in some quarters. There would be a certain attraction to being able to wipe the considerable slate clean, in the way Motherwell and Dundee had done in the past, but the new chairman insisted: 'It's certainly not something we want to see happening and we're actively doing all we can to avoid it.'

Vows, promises, pledges and headline-grabbing proclamations. David Murray had entered Ibrox with similarly strong words and lofty ambitions, albeit without the same mystery or problems to address, but ultimately he knew he would be judged on his actions. For Craig Whyte, the process would be no different. With the appointment of the administrators, the jury was sent out. The long-term verdict is unlikely to be kind.

CHAPTER 5

'I would like to find out an awful lot of things and I'm not even sure Craig would have the answers to all the questions.'

Ally McCoist, 2012

IN THE BEGINNING, all was well. Craig Whyte supported his manager; Ally McCoist supported him. Craig Whyte appointed Gordon Smith as director of football and gained the expertise of an experienced Rangers man. Craig Whyte was joined by Andrew Ellis on the Ibrox list of directors, and in turn he could lean upon a friend and ally who had trodden the path to football's boardrooms before.

Then, one by one, the trio who had worked the most closely with the owner during his brief chairmanship broke ranks to distance themselves from their paymaster as the situation rapidly unfolded in front of them.

Understandably, they had kept their counsel prior to the appointment of the administrators. After all, each had everything to lose and very little to gain from voicing any public concerns about the stewardship of the club. Besides, it would appear that they had been given little solid reason to worry since they had been kept at arm's length by the owner.

McCoist's relationship with Whyte should have been the closest. After all, David Murray and his managers had always demonstrated an unshakeable bond – even in the toughest of times.

But it was not that way. The manager, appointed by the previous regime to succeed Walter Smith, might have benefited from public protestations of unstinting backing from his chairman, but the practicalities of his job told a different story.

In Whyte's first transfer window, in 2011, funds were made available, albeit on a limited scale. Still, they enabled McCoist to put his own mark on the Ibrox squad, with the acquisitions of Australian midfielder Matt McKay from Brisbane Roar, American defender Carlos Bocanegra from Saint-Étienne, Arsenal stopper Kyle Bartley on loan, Romanian defender Dorin Goian from Palermo, American midfielder Alejandro Bedoya from Örebro, Lee Wallace from Hearts and Spanish midfielder Juanma Ortiz from Almeria. All in all, the expenditure was estimated at £4 million. It would later transpire that a chunk of the bill for Wallace remained unpaid. There was also the curious acquisition of Sone Aluko, which brought the player's claims that he had paid his own way by helping to meet previous club Aberdeen's demands for compensation. Those claims were disputed by Rangers, or at least in part.

When the second window swung open in January 2012, it became apparent that the support the manager had initially enjoyed was on the wane. The lack of transfer activity at Ibrox became a source of embarrassment for a club that continued to deny there were significant financial concerns. The lack of fresh blood was not down to money, or so the spin machine pleaded. The sale of Nikica Jelavic to Everton was, they claimed, down to the player's desire to test himself in England.

Whyte, doing his best to explain away the barren spell in the transfer market, issued an open letter to the supporters saying:

> Investment in the playing squad has been a thorny issue since I took over the club in May and is the source of endless debate, much of it ill-informed. I want to set the record straight.
>
> In the summer transfer window last year we conducted 14 different pieces of transfer business, more than any other club in Scotland. This included new signings and improvement to existing contracts with key players, increasing the players' wage bill significantly. We now have a first team squad of 30 which includes 18 full internationalists.
>
> Admittedly, there were transfer targets we did not secure but that is not uncommon. As chairman, I have supported Ally McCoist in his choice of targets and will continue to do so. The timing of Jelavic's departure so late in this window is far from ideal and efforts to improve the squad will continue until the transfer window closes.
>
> That said, we must be realistic. Media coverage of the transfer window has bordered on the hysterical. As it stands at the moment Rangers has operating costs of approximately £45 million a year and revenues of around £35 million – not including revenue from possible Champions League and Europa League participation.
>
> As we know, European money cannot be taken for granted and it doesn't take much to work out that without it there is a big financial hole to fill every year – regardless of who owns the club.
>
> I've said many times that in Scottish football we have to move on

from this mindset that you have to keep spending more and more money – that's what got this club into financial trouble before. We have to live within our means, continue to develop talent and spend wisely.

With only Mervan Çelik and Daniel Cousin, who could not play due to a registration bungle, added to the squad, and an SPL title waiting to be won, those closest to McCoist claim his public brave face was replaced by a different mood in private. The manager was, behind closed doors, expressing grave concerns about the state of his beloved club but continued to present a united front.

Speaking after the transfer window had closed, McCoist told reporters:

I'm as committed to doing this job as I've ever been. He [Whyte] wants success for this football club just as much as I do, but we've both got different ways and beliefs in how we get there.

He has to run the business. He runs the club, and the club has to be successful. My job is to make the club successful by putting a winning team on the park. So we both have the same aims and beliefs and desires. We've just got different jobs to do and different ideas how we get there.

I've got a fantastic, healthy relationship with Craig and have done since he came to the club. Like all healthy, working relationships, we don't agree on everything. I believe if we did, it would be unhealthy, but we never fall out and we don't have a problem.

McCoist, who had failed in an attempt to land Norwich City striker Grant Holt after the clubs could not agree terms, was adamant he had had Whyte's support to go out and add new faces if the price was right. He said:

I could have, yes. But I didn't feel they would really benefit the squad or the team. As manager of the club, I have to put a team out on the park that wins football games. There are lots of players out there that we could have made bids for. We didn't, simply because I didn't think they would benefit the team.

The ones that I wanted, including Grant Holt, who we put a bid in for, were just a little bit too expensive for us, which I can totally appreciate, because Craig has to run a business. The most important thing is the running and welfare of the football club. That is more important than the results, believe me.

When the administrators were appointed and some of the financial dealings began to filter into the public domain, McCoist continued to be diplomatic but began to distance himself from the man who technically remained his boss.

The revelation that Whyte had sold historic shares held by Rangers in Arsenal threatened to tip the balance, but the manager kept his cool. Those shares, gifted by the London club in the early 1900s, raised the princely sum of £230,000 when they were sold to Russian businessman Alisher Usmanov's firm Red and White Holdings in February 2012. On hearing the news, McCoist commented:

> I'm extremely disappointed in some of the things unfolding – not least the situation with the Arsenal shares. That's a particularly sore one for a Rangers supporter. I don't think me voicing any opinions at this moment in time – pointing fingers of blame or saying this, that or the other – is going to help anybody. With that in mind I'll keep my own counsel on my own views. But selling the Arsenal shares was a really sore one. Something like that is your history, your heritage. Not only that, it's a great story between the two football clubs. So that was really sad.

It was a similar story with the confirmation that Whyte had used the revenue from Ticketus to fund his takeover, with McCoist admitting: 'It came as a shock to me but not a surprise. The longer the process was going, everybody was pointing in that direction.'

McCoist said he was keen to meet Whyte to discuss the various issues connected with the administration, adding:

> I might get the opportunity to do that. I don't know what the future holds. It's not just me. Every Rangers supporter and member of staff all deserve answers to questions.
>
> We are asking the administrators a lot of questions at the moment, as you can imagine, and they are doing their level best to answer them. But a lot of them they can't answer at the moment.
>
> Hopefully one day we can sit down, whether it's with the administrators, Craig or the previous board, and get the full story. That would be what everybody would want. Whether we get it or not, I don't know. But I think everyone deserves it.

By that stage, director of football Gordon Smith had already exited his Ibrox office. Smith's appointment in 2011 had been a surprise one. He joined at the same time as director of operations and commercial activity Ali Russell, a man who had worked in a similar role in the English game at Queens Park Rangers. Smith and Russell became the first casualties of the administration when both men left their posts, without a hint of protest or bitterness. It was clear they knew the writing was on the wall and were happy to walk away as the battle for the club's survival began.

Smith, with the experience gained in the role of chief executive of the Scottish Football Association behind him, was charged with putting the contacts established during his previous career as an agent to good use in the search for new talent. He was also tasked with enhancing the youth-development strategy and with having an input in a variety of other areas of the football operation.

Like McCoist, however, he found himself isolated from the new owner. A seasoned media campaigner, Smith was just as diplomatic as the manager in public. In private moments, those who know him best reported frustrations behind the scenes.

When he eventually left the post, Smith said:

> It was a great thrill to be offered the director of football role at Rangers. As a fan it was a wonderful experience to play such a big part in our treble-winning season of '77–78. However, like my transfer in 1980, my leaving at this time comes as a tremendous wrench.
>
> I admit that under the current circumstances it has not come as a major surprise to me. I was brought in by Craig Whyte but because his control and reputation has been damaged by recent disclosures, I feel my own position has been undermined by association.
>
> However, I would make the point that I was very frustrated in my job as I was unable to fulfil the job specification which was originally outlined for me. This was to control the major aspects of the football department outwith the first team operations.
>
> These were to include recruitment, scouting, transfer negotiations and youth development. I wasn't in control of any of these activities despite constantly making it clear to Craig Whyte that this was to be my remit. I outlined my medium- to long-term strategies for the club on numerous occasions to no avail.
>
> There's no point in being a director of football unless you can control these areas, so, in that respect I'm totally comfortable with being made redundant at this time. The main thing for me is that Rangers survives and continues to operate as a great football club and I offer my full support going forward to ensure this happens.

That statement was issued in February 2012, in the immediate aftermath of the appointment of the administrators. Time has done nothing to dull Smith's sense of loyalty to the club he starred for as a player – although he has been surprised by developments since then.

Several months after his departure, Smith told me: 'Although I was appointed by Craig Whyte, I didn't know him before I came back to the club . . . and I don't know him now. It was purely a business arrangement – he told me three or four people had recommended me for the role and he hired me on that basis.

'When the administrators were appointed, friends of mine in business were quick to warn me that I would be one of the first members of staff in danger. They were right. Duff & Phelps made it clear to myself and Ali Russell that they wanted us to go, and we did that without any complaints. I left without a penny. All I wanted was to do the right thing by the club.

'I think everyone thought that we would be the first of many to leave the club as the administrators got to grips with the business, but it hasn't turned out that way. I'm surprised by that. I'm not sure I understand the logic. Surely it can't have been a money-saving thing, given only two of us left.

'Maybe it was a PR exercise. Perhaps we suffered through our association with Craig, in that he appointed us. As I have said many times, I was there purely as an employee of Rangers – not as a friend of Craig Whyte. I had never met him before. Would I like to meet him now to ask some questions? Not really. There seems little point.'

When Smith arrived at Ibrox, it was at a time of optimism. He took with him some big ideas about how the football operation could be streamlined and was looking forward to the challenges ahead. All of that changed in February 2012 with the spectre of administration.

Smith told me: 'I had no indication that administration was a likely scenario. In any discussions I had with Craig Whyte, it was always stressed that it would be a worst-case outcome, and only if the big tax case went against the club. Not before then.

'It was a huge shock when it happened. It became clear after we had gone out of Europe that we were facing a loss-making year, but I, like everyone else, was under the impression that the owner had the funds to cover that. The fact he had been able to take on the club in the first place suggested that must be the case.

'Much has been made of the fact that Rangers were reducing the debt in the years prior to Craig Whyte's arrival, that the club had been back in profit. If you break those figures down, that was purely down to the income from the Champions League group stages. Without that level of achievement on the pitch, the income simply didn't match the outgoings.

'We thought that at least some of the losses suffered because of the lack of Champions League income could be made up in other ways, with the potential for the sale of some players if necessary.

'It was part of my remit to turn Rangers into a selling club, effectively. I mean that in a positive way. We were developing a strategy that would have seen players bought in or brought through the system and sold at a decent profit, with the proceeds being reinvested in the squad by giving the manager a percentage of the transfer fees. Scotland has become a stepping stone to English football and I felt there was potential to develop that market.

'The key to making that system work is ensuring that replacements of equal quality are already identified, or even already at the club, before a player is sold. It was a strategy that could have been effective and could have given the club a solid financial footing, rather than the days of spending vast sums with no prospect of any return. There had to be a better business model than the one that had led to the debt being amassed in the first place.

'I had started to put those strategies in place and my big regret is that I did not have the time to see that through. It was a big job, a good job and one that I was really enthusiastic about. I wanted to see success on and off the park.'

The dramatic events prior to the appointment of administrators are burned into Smith's memory. He insists the rapid developments had not been predicted within the corridors of power at Ibrox.

The former director of football explained: 'I know people find it hard to believe that nobody within Ibrox knew what was going on. I can understand why people feel that way. Clearly there were very clever financial manoeuvres going on, if clever is the right word.

'Everything came as a surprise. There was the exposé by the BBC with their television programme, but even after that there were plausible explanations. Ali Russell had spoken to Craig about some of the allegations and he did admit that he had raised some money from Ticketus, but he claimed that was purely to help with cash flow. We had absolutely no idea that he had used those funds to purchase the club. None of us had any inkling that the bills weren't being paid.

'Craig Whyte is a nice guy to talk to. I didn't have many dealings with him. When I did, it was usually in the company of Ali Russell and Ally McCoist. But when I did, I found him very amenable. He is a very convincing and plausible character and spoke well about his intentions.

'The mood was naturally very low when it became clear that

administration was inevitable. There were many people who were understandably very worried about the club, but also about their jobs. Livelihoods were at stake, not just for the players.

'Meetings were called by Craig Whyte to inform the staff of the situation after he had first gone to the Court of Session to lodge the paperwork expressing the intention to consider going into administration. He addressed employees at Ibrox first and then came over to Murray Park, where I was, for two further meetings.

'The first was with the players, the second was with the rest of the staff at Murray Park. In between those two meetings, he got a call which, it transpired, was to tell him that HMRC were about to jump in ahead of him and put the club into administration. The focus changed then. He wanted to move quickly to take control of the situation himself and be in charge of appointing administrators. He dashed off to Ibrox and it then became clear that administration was happening sooner rather than later.

'I have always maintained that exiting administration would be the best outcome, that liquidation would not be in the best interests of the club. I always wanted Rangers Football Club to survive, not for a newco to emerge in its place. I care deeply about the club and nothing has changed. It is 40 years since the European Cup-Winners' Cup victory, almost 140 years since the club was formed. All of that history cannot be just cast aside.'

Just as Smith suggested he had been working with both arms tied behind his back, Andrew Ellis also broke ranks to hint that he had not been entirely happy about the facts that had come to light regarding Whyte's takeover. Don't forget, Ellis himself had tried, and failed, to succeed David Murray as owner.

There had been suspicions that Whyte was acting in cahoots with Ellis when he stepped in to buy the club, but in time the explanation that the Englishman had simply been enlisted to lend support began to appear plausible. It was in fact Ellis who had introduced Whyte to Murray and set the wheels in motion.

Ellis, speaking after administrators were appointed, was the first of the regime to apologise for the debacle. He said:

> I can only say I'm sorry to the Rangers fans. Bringing Craig to the table was done in good faith and like a lot of other people I feel let down by him. I took Craig to meet Sir David Murray in the South of France and that's when talks began and I'm distraught that it has ended up like this.
>
> My interest in buying the club had ended due to the potential

cost of the impending tax case but I had met Craig via the Cadbury family and was told by people that he was a very successful and wealthy businessman who was interested in buying Rangers. He appeared to have the money, he showed me proof of funds and told me about the numerous companies he owned. I was absolutely devastated last week to see the club go into administration with jobs at risk.

Ellis also revealed that he was taking legal instruction, claiming Whyte had reneged on a deal to hand over almost 25 per cent of his shares in the club to him in return for his support and expertise.

As events took shape, there appeared to be genuine surprise among the men recruited by Whyte to run the Ibrox show. He had, it would seem, worked very much to his own agenda and kept much of the detail of his dealings between himself and his advisors. Although a new board was in place, it did not convene regularly – with the chairman making it clear that he called the shots.

He had experience to call upon; he could have created allegiances within an inner circle desperate for the new dawn to be a bright one. He didn't, however, and when the house of cards began to fall, the manager, the director of football and the other members of the board were absolved of blame. Whyte had been bold enough to front the operation on his own, and in the time of crisis he would have to face the music, even if he did do that from his bolt-holes in Monaco and the Highlands.

The chairman, wisely, made the decision to remove himself from Ibrox after the administrators had arrived. His seat in the directors' box lay empty. It was inconceivable that the most important relationship of all, that between the chairman and his club's supporters, could withstand the turmoil his reign had become enveloped in. His entrance had been high profile, in a blaze of flashbulbs, but nobody was there to see him leave the club when the crisis took hold. For that, he could be grateful.

CHAPTER 6

'I was primarily duped. My advisers were duped, the bank was duped, the shareholders were duped. We've all been duped.'

David Murray, 2012

'NOT CONSIDERED TO be a fit and proper person.' With nine words, the Scottish Football Association had condemned Craig Whyte forever. The verdict followed an investigation by the SFA in the wake of the administration, a hurriedly convened and quickly executed probe headed by Lord William Nimmo Smith. The findings were not surprising, given the details emerging, but they were decisive.

Under its protocol, the association has the power to take action in such cases. Sanctions could be imposed or an individual prevented from bearing office at a member club if not deemed suitable. The fact that the investigation into Whyte and Rangers had taken place after he had taken control and after the club had moved into administration meant those powers appeared to be toothless. Nonetheless, it was an official verdict at least on the man who had been at the helm.

When the SFA's judicial review panel delivered its final verdict, on 23 April 2012, it was in fact the club that received the heaviest punishment.

For his part in the debacle, Whyte was hit with a £200,000 personal fine and banned from ever playing a role in Scottish football. It was of little consequence to a man unlikely to darken the game's doorstep again. He also made it clear he had no intention of paying the fine.

The club, on the other hand, was hammered – made the subject of a 12-month transfer embargo that would prevent any players over the age of 18 being recruited. With the prospect of losing several key players as the uncertainty of the situation continued, it was a body blow for the administrators as they tried to persuade potential buyers that it was a business worth saving.

In addition, there were fines totalling £160,000 for the club after it was found guilty of five rule breaches. The charge of 'bringing the game into disrepute' carried the heaviest sanction, with £100,000 of the sum relating to that offence. A further £50,000 was for going into administration and the final £10,000 for the club's apparent failure to ensure Whyte was a fit and proper official. That was despite the fact that several directors had expressed public concerns about Whyte's suitability for the role, before and after his takeover.

The measures infuriated the administrators, who were involved in delicate negotiations with the two remaining serious bidders for the club: US businessman Bill Miller and the Blue Knights consortium headed by former Ibrox director Paul Murray. The transfer embargo, and fear of further punishments either by the SFA or the SPL, would prove major stumbling blocks according to Duff & Phelps, and they immediately lodged an appeal against the SFA's judgment.

Meanwhile, Ally McCoist could not hide his fury at the punishment meted out to the club. He demanded answers about who had served on the judiciary panel and claimed their decision could 'kill' the club. For the first time, McCoist admitted he feared his beloved Rangers would face demotion to the Third Division. Hope had begun to fade.

While Whyte had escaped with a punishment that would have little or no impact, the club he had been in charge of when the walls began to close in was being pushed closer and closer to the edge.

By that stage, there were just three weeks until the season ended – and three weeks until the gate receipts dried up and the funding pot being guarded by the administrators ran dry. The last thing they needed was more bad news, but that was exactly what the SFA had delivered.

Just a day earlier, Duff & Phelps had been expected to deliver a decision on whether Miller or the Blue Knights had secured preferred-bidder status. That announcement, already delayed on several occasions, was put on hold again as they became embroiled in fighting yet another fire.

Rather than battling with the football authorities, the administration team should have been concentrating on one simple question: if Craig Whyte was not a fit and proper person to own Rangers, as had been confirmed by the panel, who exactly would fit the bill?

What Duff & Phelps had quickly discovered was that Rangers was like no other company they had dealt with. The prospect of quietly passing ownership to a third party had evaporated amid a firestorm of media toing and froing by high-profile suitors.

Many of those who had been quoted when David Murray had sold up were once again rising to the fore – and many were shouting loudly about their hopes and aspirations for the club.

Former director Paul Murray was among them, leading the wonderfully titled Blue Knights consortium, incorporating fans' groups, transport tycoon Douglas Park and, intriguingly, the wounded party of Ticketus – the firm that had inadvertently been embroiled in the whole situation and was clearly hoping to make the best of a bad situation and protect the money it had already invested.

That was just one of the unusual twists as the administrators began their search, setting a swift deadline for what they described as 'serious' expressions of interest. Calls came in from the Far East and from America as news of the club's precarious yet clearly inviting situation spread across the globe. Brian Kennedy, owner of the Sale Sharks rugby team, was another to go public with his interest.

Paul Clark said:

> Anybody who has just been talking – and there are a few out there who have done a lot of talking – we want to seek them out and, as it were, put their money where their mouth is.
>
> Let's get them round a table so we know how many parties we've got. I don't care how many bidders we end up with, but I want to know who they are, what they are and what their worth is, so then we can have more serious conversations about achieving the end goal, which is to get Rangers under new ownership.
>
> This is the problem we have got: we have one or two parties prepared to talk to the media and then you have other parties who have been quietly and slowly and diligently getting on with their business behind closed doors outside of the glare of the media, and we are taking them just as seriously as anybody who is on the front page of the newspapers saying, 'I'm going to buy Rangers, you just watch.'
>
> If somebody wants to involve the media, that's fine. And if they become the owner, then they can sit on the front page of all the papers saying, 'I did it.' But don't be surprised if that owner isn't one of the people who is media friendly.
>
> By the way, I am not ruling anybody out in this process, absolutely not. I'm just saying that nobody should assume that the only serious bidders are the ones who are in the public domain.
>
> What we've done so that people realise they need to speed themselves up is to say that we want to receive absolute proof of your funding so we understand who you are and which camp you are in, because some people have feet in various camps. We want to

know who exactly has your money. More importantly, we want some form of indicative bid, so that will distil down however many parties we have got at the moment to the final few.

The Singapore group headed by Bill Ng had been one of the most prominent in the race, but fell away as Miller and the Blue Knights moved to the head of the pack. Kennedy remained cantering alongside, insisting he would not compete with the Knights but would remain on standby to step into the breach if necessary. In the end, it boiled down to the administrators doing their homework and attempting to find the right buyer.

Bill Miller was chosen as preferred bidder and at last the end looked in sight. But it wasn't. Just days later, the American withdrew his offer and cited several reasons for the decision to back away. One was that the financial outlook at Ibrox was worse than he had been led to believe; another was that he had been made less than welcome by sections of the Ibrox support, with anti-Miller banners displayed and, he said, several derogatory emails sent to his business.

Just a few short months earlier, a similar process, save for the administrators' involvement, had taken place when Whyte had assumed control. The difference was that, while the administrators were keen for a swift resolution in 2012, the Whyte deal in 2011 had been a long time in the making.

Two and a half long and lingering years was what it took for one of the tensest and most complex chapters in the Rangers history book to be written. That was the period of time that elapsed between the first indications from Sir David Murray that the club was set to change ownership and the lodging of the documents that made Craig Whyte officially the new man in charge.

In between, there were accusations and speculation, not to mention rumour, claims and counterclaims, as the jostling for position intensified in the race to gain control of a Scottish, British and global institution.

Early in 2009, the Rangers directors were playing their cards close to their chests, with only the briefest of admissions that Murray was 'considering his options' and could be tempted to sell his stake in the club, either in whole or in part.

At that stage, there were only stabs in the dark as to who might emerge as the front-runner to take over as lord of the Ibrox manor. One candidate was Dave King. Already a shareholder who had invested tens of millions of pounds in the club, he appeared an obvious choice as successor. After all, he was a lifelong supporter who, up to that point, had demonstrated his willingness to put his money where his mouth was.

Except nothing during that period in the club's history ran smoothly, and King's involvement was no different.

He is the Glasgow boy who, on the other side of the world, rose to find fortune and, with that money, fame. The one-time milk-boy left his old life in Scotland behind in the 1970s when he emigrated to South Africa and went on to join the continent's glitterati, rising to become South Africa's richest man through his involvement in a series of enterprises.

He used a portion of his vast wealth, estimated to run into hundreds of millions of pounds, to plough £20 million into Rangers in 2000, becoming a non-executive director. Then, just two years later, news broke that King might not provide the long-term solution to the club's cash requirements.

He is a colourful figure, well connected in the sporting and financial worlds. Indeed, he took centre stage in 2008 when he caddied for close friend Gary Player at the US Masters in Augusta. However, since 2002, the exiled Scot has been embroiled in a major investigation in South Africa involving various financial charges. Those allegations ranged from tax issues to more serious financial offences and resulted in close to £119 million of assets being frozen as authorities attempted to prove claims that up to £183 million in tax was outstanding. King strenuously denied all charges and accused the authorities in his adopted country of using bullying tactics. All the same, the issue has hovered over him for years and cast a shadow – a shadow that appeared to leave his hopes of succeeding Murray firmly in the shade.

When King was pictured, alongside Ally McCoist, meeting the administrators in 2012, it looked as though the old story might be about to be revisited – although he stressed at that point that he was meeting the administrators in his capacity as a director rather than as a prospective owner.

King had appeared to be a contender in 2011, but were there any other white knights waiting in the wings, ready to ride to Rangers' aid, when David Murray was preparing to depart?

Several well-known names have been linked at one stage or another with a bid for the club, including those of Douglas Park, prior to his involvement with the Blue Knights consortium, and nightclub boss James Mortimer. Whether either would have the means to support the money-guzzling machine that Rangers had become in their own right is one thing; whether they would have the desire to shoulder such a considerable burden is another. In the end, neither emerged as a bidder in 2011, despite the rumour mill churning their names out, among others.

Murray was adamant that it would be a private investor who would succeed him, having resisted the opportunity to take the club into the public domain during healthier financial climes. In 1999, he maintained:

> I've always been against football clubs going public. To my mind, the day Manchester United went public they sold their soul. Some supporters might not agree with that, but at least they know the name over the door. I'm always concerned when money comes into the game for non-football reasons. The only thing I will ever do is raise money to go into the club. I'll never raise it for myself. I believe it's important for me personally to remain in control. We'll bring in investment, as with [new shareholders] ENIC, but I don't want the club to go public.

By the time he came to part ways with Rangers, that particular boat had sailed for Murray. Floating the cash-strapped team would have been a non-starter, so it was the private market that he turned to for a buyer, and it was a name straight out of left field that shot to the head of the list of suitors. Andrew Ellis was that man – one that nobody could have guessed. Andrew who?

Ellis, a property developer in London, had no ties to Scotland, let alone Glasgow or Rangers. Yet he was the man who fronted the bid to wrest the club from Murray's grasp.

It was early in March 2010 that Rangers confirmed Ellis had expressed an interest. Although there was widespread scepticism within the corridors of power about the financial clout of the prospective owner, the club went through the motions as they readied themselves for an offer from Ellis.

His football pedigree was not rich, but he at least had prior involvement in the game as a director of Queens Park Rangers and chairman, albeit briefly, of Northampton Town, after leading a buyout of the English lower league side.

A committee was formed with the sole remit of considering any takeover approaches. It was led by chairman Alastair Johnston and included former chairman John McClelland as well as Martin Bain, Donald McIntyre and John Greig. A statement from the club at that juncture said:

> The independent directors will ensure that any possible offer for RFC is assessed on the merits for RFC, its shareholders and all other stakeholders in RFC, including supporters.
> It is particularly important to the independent directors that any

possible bidder is able to demonstrate the capacity and commitment to provide a stable and sustainable future for RFC and the independent directors will want to understand fully the plans of any potential bidder in order to recommend the action that shareholders should take.

The independent directors exclude Mike McGill and Donald Muir, who are connected to MIH, and so have a potential conflict of interest, and Dave King and Paul Murray, about whose intentions there has been past speculation that could lead to a perception of a possible conflict of interest.

Paul Murray's potential conflict stemmed from his interest in leading a buyout in 2009; he had joined forces with Dave King and Douglas Park on that occasion. At that stage, the plan was vetoed by Lloyds, but it didn't signal the end of Murray's dream of taking control, and he re-emerged, with the club in administration, to try again in 2012.

He is a man who knows the financial world intimately after a successful career with Deutsche Bank. The chartered accountant had been appointed as a non-executive director in 2007 as the club attempted to tap into his considerable expertise.

But it was the bid from Ellis, not Paul Murray, that was open for discussion in 2010, and even Walter Smith waded into the debate. The manager's instinct, as was so often the case, proved to be right. Smith said at the time:

> The probability of a new owner coming in would be positive. However, there's a difference between expressing an interest and actually buying the club. Everybody at the club is affected by the uncertainty, so it would obviously be nice if this got settled, but I think we've got a long way to go before we see that. It's not affected the team greatly on the pitch.

What did not help matters was the looming threat of action from Her Majesty's Revenue and Customs. In April 2010, it was confirmed by the club that what was described quite simply as 'a tax issue' was being investigated. A statement issued by Rangers said:

> There is an ongoing query raised by HMRC which is part of a pending court case. On the basis of expert tax advice provided to Rangers, the club is robustly defending the matters raised. It would, therefore, be inappropriate to comment further at this stage.

The club also went so far as to issue a formal denial that future income from season-ticket sales had been ring-fenced by Lloyds to pay off existing debts. Little did they realise that such a scheme, orchestrated by Ticketus, would indeed be used by the next owner to free the club from Lloyds' clutches. That idea was not untested in football, with Newcastle United among the English sides that had effectively mortgaged their future season-ticket revenues to secure a lump sum in advance, but it was not particularly palatable.

Alastair Johnston did his best to allay fears about the 'tax issue', saying:

> It is not a new problem. It has been there for a long time, so this just hasn't come up. This is more in the holding company of Murray's. It has been one that the Murray Group has been taking care of and been involved in on a day-to-day basis in the past and I would continue to defer to them on that one.

The 'tax issue', as it was almost quaintly referred to, revolved around the use of employee benefit trusts (EBTs). A system was allegedly used whereby payments were made to these trusts and therefore significant tax may have been avoided. Again, it is a system not unheard of in top-level football but one that HMRC clearly were prepared to take a keen interest in.

For Rangers, the trusts appear to have been in widespread use between 2001 and 2010, when £48 million was paid into EBTs. These trusts are designed to allow one individual or company, for example a football club, to own an asset on behalf of somebody else, for example a player, who becomes the beneficiary. An employer would pay money into that trust and the beneficiary could take money out in the form of a loan, which would not be subject to income tax or national insurance. The term 'loan' is loose, since repayment would not necessarily be expected.

Where the lines become blurred is when the payments into the EBT become regular or contractual – which would turn them into wages, which would, of course, be subject to normal taxation rules. Painstakingly completed paperwork is vital to ensure use of the trusts remains within acceptable boundaries, and it has been suggested that this is where Rangers may have tripped up. In any case, the investigations by HMRC appear to suggest that Rangers were not using EBTs in a manner the taxman was happy with – hence the bill for £35 million in unpaid taxes and £14 million in penalties.

While the club robustly defended its conduct and insisted it was confident about winning its challenge against the astronomical bill, the situation did hamper hopes for a quick sale. Few prospective owners were likely to step forward and volunteer to take on a club, its debts and a potential tax bill running close to £50 million.

Aside from that, they would also have to satisfy the club's existing executive team that they were the right person to take on the running of operations.

Chairman Alastair Johnston was cautious when it came to the interest from Ellis. He said:

> He will have to meet with the independent committee of the Rangers board with respect to us looking at the situation, discussing with him so that we can prepare opinions and recommendations as to whether or not we believe he's got the commitment that's in the best interests of Rangers Football Club.
>
> We will be looking at it from the perspective entirely of the club, not from the perspective of Murray, the owners, or from the bank. We will be looking at it from the standpoint of the club and what he is prepared to do and what he's got the resources to do will be very much top of the agenda if and when we do meet with him.

In May 2010, as the takeover talks stumbled on with little apparent progress, Ellis went on the PR offensive. If he took over as owner, he would, he claimed, offer Walter Smith a new three-year contract and install David Murray as president of the club.

That wild statement irked Smith, who clearly had not been consulted by the prospective owner. Smith, a loyal David Murray man, said:

> For anybody thinking about buying the club to make public that they are going to offer contracts without speaking to us is not right. Buy the club first. If that's what they want to do, then do it. You get frustrated when things like that happen because the individual part, whether someone wants to offer me a three-year contract or not, it doesn't really matter. The most important thing is the football club. I stress that to you – that is the most important thing in our mind.
>
> Myself, Ally McCoist and Kenny McDowall, we are supporters and we are fortunate enough to be able to work at a club we love working at. You don't have to use my name or anybody else's to try and buy the club. Rangers Football Club should stand on its own and if he wants to buy it, then make an offer for it. He's had plenty of time to make an offer, so it's down to him.

Smith was preparing for showdown talks with Alastair Johnston as the

2010–11 season loomed on the horizon. The manager said:

> We've got a fair number of things that we need to chat about, so we
> will do that. I've said this quite consistently that we have to get this
> clarity, regardless of what it is.
>
> The main thing is just to try to get a situation where the club is
> sorted out and given a bit of direction, regardless of what that is,
> whether we carry on under the bank's rule, or new owners, supporter
> buyouts or anything like that. I don't think you are going to have a
> situation where the chairman appears, has a couple of meetings and
> then everything is clarified. It's not going to be quite as simple as
> that.
>
> My situation is probably the least important. The club's situation
> has to be sorted more than any individual's. Whether I'm in the
> Rangers dugout at the start of next season or not is really not the
> most important thing. That's just the way it is.
>
> Since January, everybody seems to be preoccupied by the fact
> that we are without contracts but we still get paid. There is no
> problem for myself, Ally McCoist, Kenny McDowall – there is still
> no problem for us working without a contract.
>
> If the club gets a new owner and he wants me to stay on, he will
> indicate that. If he wants us to leave, then we will leave. There is
> not a problem with that situation, but it would be wrong of us to
> mislead people and say we are going to do one thing or another and
> then find out that we are not.

The protracted negotiations rumbled on into the summer of 2010 with
little sign of a breakthrough being made. Ellis maintained his position
that he was poised to bid for control, while from Rangers there was a
sense of scepticism about the whole situation. It would be safe to
describe relations between the factions as strained and volleys of tit for
tat began to be exchanged as the fight for the deeds to Ibrox and
Rangers threatened to turn nasty.

After being criticised by Johnston for the lumbering attempt to buy
the club, Ellis responded with a thinly veiled swipe at the US-based
chairman by saying:

> If I have offended him, then I apologise, and I apologise if it is
> taking longer than normal. It is taking time because there are an
> awful lot of things to go through. But the next time he is back in the
> United Kingdom, then I will be happy to have a meeting with him.

Johnston, in turn, made it clear that he did not expect Ellis to see through his vow to buy the club. The chairman said:

> I don't see any imminent resolution of a new owner for Rangers. So I believe we are going to have to plan and budget on a 'no change in ownership' basis going into next season. The situation regarding Mr Ellis's proposed buying of Rangers has gone on way too long – so let's just say I am sceptical about it. Donald Muir believes that there might be something productive in this deal, but I have to say I reserve judgement on that.

Without saying as much, Johnston also appeared to imply that the prospective owner might struggle to back up his plans with the cold hard cash required. It suggested that the committee set up to vet would-be owners would not be minded to throw its support behind an Ellis bid if one was to come forward. Johnston commented:

> What I believe Rangers will need is someone who can prove capable of making a significant difference to the fortunes of the club beyond the mere buying-selling act. There has to be a means there to be able to allow Rangers to thrive beyond any dependence on the banks.

There was still a job to be done on the pitch as the takeover ball was batted back and forth behind the scenes. Walter Smith was crucial to ensuring the job was done well, although even he struggled to remain totally removed from the politics enveloping life at Ibrox.

Smith had personal talks with Lloyds bankers in 2010 in a bid to determine his own future and gain reassurances about the conditions he would be working under if he decided to see through his plans for a swansong in the 2010–11 season.

Then, in June 2010, the bombshell was dropped. The on-off state of play had shifted. David Murray, after failing to attract the type of investment required, took matters into his own hands and removed the club from the open market.

Andrew Ellis and his firm RFC Holdings were reported to be in advanced talks about taking on the club's running, but Murray had had second thoughts about selling. A statement issued by Rangers said:

> Murray International Holdings Limited has received interest in its controlling stake from a number of parties. At this time, however, the board of MIH has not been able to secure an offer which it considers to be in the best interests of the club, its shareholders and its fans.

Following on from the success of winning the 2009–10 SPL title and thereby securing participation in the group stages of the Champions League during 2010–11, the club announced that the football management team had signed new contracts.

At the same time, the board of directors of the club announced improvements in the financial position compared with the previous year, stating:

> We believe the outcome of our recent positive discussions with the bank gives us a real platform for operational stability at the club and we thank Lloyds for their support. We have a clear business plan in place and will continue to maximise efficiencies and endeavour to increase our non-playing income.
>
> The board of directors of MIH therefore considers that the interests of stakeholders are presently best served by providing the football management team and board of directors with an opportunity to implement its business plan, which is supported by Lloyds Banking Group. In these circumstances, MIH hereby announces that it is no longer actively marketing its controlling stake in the club for sale.

The nature of the plans for a change in ownership prompted the chairman, Alastair Johnston, to issue a plea for patience from supporters, who were growing tired of the lack of drive and direction at their club:

> I must emphasise to our fans that it is business as usual, and acknowledge that the board is very appreciative of their patience and support over recent months relating to the uncertainty of its future. Since the end of the season, Rangers has pursued a strategy that did not rely solely on an ownership change in order to create a funding mechanism to support our operations going forward.
>
> The executive management team worked expeditiously to formulate a business plan that was acceptable to Lloyds Bank, which ensures the ongoing financial underpinning of our operations.
>
> This facility will allow us to enhance our playing resources in the next few weeks and has already allowed us to conclude agreements with the football management team of Walter Smith, Ally McCoist and Kenny McDowall.
>
> Our chief executive, Martin Bain, and football team manager, Walter Smith, will continue to run the club reporting to the Rangers board, which in turn is responsible for protecting and representing the interests of all stakeholders in the club, especially

our supporters, who provide the lifeblood to energizing our future ambitions.

It should have put an end to what had been something of a sorry saga, played out in the media rather than behind closed boardroom doors. But it didn't. There was another twist or two left in this tale.

On 18 November 2010, there was the first formal confirmation from Craig Whyte that his interest was concrete. A statement released on behalf of the man who would be king said:

> Craig Whyte notes the articles in today's press regarding discussions between him and Murray International Holdings Limited with a view to him acquiring MIH's majority shareholding in Rangers FC. Mr Whyte confirms that he is considering making an offer and is in talks. But these are at an early stage and there can be no certainty that an offer will ultimately be made. Mr Whyte has not yet approached the board of RFC. A further statement will be made in due course.

It looked to be a positive turn of events, a welcome development. Whyte's reported personal fortune appeared to make him a genuine and credible contender for the Ibrox ownership. Although based in England, the laird of Castle Grant had retained links to his Scottish roots and certainly seemed to be, to employ a phrase used so often by the English Premier League, a fit and proper person to be entrusted with custody of the club – although Whyte's move for the club was clouded when it was revealed he had a friendship with Andrew Ellis, the man behind the abortive and at times abrasive previous attempt to relieve Murray of his shareholding.

Early in December 2010, however, Whyte's bid for the club gathered pace when he met with chairman Alastair Johnston. It came as he agreed a deal, in principle at least, with David Murray. Johnston was able to meet face to face with the prospective owner and report back to the directors with his findings.

For his part, Whyte had been able to persuade Murray that he was the man to take the club forward. Not only did he appear to have the funds, he also had the enthusiasm, but he needed to convince the independent panel that he was a person they could place their trust in.

What followed was a long process of due diligence as Whyte and his team picked through the club's accounts and negotiated the finer points with Murray, the Rangers board and Lloyds.

During that period, in April 2011, yet another tax problem appeared.

It related to the use of another method of accounting employed by the club between 1999 and 2003, this time a discounted options scheme. It had been a system employed by bankers to avoid paying tax on large bonuses and appeared also to have been utilised by Rangers to help players do the same.

HMRC caught up and closed that particular loophole before attempting to recoup taxes it believed were due, with Rangers hit with a £2.8-million bill, which included an element of interest as well as a further £1.4 million in penalties. While the penalties were disputed, the base figure of £2.8 million had been accepted and it was another chunk of cash outstanding that had to be factored into the overall financial picture being inherited by the prospective new owner. This was the wee tax case, as opposed to the more worrying big one, which was looming like a spectre over the club.

While the club's affairs were complex, on the other side of the fence there were concerns that Whyte's own plans were not transparent. As spring turned to summer, chairman Alastair Johnston, who also headed the takeover committee, issued a statement saying:

> Based on the documents we have only been able to review within the last week, we are disappointed they did not reflect the investment in the club that we were led to believe for the last few months would be a commitment in the purchase agreement.
>
> Given the requirement to repay the bank in full under the proposed transaction, there appears to be only a relatively modest amount of money available that would positively impact the club's operations, especially as it relates to an urgent requirement to replenish and upgrade the playing squad.

That notice of intention to stall the takeover came just as board member Paul Murray had emerged as the man behind a rival to the Craig Whyte bid. Murray, still an Ibrox director at that stage, was reported to have assembled a consortium of wealthy backers who would join him in underwriting a new share issue, which would provide a substantial transfer kitty to new manager Ally McCoist. As much as £25 million was mentioned as potential investment in the squad, a headline-grabbing sum that not surprisingly enticed supporters. The gloves were off in the fight for the hearts and minds of the Ibrox loyal – although ultimately the wishes of the supporters would always come second to the will of David Murray and the bank, as head ruled heart in difficult circumstances.

The Paul Murray plan would have relied on the goodwill of Lloyds, since maintaining existing borrowing would have been necessary. In contrast, Whyte's proposal was to transfer the debt away from Lloyds to an alternative company, something more likely to curry favour with the bankers as they sought to exit the high-risk world of football.

The brinkmanship finally came to a head early in May when Whyte arrived in Edinburgh for final talks with David Murray. Those ended with agreement on the sale of the club and on 6 May the paperwork was complete, the deal rubber-stamped. The months of doubt and endless discussion drew to a close. The Murray years were over; it was Craig Whyte's turn.

The rest, as they say, is history. The great things hoped for simply did not materialise. Out of both cups and trailing Celtic in the league, even before the subsequent points deduction, Rangers were cutting a sorry figure by the time the administrators began their work.

As the finger-pointing began, it was left to David Murray to call a hastily convened press conference in an attempt to clarify his own position with regard to the whole debacle. The former owner was staunch in his own defence, saying: 'I was primarily duped. My advisers were duped, the bank was duped, the shareholders were duped. We've all been duped.' He pointed to a letter from Whyte's solicitor that had pledged investment in a raft of areas by the would-be owner – from team-building to stadium maintenance, he had promised the world.

When asked why he had accepted Whyte's bid, Murray replied:

> Because he met the criteria that were in his offer document. He's quite affable and plausible. I always remember someone said, 'Does it pass the sniff test?' He was Scottish, he wasn't a foreigner, he was supposedly a Rangers supporter, he had the money.
>
> There is a stock exchange offer document there. If you can't believe that, what can you do? Craig Whyte made a statement that the club was never in better financial state when he took it over. This is a guy saying he's going to spend money on players, on health and safety, do the ground up. That is a legal offer document. You would expect that to be honoured.

Murray was also adamant that he knew nothing of Whyte's intention not to use his own funds to complete the deal but instead to rely on Ticketus to provide the necessary cash injection. Had he known that was the funding vehicle, Murray insisted, the deal would not have been done.

He was content that every effort had been made to delve into Whyte's past, even if those investigations had failed to unearth many of the issues that had since risen to the surface. He mused:

I'm not defending me – because I've made a huge mistake here. And I deeply regret, I deeply regret, selling the club to Craig Whyte now. Deeply. And if the information had been available to me at the time, I wouldn't have done it. I did it in good faith. Again, I can only apologise how this has turned out. And if I could turn the clock back, of course I would. There's not much more I can say than that.

For Murray, a man who had done so much good as Rangers chairman, it was an uncomfortable afternoon. When asked if the affair had tarnished his legacy, he added:

> Of course it has. It's 22, 23 years, and I think the first 15 or 16 were fantastic. Then we went into a tight period financially when I put a lot of money into the club. I have genuinely put just short of £100 million into Rangers in my tenure. We all enjoyed a lot of success together. Now all of a sudden it's all my fault. I accept at the end of the day I was the captain of the ship, and I take my share of criticism.

Murray himself had been visited as administrators got their teeth into the painstaking work to get to the bottom of the cash-flow situation. The results will answer many questions – but one they cannot respond to is that of who is to blame for Rangers' collapse.

Staunch supporters of the previous regime point straight to Whyte. After all, he did have his hand on the tiller when the club went into administration. Others take the opinion that David Murray was at fault, first for allowing debt to spiral during his chairmanship and second for agreeing to sell to Whyte when the chips were down.

Wherever you stand as far as the blame game is concerned, there is no doubt that each had a major part to play in the years and months leading up to crunch day. Two men, two separate reigns – but forever linked.

CHAPTER 7

'I am only the custodian of Rangers Football Club. When you walk into the trophy room at Ibrox and see the long history of achievement, you realise that's all you are.'

David Murray, 1989

IN CLOSE TO 140 years of proud Rangers history, a succession of eminent men have served the club in the role of chairman. Businessmen, doctors, knights of the realm – Ibrox has been governed by some of the finest individuals ever to grace Scottish football. While the list of chairmen is long and distinguished, the roll call of owners is markedly shorter and far more contemporary.

Craig Whyte is one. David Murray is another. The first, however, was another key character: Lawrence Marlborough. It was Marlborough who changed life at Rangers Football Club forever when he manoeuvred his way to ownership in the 1980s. Until he pushed his family's stake past the all-important 50 per cent mark, there had never been a majority shareholder.

During more than a century of the club's existence, the esteemed gentlemen who held office as chairman had to lead with authority yet manage by consensus. They may have had the casting vote, in many cases they had the largest shareholding, but crucially they never had the security of a majority shareholding.

It took years of behind-the-scenes machinations for Marlborough to rise from his position as the youngest-ever director of Rangers to become owner. There were casualties along the way, with boardroom struggles and long-standing directors moved aside, but he made it happen. And once he had made it happen, Marlborough was in a powerful position when it came to severing his ties with the club completely, negotiating the sale of his shares and, with them, control of one of football's greatest institutions.

To get a grasp of the highly charged political situation David Murray found himself in when he assumed the reins, you first have to take a whistle-stop tour through the life and times of the Ibrox boardroom.

The first chairman to serve was James Henderson, holding office for more than a decade at the start of the twentieth century before Sir John Ure Primrose had an 11-year spell. William Craig and then Joseph Buchanan were at the tiller in the 1920s and early '30s with Duncan Graham and James Bowie carrying the club through until after the Second World War when W.R. Simpson took over. Simpson was replaced by John F. Wilson at the start of the '50s. He served until his death, early in 1963, when John Lawrence was elevated to the top job.

Lawrence had first joined the Rangers board in 1954. As his standing in football and business grew, he became the obvious choice to take on the chairman's role.

Lawrence came from humble roots. Born and raised in Govanhill, he attended Calder Street School before serving his time as an apprentice carpenter. The dedication and determination that marked out his time as chairman of Rangers were evident when he was a young man starting out in the building trade, working hard to build his own business from scratch and seeing John Lawrence (Glasgow) Ltd become one of the largest building groups in Scotland. He spent a short time in America during the 1920s before returning to home soil, still a young man, completing his first housing development – a single house in Busby – and starting on the road to fortune and, through his football involvement, fame.

The strength of the John Lawrence Group stemmed from a prolific period of house-building during the 1930s. When the market dipped during and after the Second World War, the company branched out to build air-raid shelters and hospitals as well as featuring prominently in the rebuilding of Clydebank in the late 1940s and early '50s. The firm built more than 40,000 private homes and 30,000 council houses in Scotland under Lawrence's stewardship and at its peak employed 2,000 people as it grew to become a giant of the country's business world.

With success came personal wealth for the founder. By 1938, when he was still in his early 40s, Lawrence and his family settled in to Levern Towers in the Blane Valley. Nestling beneath the Campsies, the turreted mansion sits in a sprawling country estate and remains an impressive property even by modern standards. Lawrence remained based at Levern until his death in 1977.

By the time Lawrence died, he had taken on the role of honorary president at Ibrox, having stood down as chairman years earlier. The rumblings in the corridors of power at Ibrox began in the wake of the European success of 1972. Within a year of the triumph in Barcelona, the long-term future of the chairman, aged 79 by then, had begun to become a focus for public scrutiny as he himself started to hint that it was time to pass on responsibility to a younger man. David Hope, who had enhanced his credentials by his success in establishing the Rangers Pools as a key revenue generator, was the hot tip to become the new chairman, and he was the man who had the support of the current incumbent.

In May 1973, newspaper reports feverishly predicted Hope's imminent appointment, as well as the promotion of Willie Waddell to the position of managing director, with full executive powers and a remit to take control of all facets of club administration.

Waddell, who had taken on the role of general manager 12 months previously when he'd relinquished his first-team duties and passed the baton to Jock Wallace, was viewed as a man with the clout and experience to make the transition to the boardroom and bolster the new regime under Hope.

Instead, just when the headline writers were preparing to provide confirmation of the shift in power, it was left to Waddell to deliver the unexpected news that the rumoured changes would not take place. On 30 May 1973, after what sources close to the club said was a tense and protracted board meeting, Waddell delivered the following statement: 'Mr John Lawrence, despite doctor's orders to the contrary, will continue as chairman of Rangers Football Club until the end of our centenary year. This was a unanimous decision by the board.'

While the symbolic gesture of keeping Lawrence at the helm for the centenary season sounded noble – it would allow the elder statesman to continue through a programme of celebrations that was to include glamour ties against Ajax and Arsenal, as well as to reach the milestone of ten years as chairman – there were additional reasons for the decision.

It appeared that Lawrence's wish for Hope to succeed him had not won the support required at director level and, after the failure to push that plan through, the status quo remained. It was an uneasy compromise and never likely to be a long-term solution.

When Lawrence inevitably retired just weeks later, on 19 June 1973, it was vice chairman Matt Taylor who stepped up, not Hope. A statement issued at the end of a two-hour board meeting inside Ibrox read:

> At a meeting of the board of directors of Rangers FC, Mr John
> Lawrence intimated that on medical advice he was retiring as

chairman and as a director of the club. Mr Matt C. Taylor was appointed chairman of the board of directors and Mr R.H. Simpson vice chairman.

Mr Lawrence Marlborough, Mr Willie Waddell and Mr John F. Wilson were appointed directors to join Mr George Brown and Mr David Hope on the board. In recognition of his long and outstanding service to the Rangers FC, the directors appointed Mr John Lawrence honorary president of the club.

Wilson had served on the board previously, but Marlborough, who at the tender age of 30 became the youngest person ever to sit on the Rangers board, was a newcomer. Crucially, Marlborough was John Lawrence's grandson. Despite his relative youth, he was already a trusted lieutenant in his grandfather's burgeoning construction business and clutch of companies that also included the Taggart motor group.

Marlborough, of course, would become a central figure in later years. However, in 1973 the key man was new chairman Matt Taylor. It was Taylor who had led the late move to veto Hope's election to the chairman's job. According to research conducted by Robert McElroy and published in his book *The Spirit of Ibrox*, it was Taylor's last-gasp confirmation that Hope, who had developed a chain of television shops in Glasgow, had converted to Catholicism when he'd married into the religion decades earlier that provided the final insurmountable hurdle to Lawrence's succession plan. At that time, the club's policies would not allow a Catholic to take charge. The red tape left the path clear for Taylor, a wealthy haulier, to assume control of day-to-day affairs. As McElroy points out, Taylor already had the upper hand over Hope in terms of a 40,000-share stake in the club, which dwarfed his rival's holding of just 500 shares.

Both men had risen to become prominent figures in the bustling Glasgow commercial scene, but there could be only one chairman, and Taylor, revered by supporters and remembered as a gentleman and a diehard Rangers fan, won the day. His tenure proved all too brief, with his death in 1975 casting a shadow over the club.

On Taylor's death, the honour passed to Rae Simpson, a man from a completely different sphere of work but of equally prominent standing. Simpson was an eminent surgeon in his day, his passion for football matched by his devotion to medicine. He was respected in both fields and thought nothing of rolling up his sleeves to provide professional support at Ibrox. In an interview in 2008, former player Craig Paterson recalled one occasion when, as he sat in the Ibrox physio's room, Dr Simpson appeared with needle in hand to help out with the treatment.

During Simpson's stewardship, Lawrence Marlborough's influence began to grow. In 1979, at the age of 36, he was elected vice chairman, his family's historic link to the Light Blues remaining strong. His promotion came at a time when the board was evolving. The long-serving George Brown, after half a century, retired from his position as a director and was replaced by John Paton.

Paton had invested in the club and rose to become vice chairman in November 1983. His rapid climb was complete when he replaced Simpson as chairman on 10 January 1984. Paton was another dyed-in-the-wool Rangers man, one who, like Lawrence before him, had grafted his way to the top. Born in Govan, Paton was an apprentice tinsmith and worked at Boyd's spinning-machine plant before embarking on an adventure as a whale hunter in the Antarctic. It was the proceeds from that occupation that enabled him to set up as a taxi driver back in Glasgow, investing in his own cab and going on to build up a fleet.

John Paton & Sons garages sprang up across the city, and the company diversified into everything from taxi maintenance and production to finance and insurance. When in 1971 the business was sold to the Taggart motor group, a firm owned by John Lawrence, Paton was retained as a director and went on to become chairman of the company.

A decade prior to that, Paton's business acumen had earned him the privilege of a place on the Ibrox board, but his time as chairman proved short-lived as the major players continued to jockey for position behind the scenes.

He had taken on the job at a difficult time for the club, as playing fortunes faded. Paton had ambition – he attempted to persuade Aberdeen's shining light Alex Ferguson to uproot and return home to Govan – but he struggled to impose it on a giant of football that was in need of revival.

While Rangers had a proud history of gathering Glasgow's finest business brains in the Ibrox boardroom, the club had never been governed by a majority shareholder. There had never been an outright owner, a single power broker. It took a substantial amount of wheeling and dealing for this century-old situation to be turned on its head, and that happened during Paton's time steering the ship, although it was not all his doing.

While Paton attempted to guide Rangers through rocky waters, fellow shareholder and director Jack Gillespie, who had built his fortune in the motor trade through the prominent dealership Gillespie of Lenzie, was about to have an equally important part to play.

Gillespie was elected to the board in 1977, fully 24 years after buying his first Rangers share. By the mid-1970s, he was the largest single shareholder, with a 20 per cent stake that was reported to have cost £550,000 to assemble – but his bid to win a place on the board failed in both 1975 and 1976. He was aged 50 when he finally realised his ambition of making it to the boardroom, and his business portfolio had expanded from his motor interests to include two bars and a handful of other enterprises.

Gillespie clearly had desires to lead the club he loved, but he never made it to the top seat. Instead, it was his decision, during the 1985–86 season, to accept an offer from Lawrence Marlborough for 29,000 of his shares that turned the structure of the club on its head. Marlborough had stepped down from the board in 1983, but he returned two years later in a whirlwind of activity.

The deal with Gillespie gave Marlborough – or, more specifically, his firm John Lawrence (Glasgow) – a holding of 52 per cent, and that was further bolstered when he agreed to buy a batch of shares from John Paton at around the same time.

For the first time in the history of Rangers Football Club, one man had a controlling stake – and that man was Lawrence Marlborough. There had been a succession of upstanding chairmen up to that seismic moment, but never an overall owner. Marlborough could call himself that, and no matter how many follow, he, as the first-ever owner of Rangers FC, will always have a place in the rich history of the club.

Paton was the biggest casualty of the deal between Gillespie and Marlborough. Once the majority shareholding was in place, the new owner decided he wanted his own man in the chairman's seat, and that man was David Holmes.

It was announced on 11 November 1986 that Paton was stepping down from his Ibrox role and severing all business ties with Marlborough, resigning from his post as chairman of the Taggart group and various other boardroom positions with the motor group's subsidiary companies.

He was left to regroup at home in Newton Mearns and to reflect on what life after Rangers would hold. Although he remained an ardent supporter of the Glasgow club, Paton joined the board at Kilmarnock in 1989 and went on to serve as vice chairman until his death in 2001. At the time of his departure from Ibrox, Paton, then aged 63, said: 'I'm sorry it happened this way – but there are no recriminations. We are all still friendly. I have supported Rangers for about 50 years and I don't see why I should stop now.'

Months earlier, in February 1986, there had been a trio of resignations from the board as the new structure began to take shape. Rae Simpson, who was the longest-serving director, bowed out at the same time as Tom Dawson and James Robinson as Marlborough's new broom began to sweep clean.

David Holmes, who was chief executive of the John Lawrence Group, was given the task of putting a fresh slant on the business of the football club. He did not arrive alone; Freddie Fletcher also pitched up at Ibrox as full-time commercial director. Fletcher is perhaps best known for his involvement with Newcastle United, steering the club from the verge of administration to the heights of the Premier League, but he cut his teeth with Rangers.

Fletcher, who had held various posts under Marlborough in the Lawrence group of companies, was managing director of the private housing division when he made the switch to Ibrox. He threw himself into his new world, becoming treasurer of the Scottish Football League.

With Marlborough based in the USA, the day-to-day running of the club was left to the team he had put in place. Graeme Souness was appointed as manager, replacing Jock Wallace, and an influx of big-name signings began. It was the leadership of Holmes, with the backing of Marlborough and his financial clout, that allowed Souness to begin building a formidable squad, peppered with household names.

The new regime spent two years imposing its up-to-date, modern ideas before the club's first owner handed control to the second: David Murray.

Murray, who had failed in an attempt to buy Ayr United prior to his involvement with Rangers, had vowed to leave football alone. The Ayr experience in the 1980s had dampened his enthusiasm, but that changed when the prospect of the Ibrox deal emerged. The source was Graeme Souness, a man Murray classed as a friend rather than a potential future employee.

It was Souness who sowed the seed in Murray's mind, the idea that he might take control of Rangers. It was no secret that Marlborough was looking for an exit strategy, with his role as absentee owner proving difficult to marry with the demands of running a club of such proportions.

Robert Maxwell was reputed to be circling. He had cut his teeth in somewhat controversial circumstances as Oxford United owner and then failed in a bid to take control at Manchester United. Souness, with apparently flawless foresight, sensed that Maxwell would spell only trouble for the club the former Liverpool player had been charged with reviving. Murray, the manager felt, would be a much safer bet.

Time would prove that Souness was a shrewd judge of a prospective owner. Maxwell's Mirror Group had begun to crumble even before his death and the subsequent revelations about the real state of his affairs; his media empire turned out to be a pack of cards ready to collapse in the slightest breeze. Had Rangers been part of that, the club could have been severely affected along with the *Daily Mirror* and countless other strands of Maxwell's business.

When Maxwell began to take an interest, Souness sprang into action and gave Murray the nudge required to send him in the direction of Rangers. And so the wheels were set in motion.

The idea that Murray might buy control of Rangers had been a topic of discussion between the two friends for some time, but it began to gather momentum in the autumn of 1988. It was Souness who instigated the negotiations, alerting chairman David Holmes to Murray's interest in October that year.

It took less than a fortnight for that initial expression of interest to turn into a serious proposition, with Marlborough receptive to the overtures from the Murray/Souness partnership. It took a series of meetings for the owner to be convinced that the man he would pass the baton to was befitting of the honour, but Murray clearly made a big enough impression to convince Marlborough that it was time to sever the family's long-standing link with the club.

One remarkable facet of the whole takeover story was that it did not leak to the media. This was the result of a carefully orchestrated effort to maintain complete discretion and confidentiality on all sides. The negotiations came to a conclusion on 22 November 1988, when the parties gathered in the Ibrox boardroom. It was not all plain sailing, with final amendments required to the documentation and legal talks rumbling on late into the evening.

As rumour had suggested there might be, there was also an attempt at a late intervention by Robert Maxwell. The media tycoon made an approach to Lawrence Marlborough through the merchant bankers who were brokering the sale, and Murray's feathers were ruffled; he was anxious to ensure that he was not tripped up at the eleventh hour.

By the time the contracts of sale had been ironed out, the clock was running down. Midnight was the deadline; any delay beyond that point would have required the paperwork to be redrawn in line with the change of date. Pen was eventually put to paper at 11.57 p.m. – the deal was done, signed and sealed.

More than £6 million changed hands between Marlborough and Murray, with the new owner inheriting not only a football club but also debts and an overdraft reported to total £8 million.

A press conference was called for the following afternoon, when the new owner was introduced to the nation. If they didn't know David

Murray before, everyone in the country was aware of the young businessman now.

Marlborough was present, outlining the emotional dilemma he'd faced when deciding to sell. He told the assembled press and broadcasters: 'I am delighted that the new custodian is such a personable and dynamic young man, that he is Scottish-based and that he is a Rangers supporter.'

Simple words, but it was clear that Maxwell's attempt to parachute himself into a great Scottish sporting institution had been entirely futile. Money was not everything when it came to finding a new keeper for the Rangers name. Murray pressed home the point, stating:

> I am delighted that this takeover means that a Scottish institution remains in Scottish hands. We intend to provide a strong case for the continuing development of the club and its business aspects. I see Rangers as the leading club in Scotland and I believe it will become a major force in the game in Europe. We want to take Rangers forward into a new era of achievement.

After the last flashbulb had popped and the microphones had been packed away, the new owner could sit back in the confines of Ibrox, his stadium, and begin to let the dramatic events of the previous months sink in. What had started as little more than an idea, a seed sown, had blossomed into a fully fledged takeover of one of the highest-profile businesses in Scotland. Despite the scale of the deal, in many ways it was the easy part. The decades that followed were to be the real challenge.

Wall-to-wall media coverage followed in the days after the announcement, pressing home the finality of it all. Murray was in charge, at last. The process was complete on 26 November when he took his seat in the directors' box at Ibrox for the first time, receiving a rapturous reception from the crowd and treated to a victory on his debut when Richard Gough scored the winner against Aberdeen. The result extended the team's lead at the top of the table to four points, and the match was played in front of 42,239 people – the biggest crowd not only in Scotland but in Britain that day.

Murray could afford to sit down and reflect on a satisfying start to life in football, knowing it was only the beginning of a long journey. Perhaps it was only after the rush of that first game had passed that the scale of the challenge began to sink in for the new owner. Speaking shortly after taking control, Murray was clearly aware it was like no other business deal he would ever conclude. He said:

I am only the custodian of Rangers Football Club. When you walk into the trophy room at Ibrox and see the long history of achievement, you realise that's all you are. That's why Lawrence Marlborough thought it was great during our negotiations that I was going to take over the club, for there were so many rumours at the time about others in the running.

He was already finding that the unique nature of the club also brought commercial benefits. He said:

So many people want to be involved with Rangers it's amazing. We are going to announce some major sponsorship deals in the summer, involving millions of pounds. I just can't believe some of the offers we have had. I'm trying to use some of my business skill to try and maximise income so that we can continue to bring the best players to Ibrox.

He insisted he would not use his financial clout to influence team affairs, claiming:

Graeme Souness will ask me things and I think he'll appreciate my advice, but whether he listens or not is his decision. He has his strengths and I have mine. There's no point in me telling him to do his job. We have a good personal relationship and I'm happy to let him get on with it.

There was no sledgehammer approach from Murray International Holdings following the takeover in the winter of '88. Holmes remained in his post as chairman during the extended handover period, not being replaced by Murray until June 1989. Holmes was praised for his contribution, although presumably Murray was eager to begin implementing his own ideas, free of the shackles of throwbacks to the previous ownership.

In a statement announcing Holmes' removal from the seat of power, Murray said:

David Holmes arrived at the start of a period that has seen the ambition of Rangers grow tremendously in the eyes of not only the Scottish footballing public but throughout the UK and indeed Europe. I and my fellow directors at Ibrox thank him most sincerely for all he has done for the club.

Murray stressed that his focus was on taking Rangers to a new level domestically and in Europe, adding: 'This is a challenge that the directors and board of Rangers seize with no shortage of confidence or determination. My colleagues and I believe that only success at the highest level will do for Rangers and our supporters.'

It was a rallying call by Murray, who had eased himself into football club ownership but was clearly ready to make an impact. He was careful not to alienate the present from the past, with vice chairman Jack Gillespie remaining in place on a board that also had a seat for manager Graeme Souness as well as chief executive Alan Montgomery and Hugh Adam, who was managing director of the Rangers Pools.

After being nudged out of Ibrox, Holmes resurfaced in football as chairman of Falkirk, before being appointed as vice chairman and managing director of Dundee at the start of 1992, as part of Canadian owner Ron Dixon's major changes at Dens. He was replaced as vice chairman by Ron Hutchison just months later.

Marlborough's exit from football was even swifter. Already living and working in America when he sold the club to Murray, little has been seen or heard of the exiled Scot since he ended the Lawrence family connection with Ibrox in the 1980s. That effectively severed his ties with the country, with John Lawrence (Glasgow) eventually coming under English ownership, in the shape of industrial investment firm Gidney Securities, and falling into administration in 1997.

Marlborough had relocated to the US while still heavily involved in Rangers, incorporating John Lawrence in California in 1980 as he expanded the firm to become a global operation. While the name John Lawrence Inc. can be tracked back to property developments in the late 1980s, Marlborough's public profile has been non-existent. He is believed to be living a quiet life in Nevada, over the border from California and with a more relaxed tax structure, having established the Reno area as his base while he was still in his 30s. It is thought that the upmarket Lake Tahoe resort of Zephyr Cove has become home to the Marlborough family.

It took only a matter of years for Murray to begin putting his own stamp on the make-up of the board of directors at Ibrox as the remnants of the traditional hierarchy were brushed away. Hugh Adam was the highest-profile casualty, ousted from the board during the 1991–92 season after finding himself at loggerheads with the recently introduced owner. Adam, who by that stage was chairman of the Rangers Development Fund, had been critical of the chairman – labelling Murray a 'football carpetbagger' in an interview with *The Herald*.

At the AGM in 1991, Murray had vowed to remove the club's

£1.2-million overdraft completely within 18 months, but was forced to concede defeat just a year later when he admitted that Rangers would remain in the red for at least a further four years.

At that time, he was also involved in a Court of Session bid to lever Jack Gillespie's remaining 15 per cent stake in the club from the motor dealer's grasp, even though Gillespie at that stage remained a director.

As the likes of Adam and Gillespie, the old school, were edged out, there were new faces appearing in the boardroom. Donald Findlay QC was one of Murray's men and Ian Skelly was another. Walter Smith, after succeeding Graeme Souness as manager in 1991, was also promoted to director level.

Skelly had sold his group of car dealerships to Appleyard in 1989 for £18.3 million, although he did retain an interest in the motor trade and did not sell his last garage, in Motherwell, until 2001. He had started the group on a derelict site in the East End of Glasgow in the 1980s and had quickly built it into the largest Volkswagen and Audi franchise in Europe. Appointed as one of Murray's directors at Ibrox in 1992, he retired in 2003 at the age of 69 with the promise that he would offer his 'lifelong support' through the members club.

Other notable boardroom comings and goings during the Murray years included John Greig, appointed as a director during the festive season in 2003, having initially been taken back to the club in a public-relations role. It was when Whyte took over in 2011 that Greig took the decision to stand down, hinting that all was far from well behind the scenes.

A succession of others also joined during Murray's tenure and became pawns in the takeover games that unfolded as the Murray reign drew to a troubled close. Just as Murray's arrival as owner in 1988 had been credited with ending boardroom unrest, his departure more than 20 years later ironically resulted in the same sort of turbulence that he had been brought in to end.

CHAPTER 8

'I've had a roller-coaster of a life, with good
fortune and bad, but I think I'm good under
pressure.'

David Murray, 2008

BUSINESSMAN, FATHER, HUSBAND, sporting impresario, risk-taker, spin doctor, competitor, hero, target. David Murray has been all of those things and more as he has scaled the highest heights, stared adversity in the face and tackled challenges of the type that would push most ordinary men to the limit. But then Murray has never been ordinary; it is not a quality that is in his make-up.

From his earliest days as a young entrepreneur, there was a drive and determination that set him on the road to fame and fortune – not necessarily in that order, with the public profile following after the trappings of a career in industry that opened the door on a whole new world for an Ayrshire lad with grand ideas.

He has become a heavyweight in spheres as diverse as football, property, fine wine and politics, with influence extending far beyond the confines of the metals trade that edged him onto the first rungs of the millionaires' ladder.

One of Scotland's most instantly recognisable figures, Murray worked tirelessly to build a life that brought rich rewards in every sense. Materially, the fruits of his labour have been plain for all to see; so too have those riches that money simply cannot buy.

Mr Murray entered the Palace of Holyrood House in July 2007 for a date with the Queen; he emerged as Sir David. The summer investiture in Edinburgh marked the ultimate rise for the one-time King of Ibrox as he joined the knights of the realm and took his place among society's elite.

In the New Year's honours list at the end of 2006, the name David

Murray sat alongside the likes of inventor James Dyson on the roll call of those awarded knighthoods. When the time came to be bestowed with the honour, he was the model of decorum after the ceremony in the palace's picture gallery. Aside from a handful of obligatory photographs after receiving his honour, Murray maintained a dignified silence about the event. However, it is safe to assume that more than a flicker of pride burned within. The boy had done good.

It all began for him on the west coast. He grew up in Ayrshire, son of a coal merchant and part of a family enshrined in community life. His had the hallmarks of a privileged upbringing, with a public-school education as a boarding pupil at the prestigious Fettes College in Edinburgh supported by the Murray silver. Yet he also had lessons in the value of money, thanks mainly to his father's gambling and subsequent financial struggles, which led to a shift away from the fee-paying college to the neighbouring state-run Broughton High School. He completed his studies at Broughton, leaving school at the age of 17 with five O levels to his credit.

When he left school, having spent summer stints working as a barrow boy and cattle-mart assistant, Murray found himself thrust into the big bad world with only that handful of qualifications and his inbuilt enterprise to rely upon.

In 2008, Murray's list of accolades grew when Edinburgh University awarded him an honorary doctorate. Recognition from the city's esteemed seat of learning came 20 years after he had first walked through the boardroom door at Ibrox and even longer since he had completed his school studies. Rivers of water had passed under the bridge and Murray, a self-taught businessman, could be proud of his achievements after modest educational accomplishments in his youth.

Nowadays Murray's image is very much that of the dapper city gent. In those early sink-or-swim days, it was as a purveyor of menswear, rather than a consumer, that he hoped to make his way in the world. Buying and selling shirts was just one of the ventures the youngster attempted as he searched for the niche that would keep him in the style to which he wished to become accustomed. Sandblasting houses was another of the businesses that drew his attention.

Eventually, the answer was discovered closer to home, although not in the coal yards that had been home to his dad's business empire. Instead, it was his uncle Ken McLeod who held the key in the late 1960s, with his enthusiastic nephew reporting for duty at his scrap-metal business as he embarked on a career that would lead down paths that nobody would have dared to predict. Murray has said in the past that his Jaguar-driving uncle was a major influence, not least because he 'looked affluent' and exuded the successful image he himself craved.

To get where he wanted to be, there was no time to waste. Murray progressed to a £7-per-week position with Scotmet Alloys, working as a trainee salesman, and stayed with the firm until it was bought by a competitor.

Aged 22 at that stage, the young gun took the opportunity to make a clean break and branched out on his own. It was a brave decision and, true to form, it was a risky one. He had surrendered the security of a staff position for the slings and arrows of self-employment. Setting up shop in the centre of Edinburgh, he rented a yard on Alva Street to launch his own metal business. One large contract win later and Murray International Metals was on the map. He had gone overseas to source the material to fulfil the order, finding an agreeable steel price in Belgium, and had shown a willingness to go the extra mile, quite literally, to make his business profitable.

And it was. In the first year alone, his fledgling enterprise is reported to have turned over in excess of £2 million and generated £100,000 profit. In the early 1970s, those represented significant figures and made the upstart a face to watch on the Scottish business scene.

Murray had been a keen athlete as a teenager, an avid rugby fan and player as well as a strong cross-country runner, and he continued to pursue his love of sport after he had left school behind. The budding businessman juggled his growing work commitments with his weekend pursuit of playing the oval ball game for Dalkeith.

In 2007, the Scottish Rugby Union confirmed a £2.7-million sponsorship deal with Murray International, with the three-year contract seeing the Murray logo replacing the Famous Grouse on the national team's shirt and reaffirming his passion for the sport.

That love of rugby played a part in the biggest single life-changing moment for Murray. It was during a journey back from a match in 1976 that the tyre of his Lotus Elite blew out and sent the sports car careering off the road and into a tree. It was a serious accident and, as a result of his injuries, Murray, aged just 23 at the time, lost both legs. He had saved his own life by tying makeshift tourniquets around his damaged limbs. As if he did not have enough to contend with, just months later his father died. He once claimed: 'It made me tougher, more focused. You learn in the tough times and I am now reasonably fearless.'

Already the father of two young children by then, he refused to be beaten by his disability and threw himself back into work. Murray's social life was put on hold; he abstained from alcohol for a sustained period and immersed himself in his professional life in the wake of the accident. He dedicated himself to building an already successful

93

business into something much bigger, with his metals firm mushrooming in time to become one of the country's biggest private companies, with an incredible turnover.

His own commitment to making the most of opportunities has not always been mirrored by his employees in the football world. Just as in business life, he took defeat to heart in the sporting world and was irked when players did not share his own feelings. When Barry Ferguson was involved in a confrontation outside a hotel bar after a 6–2 Old Firm mauling in 2000–01, Murray noted:

> What concerned me most as Rangers chairman was that, after what went on during the day, Barry Ferguson should even be in a pub at night. I knew on Sunday night after the game that I did not want to be out and about. The place to be at times like that is in your own home and I hope that Barry learns his lesson. I'm sure he will.

Murray's own lessons in life were far harsher than any footballer could relate to. He has reflected in more recent years on the impact that the effects of the car crash have on him day in and day out, telling the media:

> When I get up every morning I have to face things that none of you have to face. So never worry about my motivation or dedication – I have as much of these as anyone. I've had a roller-coaster of a life, with good fortune and bad, but I think I'm good under pressure.

Murray's disability has also brought to the fore the softer side of the hard-edged businessman. His empathy with fellow amputees has been genuine and heartfelt, and he has lent his support to a number of groups dedicated to supporting those in similar situations, proving a driving force behind the establishment of organisations the length and breadth of the country.

He has often made hospital visits to patients who have suffered similar injuries, not seeking publicity but making long trips to offer support. In 1996, he launched the Murray Foundation, a charity offering support services to those affected by limb loss or absence. His work with amputees has been done quietly and under the radar, with publicity furthest from his mind during his commitments to a cause close to his heart.

Family has naturally also been a major part in the life and times of Sir David. His sons have been part of the family business throughout their adult life, with David and Keith featuring in various roles. The boys' mother, Louise, died in 1992 after being struck by cancer. She had been Murray's childhood sweetheart.

After the pain of her death, their father has since found happiness once more with his second wife, Kae Tinto. Murray married Tinto, a lawyer turned photographer twenty years his junior, in summer 2011 after a five-year engagement. The pair had been in a relationship for two years before laying wedding plans. The champion showjumper, based near Glasgow, has twin daughters from her previous marriage to property developer John Sim.

Murray proposed during a visit to Jersey, with the island significant to him as home to one of his many properties over the years, providing a favourite bolt-hole from which to conduct Rangers business. He used the luxurious base as an impressive venue for important discussions, including entertaining prospective new signings. He had first fallen in love with Jersey during a visit in the 1960s and returned, cheque book in hand, when he had the funds to secure a property on the island. He owned a sumptuous house at St Brelade's Bay, Jersey's picturesque millionaires' row, for 15 years until placing it on the market in 2003. The house had a £4.35-million price tag when he departed, favouring a new holiday home in the sunnier South of France, swapping the sedate surroundings of Jersey for the playboys' playground of Cap d'Antibes, a short hop along the coast from Monaco.

While he chose Jersey for the engagement, it was another part of his property portfolio that won the day when it came to the decision on a wedding venue. Murray and his wife-to-be opted for the Dunbarney estate as the location for their nuptials.

It was in the late 1990s that he added to his assets with the acquisition of the 290-acre estate in Perthshire. Boasting an eighteenth-century 11-bedroom mansion and a price tag reported to be in the region of £2.5 million, it provided a tranquil weekend retreat as well as a hunting and shooting base to entertain guests. It was also utilised as a venue for Rangers business, with summit talks between Murray, football management and his directors staged at the countryside retreat as he sought to get away from prying eyes. He had bought the sprawling country estate from Lilley Construction Group chief executive Bob Rankin.

While Perthshire has provided an escape to the country, the capital city has been Murray's permanent residence and business base from his earliest days as an entrepreneur. He settled in the plush surroundings of Murrayfield in the 1980s. In 2004, he won permission to demolish his house and build a new, art-deco-style home, complete with pool, spa and orangery, on the site. Two years later, he invested in Woodcroft, a B-listed mansion in the exclusive Barnton district with a £4.5-million price tag. Within a year, he had sold the property for a fee reported to be touching £5 million. It was a new record price for a Scottish residential property.

His taste in homes is not Murray's only indulgence, with fine wine and art also on the agenda. Murray's office is in the Georgian confines of Edinburgh's plush Charlotte Square. Hanging from the walls of his first-floor office, above trophies and trinkets from his career in business and sport, are canvasses by the renowned colourist Samuel John Peploe, a refined and expensive collection housed in elegant and understated surroundings in one of the capital city's best addresses.

Vintage goods sit side by side with more modern inventions on the inventory, with the former Rangers owner also boasting a private plane, which was used to whisk signing targets to talks during his tenure at Ibrox.

In 2000, a Learjet owned by Murray was involved in a tragic accident. The aircraft crashed at Lyon, killing the two pilots but leaving passenger David Coulthard shaken but uninjured. The plane was operated by Northern Executive Aviation at the time of the accident, leased to the company by Murray for hire, and it emerged in the weeks that followed that it had been using loaned engines as its regular power plants were being serviced at the time.

Private planes were just one of the trappings of success for a man who had established himself as one of the country's highest-profile businessmen. If Murray gained notoriety on the way up Scotland's ladder of the super-rich, the headlines were not as big or bold when his fortunes took a turn for the worse. Murray has been quick to stress that the blip is temporary, that his group remains strong and capable of weathering the global financial storm, but there is no denying there has been a dramatic shift in recent years.

The dawn of the 1990s brought the advent of the *Sunday Times* Rich List. For the first time, Britain had a league table of the super-rich, and the list monitoring the highs and lows of the upper echelons of society became an annual event, unveiled with great fanfare.

The Murray star was very much in the ascendant in the 1990s and when the first rich list of the new millennium was published his was a name that sat near the top of the table of Scottish high earners. With a personal fortune estimated at £300 million in 2000, Murray was, according to the *Sunday Times*, the third-wealthiest person in Scotland. Stagecoach founders Brian Souter and his sister Ann Gloag, with a combined fortune of £565 million, were at the top of the national pile, with Sports Division founder Tom Hunter, worth £400 million, in second place, followed by Irvine Laidlaw, owner of the Institute for International Research, also at number three, with his £300-million fortune enough to equal Murray's.

In terms of annual pay, Murray sat fourth on Scotland's leaderboard. J.K. Rowling, with her £25 million haul for the year, was the nation's best paid, while construction magnates Sir Fraser and Gordon Morrison took home £23.21 million and £23.08 million to finish second and third. Murray, with an annual salary of £8.6 million in the year prior to the publication of the list, was just above Brian Souter on £6.31 million.

As the champagne corks popped and the bells rang to bring in the year 2000, prophets of doom braced themselves for the Millennium Bug to strike and take the world's computer systems to their knees. Those predictions proved to be sensationalist and instead it was a different type of collapse that would make its mark on the decade that followed. When the world's financial markets crumbled, the ordinary man on the street saw borrowing dry up and the cost of living soar. But what of the extraordinary man?

Well, fast forward to the *Sunday Times* Rich List of 2010 and a picture begins to emerge. According to the paper's research team, Murray was one of the biggest losers, as they sliced £390 million from his estimated personal fortune – a staggering 78 per cent reduction from the previous year's figure of £500 million. It saw him tumble from 88th place on the overall British rich list to 596th. There was a new kid on the block in Scotland, with Mahdi al-Tajir and his £1.5-billion fortune dwarfing the nation's established elite thanks to his success in the metal, oil and bottled-water industries. Philip Beresford, responsible for compiling the annual list, said:

> In the past, Murray has been able to do well when there has been a downturn because if one section of his business did badly, he could rely on the others. But this time they have been affected at the same time. Murray's major investments – steel, commercial property and football – all went down at once. The latest accounts have been delayed and the business is weighed down by £759 million of debt at the last count. However, Murray is a tough entrepreneur and will bounce back.

Murray, for his part, came out fighting – just as Beresford had predicted. In an interview carried in *The Scotsman* in the spring of 2010, he admitted:

> There were factors outwith my control. But I have to take

responsibility for taking on property loans and buying so much metal at the worst time. We all borrowed too much money. We got it wrong. And we have paid the price for it. But much of the fall in property values has recovered.

His group had undergone major restructuring as bankers Lloyds increased their stake to 24 per cent in exchange for wiping £150 million of debt from the balance-sheet, still only making a small dent in the overall deficit. In a single year, MIH posted pre-tax losses of £174 million to fall deeper into the red.

Having said that, millions are the equivalent of loose change when you consider that in a single property transaction, the sale of a Glasgow office development, a healthy £66.5 million in revenue was recouped.

Murray was full of praise for the support he and his company had received from Lloyds through challenging times, adding, 'Throughout the restructuring, the approach of both parties has been one of mutual cooperation and pragmatism.'

With property prices recovering and metal, particularly steel, also bouncing back strongly, he was confident of steering his group back into profit and negotiating the choppy waters created by the waves that had cascaded through the world's major financial centres. In Edinburgh, home to the wounded RBS, nobody had to look far to appreciate the severity of the situation.

Murray knew as well as most the extent of the situation and the impact it could have on his personal position. His salary fluctuated in line with the company's performance. For example, in 2003 he took £903,000 in wages from Murray International, compared with a salary of £2.6 million the previous year.

His salary might have been reduced, but, particularly when dividends are added on top of that annual wage, a picture of a man of means is painted. Not only means but power too. Murray has made sporadic and relatively subtle forays into the political world. Given his influence and wealth, the former Rangers owner has had access to the most powerful players on the British scene and was granted an audience with Tony Blair, amongst others.

Having extolled the virtues of the Union prior to the establishment of the Scottish Parliament, he then conceded that Holyrood had a part to play – while all the time maintaining the need to ensure devolution did not lead to independence. Speaking in 1999 he said:

Separatism could put jobs at risk. There's an old saying: 'If it's not broken, why fix it?' and that applies here. The best way forward for this country is a devolved parliament within the UK. Separatism could leave Scotland a cash and carry economy. I do not see the benefit of independence as a businessman and I don't think the repercussions of it have been properly thought through.

Labour seized upon Murray as a figurehead, using him alongside fellow football personalities Alex Ferguson and Billy McNeill to draw attention to fears over SNP plans for a 'tartan tax'.

Accordingly, Murray found himself at loggerheads with one of Scotland's other most recognisable public figures in the shape of Alex Salmond. The Ibrox chief went as far as accusing the SNP leader and his party of bullying tactics in the run-up to the 2007 Scottish elections. He reiterated his long-held view that an independent Scotland would be bad for business and bad for individuals, claiming taxes would soar.

Four years later, in a remarkable turnaround, Murray performed a rare U-turn and publicly endorsed Salmond and his party as they put the finishing touches to a campaign that returned them to power. Murray stated during that race for Holyrood power:

> Over the years I have been asked on numerous occasions my views on Scottish politics. I now intend to make my present views clear, but have no intention to make any further political statement or to become involved in party politics.
>
> As people know, although I have never been party political, my views have always been in favour of the continuation of the Union. They still are. However, the SNP under Alex Salmond has demonstrated that they can run a competent government and Alex Salmond makes a fine First Minister. I think Alex deserves a second term in office, and he is the best choice for Scotland during these difficult times.
>
> This is not a political statement – it is support of an individual who I admire and think is the best man for the job. I've never discussed who I'm voting for, but I'm backing Alex for First Minister.

Salmond was like the cat that got the cream as he revelled in the backing of a staunch Unionist. It came hot on the heels of a vote of support from Stagecoach millionaire Brian Souter, who also injected £500,000 into the SNP coffers. The party, with backing from big business, went on to win by a landslide. The support of the country's most prominent industry leaders undoubtedly had a part to play in that triumph, illustrating the reach of those individuals.

For Murray to have risen to a position of power and influence in the face of the incredible adversity in his early life says much about his strength of character, perhaps the second most important element in his stewardship of Rangers over the course of more than two decades.

The most important would be financial clout and the ability to find and generate finance for the club, as even the most cursory glance at the events at Ibrox during his ownership would show.

Murray brought energy and drive to the boardroom, but that would have counted for little had he not been able to support his grand plans with cold hard cash, even if it did lead to spiralling debt during the latter years of that period as individuals and institutions pumped in the money required to keep the machine rolling. They did that because the man at the top provided a convincing and compelling argument to do so.

Businessman, father, husband, sporting impresario, risk-taker, spin doctor, competitor, hero, target. Perhaps 'salesman' should be added to that growing list.

CHAPTER 9

'I cannot think of another Scottish private company
as big and diverse as ours.'

David Murray, 2006

ONE BILLION POUNDS. For most, it is a figure difficult to imagine, but that was the magic number for Murray International Holdings – the dream annual turnover. The ambitious target was mentioned in dispatches by the top man long before the world span into financial meltdown, but it is an indication of just how high sights have been set from the top right through to the bottom of an organisation with tentacles stretching in all directions.

From the heavy industry of metal to the refined environs of vineyards and back again to bus manufacturing, David Murray has turned his hand to many and varied business challenges and created a complex web of companies falling under his MIH umbrella.

The entire group is built on the foundations of the metal business built from scratch all those years ago. In the early 1970s, his metal enterprise was turning over £2 million and generating £100,000 of profit.

Thirty years down the line, by 2002, that turnover figure for the MIH group had increased by 100 times to sit at £200 million, and the annual profits had increased 50-fold in the same period to reach £5 million. Metals made up £142 million of the turnover, with property and mining among the other significant contributors. Major contract wins in the offshore oil industry, supplying material for fabrication, helped bolster the balance-sheet. The £1-billion turnover target was proposed as achievable by 2010, although the reality of the world's finances conspired to ensure that that deadline passed without the goal being accomplished. Never mind. There's always 2020.

The business established on the back streets of Edinburgh has mushroomed to an incredible extent thanks to vision, unrelenting drive and, in no small part, a willingness to take calculated risks in the pursuit of greater riches and returns.

What has been evident in Murray's business dealings has been an ability to separate heart from head when necessity strikes. That was most patently reflected late in 2005 when news filtered through that Murray International Metals, the business baby born at the very start of the journey, had been sold to an overseas enterprise that clearly saw the worth in a brand and organisation that, from humble beginnings, had risen to become one of the biggest players on the global stage.

It was in December that the sale was announced, with Murray International Metals commanding a £112-million fee. MIH insisted the deal was nothing to do with the group's net debt, which had risen to £556 million, although it would be impossible, surely, to argue that the injection of more than £100 million would not be greeted with some satisfaction by the group's bankers – even if the sale was followed by the promise that the Murray group would set off on the acquisition trail after landing its windfall, with a renewed vigour in the pursuit of property pounds.

The international business supplied steel across the world and was bought by US firm Jefferies Capital Partners, a private equity house, for that weighty sum. The operation was rebranded Edgen Murray Europe as it was integrated into its new owner's portfolio, and it went from strength to strength – raking in £18 million profit for the Americans in their first year of ownership alone.

For Murray, time proved the great healer when it came to the wrestling he must have done with his conscience in the build-up to setting Murray International Metals free. In a *Sunday Times* interview in 2006, a full year after MIM's sale, he admitted:

> The success of MIM funded all my other businesses, but I got a great offer and it took four or five months to complete. So when it went public, I had wrung all the emotion out of it. The real test will be what we do with that money. If the £100 million is only worth £200 million in ten years, then we've not done our job well. For every £1, you can leverage £3–4 in property.

Still, the competitive streak is never far from the surface even in times of quiet reflection. In the same interview, Murray was at pains to stress: 'We still have another metals division, which is worth £250 million, twice the value of MIM.'

And he was right. The disposal of MIM did not signal the end of

Murray in the business he knew best, with the Murray Metals Group parent company continuing to trade as part of his portfolio despite the sale of the international arm.

Murray Metals included the firms Austin Trumanns, Apollo Metals, Ireland Alloys, Premier Alloys, Multi-Metals, Forth Steel and Northern Steel Stocks. Between those various companies, he employed 750 people to generate a turnover in the region of £250 million. It is fair to say Murray was remaining firmly entrenched in metal, although the Apollo branch was sold in the winter of 2007 for an undisclosed sum.

Apollo, a supplier to the international defence and aerospace industries, with clients including Boeing and Airbus, was snapped up by German outfit ThyssenKrupp and represented a success for the Murray staff.

He had bought the Birmingham-based business in 2004 when it was making multimillion-pound losses, and he succeeded in returning it to profit and almost doubling annual turnover to in excess of £120 million. After that work was done, it was time to recoup cash and move on to the next project, bolstered by the proceeds of the sale.

What the millions made from metals over the decades had allowed Murray and his group to do was establish a sound financial footing from which to launch themselves into the property world. The move into property was an opportunity to reinvest profits and proceeds from sales of other successful companies, and Murray's impressive track record in business also opened the door to vital support from the banking sector to provide capital for a series of bold and ambitious projects.

As with any self-respecting entrepreneur, property has become a key part of Murray's business life. The Premier Property Group was established to handle that area of his dealings. A bid for the site of Edinburgh Zoo in the late 1990s was among the high-profile enterprises that arm of the empire was involved in, although ultimately the zoo chose to remain at its valuable Corstorphine base, despite interest from Murray and seven other developers.

He was also involved in plans to create a tartan Hollywood in Edinburgh when a green-belt site his property firm owned on the outskirts of the capital was earmarked by Sean Connery and Sony to house a £250-million film-studio complex. The plans for the Aberuthven development were scrapped due to planning red tape, despite having the backing of Edinburgh-based financier Sir Angus Grossart. The name Grossart crops up in more than one of Murray's business dealings.

Murray Estates, another property vehicle under the entrepreneur's umbrella, has even been involved in Hearts' consideration of a move away from Tynecastle. The firm developed plans for a greenbelt site near Edinburgh Park, to the west of the city, which included 3,500 homes as well as visitor attractions and a 25,000-seat sports arena. Edinburgh Rugby and Hearts were the preferred tenants for the stadium, and the Jambos were open to discussions. In truth, the sporting element was just a drop in the ocean for the £1-billion development scheme Murray was plotting. As always, ambition was not in short supply.

He was also reported to have made a £90-million bid for the Gleneagles Hotel in 2001, failing to prise the prestigious golf complex away from Diageo's grasp as he attempted to dip a toe in the hospitality trade, which had tempted the likes of *Dragons' Den* star Duncan Bannatyne to part with hard-earned cash with a view to making a long-term return. Gleneagles would have been far from a low-key entry into the hotel sector if Murray had succeeded in getting his hands on one of the nation's gems.

While it would have represented a property trophy, Gleneagles is not typical of the type of target pursued by the experts on the Murray staff. Commercial real estate has been very much at the heart of the enterprise and the reach extends far beyond the confines of the Scottish border.

For example, in 2004 Premier Property Group splashed out more than £20 million on an office complex in the less-than-glamorous surroundings of Leeds – clearly suggesting the rising debts at Rangers were not a sign of difficulties in other sectors of the Murray empire.

In the same year, it went on to clinch its largest purchase to that point with the acquisition of the International Press Centre in London for more than £40 million, with support from the Bank of Scotland. The 18-storey building put PPG firmly on the capital city's real-estate map and took its London interests past £100 million.

Office accommodation was the key focus of the group, led by managing director Ian Tudhope, and profits were strong as the sector rode out the worst of the economic slowdown. In 2003, for example, the surplus was in excess of £13 million.

As well as commercial property, Murray's PPG arm has had an interest in residential developments. Among those ventures was a partnership with the house-builder Burrell, to form Premier Burrell, which resulted in a number of restoration projects and urban-regeneration schemes at historic sites throughout Scotland.

To return to the Duncan Bannatyne comparison, the two Scottish entrepreneurs do share a passion for opportunism. While Bannatyne's investments in 'The Den' have been high profile, Murray's venture capitalism has been on a far larger if less public scale, through his Charlotte Ventures organisation.

Spearheaded by his son David junior, that arm of the Murray group has been responsible for ploughing tens of millions of pounds into a diverse range of companies in exchange for significant equity stakes. It has seen the Murray family leap into business bed with some of the country's other best-known, and most well-heeled, figures.

In 2004, Murray joined forces, through Charlotte Ventures, with Stagecoach founders Brian Souter and Ann Gloag to rescue the TransBus International bus-building company, subsequently renamed Alexander Dennis. The £90-million deal saved 1,000 jobs at the firm's bases in Falkirk and Larbert. Murray and investment group Noble Grossart were named as the majority shareholders after buying the company out of administration. Funding came from the Bank of Scotland. Within two years, it had been announced that Alexander Dennis had grown to become a world leader in the bus-building industry, with an annual turnover in excess of £170 million and profits breaking £10 million.

Charlotte Ventures was not totally removed from football involvement. In 2001, it made a £14-million injection into Vida, the Edinburgh-based chain of five-a-side football and leisure complexes. The firm, which made £700,000 in profit in its first year of trading, had around a dozen centres throughout the UK and was sold by Charlotte in 2003 for £30 million when Tom Younger, the son of Hibs legend Tommy Younger, led a management buyout. A year later, Vida went into administration with debts in the region of £15 million, with administrators Ernst & Young citing an 'aggressive' roll-out strategy as the root cause of the collapse.

Another football-related business supported by Charlotte Ventures over the years has been Azure Support Services. Sound familiar? It should do, since Azure has in one way or another been part of the furniture at Ibrox and Rangers Football Club over the past decade.

Going right back to the start, Azure Support Services was founded in the post-millennium haze of 2000 by Caroline Black and business partner Lawrence Morison as an independent catering operation. They received financial backing from Charlotte Ventures to get off and running. In return, Charlotte Ventures took a 70 per cent share in the business and left the founders with the remaining minority stake. Nobody said it would be easy in the real-life *Dragons' Den*.

In a whirlwind of activity, Azure became established as a stadium caterer with significant clout. The company went on to win the rights to provide food and drink at the grounds of clubs including Nottingham

Forest, Stoke City, Birmingham City, Edinburgh Rugby and Durham Cricket Club and at Kempton Park racecourse ... and, perhaps predictably, given the Murray money propelling the rapid expansion, at Ibrox.

Turnover quickly soared past the £10-million barrier, and, typically for a Murray-backed firm, Azure swallowed up potential competitors. Le Bistro, an Edinburgh-based contract caterer with a blue-chip clientele, was snapped up in 2001 and through that firm the burgeoning Azure claimed the rights to cater for the corporate market at the Champions League finals in Glasgow and Manchester in 2002 and 2003. The rights to provide catering at Rangers' Murray Park ground were added to the CV, amongst a myriad of others, which included catering on board the Royal Yacht *Britannia*.

In 2004, Charlotte Ventures sold a significant chunk of Azure to Elior UK, the British arm of a French catering giant. By that stage, turnover was in excess of £15.2 million for Azure. By the start of the 2008–09 season, it had agreed a deal to transfer the remaining 49 per cent of the business to Elior – who clearly liked what they had seen after becoming involved four years previously.

The severing of the Murray connection with Azure did not signal the end of the relationship between the firm and Rangers. Quite the contrary, in fact. One of the first acts of new club owner Craig Whyte and his business team was to award a nine-year extension to the catering contract at Ibrox and Murray Park as well as signing a new five-year agreement for cleaning services at the stadium and training ground. But more on that deal later, in the context of Whyte's stewardship of the club.

The intertwined dealings between an offshoot of David Murray's empire and the football club were not unique during his tenure as owner of the Gers. Response Handling Limited, a call-centre business established with Charlotte Ventures backing, dealt with calls relating to the Ibrox debenture scheme in the firm's early days. In a short period of time, it was cashing in on the boom in remote call-handling services.

RHL also won the contract to handle calls for Rangers early in its existence – and was even based at Ibrox, taking over the office space at Edmiston House in the shadow of the stadium. Services provided for the club included fielding phone orders for merchandise and calls related to the Rangers credit card.

The firm became a key part of the Murray empire and expanded substantially in 2004 when it created 450 jobs at its existing bases in Glasgow and its new centre in Clydebank. The company's clients included BSkyB, Scottish Power and the Student Loans Company.

Turnover at that stage was expected to break through the £18-million barrier. Later that year, the RHL success story continued when it snapped up three contact centres, employing almost 1,000 staff, from Thus Group for £4 million. It added the likes of Hewlett-Packard and Kwik Fit to the list of clients, although the three new call centres had been loss-making for their previous owners.

The chairman of RHL was none other than John McClelland, chairman of Rangers FC. He was appointed by the call-centre firm early in 2003 and joined a team led by managing director John Boyle, Motherwell's one-time owner and erstwhile benefactor. Who says Scottish football's web is not a tangled one?

Football-related activities have, of course, represented only a slice of the Charlotte Ventures pie. They are the headline-grabbing deals, the ones that capture the attention of the fan on the street, and particularly the Rangers fan on the street, given the Murray involvement.

For example, while many Ibrox supporters would know about Murray's involvement in Azure catering or the Response Handling call centres, few would be aware of Charlotte Ventures' investment in award-winning medical technology firm Optos, whose innovations include a device for providing high-resolution images of the retina to help diagnose sight problems. Just another string to the family's bow through the maze of firms it has either supported, created or taken a stake in.

There are few sectors that haven't been touched, but sport is a recurring feature of the business track record. Carnegie Worldwide was another one of those offshoots. The firm specialised in sporting sponsorship and brokered several high-profile deals, including the Bank of Scotland's link with the SPL in 1998. It also arranged lucrative deals involving Leeds United, as well as working with the shinty governing body to gain the backing of Glenmorangie for the Camanachd Cup. Carnegie Worldwide also majored in the corporate-hospitality sector, booming during the pre-recession years when big business had big money to spend wining and dining staff and clients.

In 2003, Carnegie Worldwide became the latest branch of the Murray tree to separate from the core business, bought out by management. The group did retain a 20 per cent stake in the company, which was another that had been owned by Charlotte Ventures.

Management buyouts were a popular route for the disposal of less profitable arms of the business, allowing staff to take a project and run with it when the returns proved not befitting a group with billion-pound aspirations.

For example, in May 2000 the firm Carnegie Public Relations was sold to its management by Murray International Holdings and was subsequently renamed Atlantic Public Relations. Murray retained a 15 per cent stake in the Edinburgh-based media outfit, which included St Andrews Bay golf resort and KLM UK among its clients.

The PR company was typical of the diversity of businesses under the Murray banner, with spates of rationalisation taking place along the way as the group was slimmed down and focused.

Not surprisingly for an organisation with an almost unfathomable range of businesses, there have been downs as well as ups. Because of the structure of his company, the faltering fortunes of Rangers had an impact on Murray's wider interests. In 2003, for example, he was forced to knock millions off the value of Murray International Holdings due to the financial struggles at Ibrox and the diminishing worth of MIH's stake in the club.

Similarly, profits have not always been guaranteed. For example, in the year to the end of January 2003, the Murray International Holdings group posted annual losses of £2.38 million, although it bounced back with £18 million of profit for the following 12-month period. That is just one demonstration of the huge swings in fortunes experienced by the group, and the move into property, bringing with it substantial borrowings to fund that cash-hungry commitment, only added to the unpredictability.

So where does Murray International Holdings stand today, in the days after the Rangers adventure has ended? It is certainly a leaner and, presumably in the eyes of its owner, a meaner operation. There are five key strands to the group in its current guise.

First, as already touched upon, there is Murray Metals. Steel is at the heart of the business, although specialist metals are also traded. The company boasts of its knowledge and expertise, particularly in the engineering of metals to order, and has a global reach through the companies that fall under its banner.

The second strand to the group is Premier Hytemp, based on the outskirts of Edinburgh. The business is among the market leaders in the supply of engineered metals, including alloys. Clients include the oil and gas industry, the renewable-energy sector and even the nuclear industry. With bases in North America and Asia, Premier Hytemp is another with a worldwide presence.

Third is the Premier Property Group, the commercial-property branch of the empire. Having developed in excess of two million square feet of commercial property since bursting into life at the start of the 1990s, it has become integral to the Murray group finances. The land bank credited to PPG is among the group's most tangible assets.

Fitting hand in glove with the commercial-property interests is Murray Estates, the fourth piece in the Murray International Holdings jigsaw. It is Murray Estates that holds the portfolio of property and land deemed to have residential potential. With high hopes for a 600-acre swathe of land to the west of Edinburgh, as well as land banks in Fife measuring 130 acres and in Lanarkshire standing at 80 acres, the Murray Estates division has huge potential if the storm in the mortgage and borrowing markets can be weathered.

The fifth and final major strand is the company now known as RESPONSE, rebranded in 2007. The call-handling business now employs more than 2,000 people.

While those five businesses are at the core of Murray International Holdings, that is not to say that there are not many other interests bubbling away under the surface. Some could be seen as being as indulgent as the Rangers exercise, although the group would argue that all have been embarked upon with a business hat firmly on.

Even when times have appeared to be tough, most notably when the banks were circling and putting pressure on Murray for a solution to the long-standing problem of negotiating a future path for Rangers, he has kept an eye open for opportunities. On occasion, those have arisen from the plight of other businesses.

When Cockburn's of Leith, Scotland's oldest surviving wine merchants, went into administration early in 2010 it was the Rangers owner who stepped into the breach. He bought the brand and customer list to fall under the umbrella of his existing wholesale business, Wine Importers. Cockburn's had served Sir Walter Scott and Charles Dickens, amongst other well-known figures, so it was a brand with clout.

Murray had been approached by administrators who were well aware of his interests in the sector. He was reported to have invested around £10 million in wine businesses, with Château Routas in Provence and Domaine Jessiaume in Burgundy his prized vineyards. He paid £3 million for Domaine Jessiaume, in the village of Santenay in the south of the prestigious Côte de Beaune wine region. Château Routas, a 630-acre wine estate and five-acre truffle bed in Coteaux Varois, cost £5.5 million.

Murray added Wine Importers to his stable in 2006 when he bought the firm for more than £1 million, and three years later he moved swiftly to acquire the firm T.M. Robertson, another of Scotland's long-established wine merchants, when that famous name was set to disappear from the business scene due to a restructuring of its parent company. Other, smaller merchants that have been welcomed into the

Wine Importers stable include Harris Fine Wines and Irvine Robertson, as the company attempts to corner the market of supplying to restaurants and exclusive clubs the length and breadth of the country. Cockburn's of Leith represented a good fit with that aim.

In a sense, wine could be seen as the new sport for Murray – a passion that has transcended the boundaries between personal life and the business world he operates in. In an interview with *The Scotsman* in 2006, on the back of his substantial investment in his Burgundy plaything, he said:

> We wanted to be in Provence and we are, we wanted to be in Burgundy and we are. We will keep looking at the Rhône and perhaps in the future Bordeaux. We are endeavouring to build a broad wine business.
>
> I would like to have a portfolio of three to four premium-end vineyards, which would give me between 20 and 30 brands. I have had an interest in wine for more than 20 years. I've read all the reference books and invested heavily in fine wine. But it's not until you actually get into the vineyard, work with the winemaker, experience the seasons, that you really begin to understand what it is all about.

With a significant personal collection of wine, reflecting what experts describe as 'sophisticated' taste in wines from the traditional vineries of the French heartlands, Murray has cultivated an interest in the subject since first becoming fascinated by the trade in the 1980s. Only in latter years has that interest manifested itself in his professional life, and since then the familiar traits have materialised – with wines from his vineyards winning medals at prestigious international events. Will they ever make it nine gold medals in a row? Only time will tell as Murray leaves football behind and settles into life with a new, more refined, focus.

CHAPTER 10

'I stood on the terraces [at Ayr United] as a boy
and I wanted to put something back into the club'
David Murray, 2002

IT IS NO secret that Rangers were not David Murray's first choice when it came to finding a football home for some of his hard-earned pennies. But what would have happened if he had got his way and it had been Sir David Murray of Somerset Park, not Ibrox, who made his mark on the Scottish game?

For one thing, life for the blue half of Glasgow's football fraternity would have been very different. No Murray would have meant many things. Who knows who would have taken over from Lawrence Marlborough when the time came for a change in ownership? When Murray took control, he was unopposed and unrivalled, publicly at least.

Working on the presumption that there was no multimillionaire waiting in the wings, it is fair to surmise that there would have been no major investment in a club that, despite attracting a star manager in Graeme Souness, was in obvious need of reinvigoration.

Would there have been nine in a row without somebody with Murray's financial clout raising the funds to bankroll Souness and then Walter Smith? Probably not. Would another chairman have broken the mould with the audacity displayed to tempt Maurice Johnston across the great divide? Probably not. Would another chairman have had the clout, charisma and unshakeable self-belief to lure Brian Laudrup and Paul Gascoigne to Scotland? Probably not. Would another chairman have broken with tradition and turned to a foreign manager with the stature of Dick Advocaat when it came to the changing of the guard? Probably not. And would another chairman have racked up debts running into tens of millions of pounds and left

111

the club nervously facing an uncertain future? Probably not.

In ways good and bad, life without David Murray would have made Rangers in the 1980s, '90s and beyond a very different club to support.

Conversely, what would life for Ayr United fans have been like if, in their wisdom, the directors of the Honest Men had seen fit to accept an approach from Murray to buy into their club in the late 1980s?

While Rangers went on to scale the heights under Murray's stewardship, sweeping all before them to win nine in a row and coming close to European success on more than one occasion, the Somerset Park side have dotted around the lower reaches of the Scottish game for decades. They reached the League Cup final in 2002 and returned to the First Division in 2011, under the management of Ibrox old boy Brian Reid, but top-flight football has remained the preserve of others, not least fierce local rivals Kilmarnock.

Had Murray succeeded in getting his feet under the boardroom table at Somerset, perhaps some of his drive and ambition, not to mention financial muscle, would have helped them find a way back up the football ladder that has otherwise proved frustratingly slippery over the years.

The steel magnate's attempt to buy Ayr United in 1988 was no flash-in-the-pan, half-hearted effort. It was a carefully thought-out move fuelled by the passion of a home-town boy made good. His links to the Honest Men are rooted deep in his family's heritage; his grandfather, of the same name, had served as president of the Ayrshire Football Association in the late 1930s and also sat on the board at Somerset Park, receiving the title of honorary secretary in 1940. As a boy, Murray had cheered on the team from the terraces.

Having joined the elite club of the country's millionaires, Murray returned to his old stamping-ground aiming to come to the rescue of an ailing club, which, despite its on-field struggles, was widely recognised as having the potential to achieve far more than it had in the preceding years.

The side had produced a string of Scotland internationals, including Steve Nicol and Alan McInally, but there was a distinct lack of collective glory for the Honest Men in the 1980s. Not even the return of the talismanic manager Ally MacLeod, who checked in for a third stint in charge late in 1985, could spark an immediate revival, and Ayr sank like a stone to the foot of Scotland's league structure.

The 1987–88 season saw MacLeod inspire his men to greater things, and the Second Division championship was won, coinciding with Murray's offer of assistance to continue the progress being made.

Ayr United were enjoying a free-scoring season when the Edinburgh-based businessman first made his move for the club. MacLeod's cavalier side, which was built around the exciting strike force of Henry Templeton, John Sludden and Tommy Walker, was winning fans not just with its results but also with the manner in which it was achieving them. Ayr might have been only a part-time club, but they were playing exhilarating football.

There had been no hint on the terracings of a takeover bid until in February 1988 a Sunday newspaper broke the story that Murray wanted to buy over his home-town team. His name was unknown to most United supporters, but it was one with which they were quickly to become familiar. Murray was quoted as saying: 'I'm an Ayr United supporter. I followed them as a boy and I've seen them half a dozen times this season.'

The takeover saga was to split the fans, and it was the subject of much debate in the *Ayrshire Post*, where Murray was to take out a full-page advert to publicise his plans for the club and garner support.

For Mike Wilson, the *Post*'s sports editor, it was the start of a long-running debate that carries on even to this day. Wilson told me: 'Initially, there was great excitement among the supporters, who believed a Murray takeover would mean a much-improved stadium and pots of money for Ally to use to strengthen the team.

'However, the board of directors were immediately cautious and were very guarded in their initial response. It soon became clear that Ally was firmly against the takeover. He came out strongly in support of the directors and there were hints that he would quit if Murray got his way.

'Some fans were of the opinion, however, that Ally knew his position would be in jeopardy if Murray took over because a new man at the helm would, in all probability, want to install his own manager.

'The team's results on the park meant the fans were all behind Ally, who will forever be revered as the greatest manager in the club's history.'

On 22 March, chairman George Smith spelled out the directors' opposition to the takeover in a letter to shareholders. He claimed Murray's original proposal specified a cash injection of around £90,000 (later increased to £112,000) plus a repayable loan of £500,000 in exchange for 75 per cent ownership of the club by way of new shares to be issued to him. He said Murray also proposed to pay £10 per share if all 467 shareholders sold out to him.

Smith, a Girvan farmer, was well liked by fans and many took on board his reasoning. He wrote:

Mr Murray's latest proposal is to inject the whole £500,000 into the club not by way of a loan but by way of new shares to be issued to him again on the basis that he gains 75 per cent control.

While I accept that the injection of the £500,000 into share capital rather than by way of loan demonstrates a more permanent financial commitment by Mr Murray, it seems to me that his latest proposal, from the shareholders' point of view, has gone down rather than up.

Shareholders will bear in mind that in seeking to acquire 75 per cent ownership, Mr Murray would secure for himself not only 75 per cent ownership of the whole club as it stands but also 75 per cent of his own investment of £500,000, howsoever that was later spent.

By that argument, it could be said that Mr Murray is only prepared to divest himself of £125,000 to put himself into 75 per cent ownership and the virtually unassailable position of one-man control.

I suggest to you that this is a nonsense figure in relation to the value of your club.

Indeed, your manager, Mr Ally MacLeod, assures me that one or two of our players alone might well be worth more than that.

And then what about the value of the rest of the players and the five acres or so of ground, buildings and facilities?

Smith assured supporters that the club's future was looking very good, with First Division football just around the corner.

The board unanimously rejected Murray's proposals. And when it went to a vote of the shareholders, 56 were in favour and 60 were against.

In November that year, Murray acquired a controlling interest in and subsequent chairmanship of Rangers. Meanwhile, Ayr's shareholders raised around £250,000 to build a family stand and to finance full-time football for two years in a bid to reach the SPL.

Twenty-three years on, however, the debate about Murray's attempted buyout still rumbles on in the auld toon of Ayr. Mike Wilson, who still heads the sports team at the *Ayrshire Post*, says: 'Even to this day, many fans still wallow in what might have been. If Murray's bid had been successful, would he have ploughed the cash into Ayr that he later invested in Rangers? Or would he have turned his back on Ayr when the chance to buy Rangers came up?

'Would he have transformed Somerset Park by building at least one new stand and leaving a legacy for all to see? Would he have splashed cash on new players and tried to take the club to the next level?

'No one can safely say they know the answers. Many still wonder how a club like Ayr could afford to turn down an offer from a businessman of the status of David Murray. But others insist the directors at the time got it right. Handing over control of the club to one man was a risk they were not prepared to take.'

George Smith, who remains a director at Ayr, was the chairman who presided over that crucial decision. In 2002, when Rangers and Ayr were drawn together in cup football, Smith reflected on the logic behind what, to outsiders, appears to be one of the game's great imponderables. Why on earth did a part-time team rebuff the advances of a man who went on to become of British football's biggest personalities?

For Smith, there was not even a pang of regret. He was adamant that the path would not have been littered with gold, or, more crucially, silverware, if he and his club had walked it hand in hand with their wealthy supporter, which, to be fair, is a sentiment shared by Murray himself, since his intention was not to blindly plough money into Ayr United with little prospect of a return from what will forever be a provincial club. Smith told *The Scotsman*:

> What Murray has done at Rangers certainly could not have been done at Ayr. The money was not available for that, and neither was the fan base. He never put any figures on the table. It was only really a proposal. It was nothing concrete. He didn't really value the club properly if I remember.

The mists of time have left detail scant, but the recollections of those who covered the takeover attempt for the media at the time suggest the Ayr United approach was made with head as much as heart. While Murray harked back to his days as a boyhood fan at Somerset Park, he did not arrive in town with an open cheque book after making his millions in the metal business. He made an offer of backing rather than a promise to spend with gay abandon. As the voting figure testifies, the shareholders of the Honest Men were not sure what Murray's intentions were. Did he want control of the club or simply to be a generous supporter with an influence in the boardroom? As it turned out, they did not wish to take a chance and find out.

Perhaps a throwaway remark from George Smith hints at the motivation behind at least some of the 'no' votes. Speaking to *The Scotsman* in 2002, Smith said: 'David Murray says he is an Ayr fan, but he always had a soft spot for Rangers.'

Bluenose or not, it was Ayr United that the would-be benefactor had turned to first. In his *Post* advert, Murray had vowed to put Ayr United's name up in lights and emulate the achievements of other provincial sides that had challenged the more established teams. Dundee United, after all, had just scaled the heady heights of the UEFA Cup final, and the support base and enthusiasm for football in Ayr were arguably at least equal to that enjoyed by the Tannadice side. Full-time football and a new stadium to replace the tired facilities that had changed little from his days as a schoolboy fan were among his plans.

Murray would be cautious when it came to vetting potential Rangers owners when he stepped aside in 2011, and those who served as custodians at Somerset were equally sceptical when their own white knight rode into town. Among the office bearers was Bill Barr, secretary at the time and a businessman who would go on to make a career in stadium development as well as becoming chairman at Ayr United. Barr, it has been reported, was among those not convinced that Murray had the clout to back up his plans for the club.

The bid for control of the club was not entirely without support, however. Fans are reported to have begun chanting Murray's name at one game during the negotiations, earning a swift rebuke from manager MacLeod as he pinned his colours to the mast of the ship being steered by the incumbent regime.

Some time after his publicity campaign failed to bear fruit, Murray went on the offensive in another media outlet. Although he was by this time firmly ensconced in the Ibrox seat of power, he wrote an open letter to supporters, using the new fanzine *4–1* as his vehicle. The issue was a sell-out and readers were treated to Murray's thoughts on the rejection of his approach, which clearly rankled, as he branded it a 'disgrace' and stressed that his attentions had only turned to the opportunity to take over at Rangers after he had been shown the exit door at Somerset Park.

Even the sands of time have not totally buried the disappointment of the rejection by the Ayr shareholders. Murray remarked in later years: 'I stood on the terraces as a boy and I wanted to put something back into the club. If you want to analyse it, I suppose you could call it an emotional thing.'

Still, time has proved to be a healer of sorts. In the build-up to the 2002 League Cup final showdown between his side and Ayr, the club he had at one time wished was his, Murray mused in *The Scotsman*: 'What is meant to be is meant to be. Remember, there is no guarantee that I would have taken them to their first-ever cup final.'

It seems a fair assessment of a decision that changed the course of

Scottish football history. Had Murray taken control at Ayr, the course Rangers charted in the subsequent years would undoubtedly have been very different. Votes cast by a smattering of Ayrshire shareholders had a huge impact on events at Ibrox in the 1990s and beyond.

Whatever the United power brokers thought at the time, they would have been wrong to suggest that the Murray approach was made on a whim or without thorough consideration on his part. He knew what he was preparing to get into and already had first-hand experience, albeit in a totally different ball game – quite literally.

The courtship of the Ayr United shareholders was not Murray's first venture into sports-club ownership. The team that can lay claim to that honour is Livingston, or Murray International Metals Livingston as they became known. The MIM Livingston moniker is not one familiar to Scottish football fans, mainly because football was not their game: it was basketball.

Murray's first flirtation with running a sporting institution was in the high-paced world of professional basketball in the 1980s as he took the helm of a club that he steered to the pinnacle of the British game. Not content with one top-level team in the National Basketball League set-up, in 1988, after landing his first football club in the shape of Rangers, he spent £100,000 to buy the franchise of the Kingston Kings.

His intention was to relocate the team to Scotland, and it duly happened, with his new acquisition being renamed Glasgow Rangers and taking their place alongside Livi in the British top flight. The two dominated the 1988–89 season, their first as rivals. It was the new men from the west coast who came out on top, winning the league as part of a string of trophy successes in their maiden campaign.

It proved to be a one-hit wonder, as the basketball experiment was wound down after just a single season. MIM Livingston also folded, with the popularity of basketball in Scotland traditionally insufficient to provide adequate support for full-time teams.

The creation of the Edinburgh Rocks in 1998, this time with no Murray involvement, marked the reinvention of the pro game north of the border. Since rebranded as the Scottish Rocks, the team switched to the west coast to once again attempt to attract a Glasgow support, and it has demonstrated admirable staying power. Still, with crowds averaging somewhere just north of 1,000, it is a difficult sporting business model to sustain and it was that lack of appetite that saw Murray turn his attentions elsewhere in the late 1980s.

Murray's basketball team is not the only one from another sport to have worn the Rangers badge over the years. In 2008, the club announced its intention to race in the Superleague Formula motor-racing series. Around 20 clubs from across the world put their name to a team for the series, which was to be contested by cars displaying the colours of 'their' club.

Rangers explained at the time that the diversification into circuit racing was viewed as a means to expand the Rangers brand and take the club to a wider audience around the world. It also proved to be another opportunity to get in ahead of Celtic, as Rangers could boast of being the only Scottish team in the new series, which was due to be beamed live across the globe, with football and motorsport coming together in a television- and sponsor-friendly format.

Nothing ventured, nothing gained appeared to be the mantra trickling down from the top as the club turned over every rock in an attempt to gain an advantage during a period in which any opportunity to generate revenue was embraced with open arms. The first season brought strong showings from the Ibrox car, resplendent in blue, and ripples of interest from Rangers fans, with a small but loyal band of followers attaching themselves to the race team.

The racing venture was a minor distraction, nothing to rival the complexity or the passion involved in running one of the world's biggest football clubs. Basketball, motorsport . . . neither had captured Murray's imagination in quite the same way as football had, and over the years one club proved not to be enough to quench his thirst for the beautiful game.

Even after securing Rangers, Murray remained on the hunt for further football acquisitions, and in 1998 he was involved in talks regarding a move for Manchester City. A £25-million offer was weighed up by the Scot after he was approached by City power brokers, but the proposed takeover was abandoned when it became clear that UEFA would frown upon two clubs operated by the same man competing in its premier Continental competitions.

Had Murray gone through with the purchase, he would have been faced with the prospect of having to withdraw one of his two clubs from European competition if they had both qualified in the same season. Given that City were languishing outside the top flight at the time of his interest, he clearly had grand plans to invest heavily to restore the sleeping giants to their former glory.

He sought the counsel of trusty SFA secretary Jim Farry during the time of the negotiations with City and was advised by the Hampden official that the road ahead would be fraught with danger. The prospect of having UEFA breathing down his neck and attempting to knock Rangers off the European course he so passionately wished to follow was, for once, enough to convince Murray he should go against his instincts.

He refused to take a gamble that could have been detrimental to 'his' club and was instead left to rue the missed opportunity and reflect on what might have been. Murray said at the time:

> Sometimes football clubs are more than football clubs – they are a cause; they are what makes people tick. Everybody supports their club passionately, but Manchester City have done a lot of good for other clubs in the Second Division with the supporters they take away. They shouldn't be in that division. They are meant for better things, and I hope that through me or through someone else they will get that at the end of the day.

And there we are, back at the Ayr United scenario. Manchester City supporters could have been forgiven for wondering what might have been as their foundering club missed the Murray boat in the late 1990s; it looked as though a golden opportunity had sailed for the Maine Road side. Skip forward a few unremarkable decades to the arrival of billionaire owner Sheikh Mansour and all of a sudden Murray's millions look like small fry. Those are the swings and roundabouts of football's league of wealth.

It was shortly after his discussions with Manchester City that Murray admitted he was still learning the ropes as a club owner, more than a decade after taking the seat of power at Ibrox. He stated:

> You can't just throw money at a situation. You have got to have experience. People have bought football clubs and then not realised what they are taking on thereafter. We've been at it 11 years – we have got a few things wrong, but we've got more right. I felt I had a lot to offer Manchester City. Obviously, my priorities lie with Rangers and will always remain with Rangers. But I felt it was a good opportunity, although, regretfully, not at this time.

Of course, City eventually got their white knight and revelled in the type of riches that others could only dream of. Unlike Ayr United, it appears that City got the better deal when their dalliance with Murray hit the rocks.

In 2000, two years after the flirtation with the English game, Murray did broaden his football horizons substantially when he made an investment in excess of £1 million to take a controlling interest in Australian team Northern Spirit and support them financially.

With Socceroos stars Craig Moore and Tony Vidmar already on Rangers' books, the Ibrox supremo hit upon the idea of recruiting more talent from Down Under by using Spirit as a feeder club. It circumnavigated the thorny issue of UEFA rules by branching out to another continent. It also marked a move towards a strategy of globalisation, as Murray looked to take the Rangers brand to new and captive audiences overseas.

Northern Spirit had previously been owned by Mark Goldberg, the high-profile owner of Crystal Palace. Goldberg, who had reputedly ploughed more than £20 million of his fortune into Palace with little reward, took a 70 per cent stake in Spirit in 1998 and promised to stump up more than 2 million Australian dollars to develop the Sydney-based club. Soccer Australia, the game's governing body, were delighted to have attracted British interest, viewing it as an endorsement of their club scene.

Hopes were high for the vibrant new side, but soon the dream turned sour for the London businessman as he discovered that the large crowds attracted initially, with the home ground selling out, could be attributed to a honeymoon rather than a long-lasting love affair with soccer.

Goldberg made his exit and it was Murray, and Rangers, who stepped into the breach. Shortly before he moved into the Australian game, Murray had been looking tentatively at possibilities to establish himself in the blossoming American soccer scene. Instead, he turned his attention Down Under.

The new addition to the Rangers family was taken seriously, as you would expect after an £800,000 outlay for a 51 per cent stake in the National Soccer League outfit. Accountant Colin Mitchell was parachuted in from Murray headquarters in Edinburgh, installed as general manager and charged with turning potential into profit, or at least sustainability, for a fledgling side that had already endured financial difficulties.

The tie to Rangers was expected to attract a following among Sydney's band of exiled Gers fans, but that was not the focus of the business plan. Instead, Mitchell aimed to raise the club's profile and try to claw back the supporters who had given Spirit an average gate of 15,000 in their debut in the NSL. For their first-ever game, in 1998, Spirit had pulled in 18,000 people, and no doubt that potential had registered back at Ibrox when the move into Australia was under consideration. However, by the time Murray took control, less than half that number were regularly attending.

Improving quality was key to bringing back the absentee fans, with coach Graham Arnold sent to Ibrox to learn tricks of the trade from Dick Advocaat and his staff, and attempts made to take Gordon Durie over the ocean to bolster attacking options. In the end, Durie opted for the less clement surroundings of Edinburgh and joined Hearts.

With average wages for players in the NSL sitting at less than £40,000, it should have been easy to supplement the playing squad without massive investment.

Mitchell and Murray dreamt of the day when the Australian NSL would thrive and could join forces with the burgeoning Asian competitions to create a new Champions League-style competition with global appeal. They longed for a time when a flow of talent would take the new Harry Kewell or, dare I say it, Mark Viduka from Northern Spirit's youth academy straight into the Ibrox first team.

In 2001, a year after their first involvement, Rangers bought the remaining 49 per cent of shares in the club to give them complete control as they prepared for a revamp of the Australian game that would cut the elite league from 15 to 12 teams. With the high-profile backing of Rangers, Spirit looked assured of a place at the top table and the future would, surely, be bright.

But the dream and the reality proved two very different things and in 2002 the decision was taken to sell off the Australian interest, with Antonio Gelonesi stepping in to buy the club from the Murray stable. Attendances had not picked up in the way it had been hoped they would, and making an Australian club financially viable was not easy in a climate in which sponsors were not flocking to become involved. According to reports, sporadic crowd trouble at Spirit games had not helped with the charm offensive required to bring the city's business community onboard. All in all, it was time to cut the losses and hand over to a new owner – one who was closer at hand to oversee the running of the Sydney side.

It marked the beginning of a rocky road for Spirit, and the following year the club was placed in liquidation, although hopes were high that fixtures could still be fulfilled despite what was a major setback. At the time, Gelonesi was quick to lay blame at the door of Rangers, which he accused of failing to meet financial obligations to Spirit under the terms of an agreement he claimed had been made when he had taken over. It smacked of looking for a scapegoat, and it was on Gelonesi's watch that Spirit kicked their last ball. The whole affair was the subject of much intrigue and interest in Australia as the soap opera unfolded.

The Northern Spirit experiment, which proved to be Murray's only other football involvement outside of Rangers, despite interest in other ventures, would be put down as a failure due to the relatively high costs in comparison with limited returns.

In a country steeped in the traditions of rugby and cricket, not to mention Aussie rules football, the plans to catapult soccer to the forefront of the nation's sporting consciousness had stalled. Northern Spirit were just part of that wider picture, one of several clubs that had started life with high hopes but had had to reassess their aspirations as time wore on.

What had started as a bold and bright new innovation in diversification at Ibrox, heralded in the pages of the *Rangers News* and the wider media, had slowly been allowed to disappear from the Ibrox agenda.

In true Murray style, it was a case of nothing ventured, nothing gained, and, in the case of Northern Spirit, it was very much nothing gained – save for the lesson that football-club ownership is an occupation littered with pitfalls. On paper, it had looked like a sound proposition; as we are forever being told, football, unfortunately, is played on grass.

CHAPTER 11

'I think Sir David will be remembered as the greatest chairman Rangers ever had.'

Graeme Souness, 2009

THE RELATIONSHIP BETWEEN chairman and manager is arguably the most important at any football club, and when David Murray joined forces with Graeme Souness at Ibrox, the bond between the two men was stronger than outsiders could ever have imagined. Friends first, colleagues second, the partnership had begun long before Murray had signed to take over guardianship of the Light Blues.

Lawrence Marlborough was the owner at Ibrox and David Holmes the chairman when Souness, the national-team skipper, swept into Scotland to send a jolt through our game. It was the spring of 1986 when the Sampdoria star was persuaded to move lock, stock and barrel back to his homeland and take on his first managerial appointment.

He was many things. Bold, to the point of arrogance many would argue, and unerringly determined. But the one thing the new player-manager could never be accused of was being unintelligent.

He was cute enough to make the decision right at the start of his tenure to remove himself from the line of fire and chose Edinburgh, not Glasgow, as his home. He built a mansion in the plush Colinton area, a house bought in more recent years by former Royal Bank of Scotland chief Sir Fred Goodwin. Given Fred the Shred's reputation, it is fair to say the Rangers manager had expensive taste. Rather than being embedded day and night in the frenetic world of the Old Firm and its supporters, the new Ibrox boss was free to move in the capital city's social scene and step out of the line of Glasgow's football-generated tunnel vision.

It was while settling into life in Edinburgh that he was first introduced to David Murray. Flamboyant, successful, with an unshakeable will to win – in describing one, you could just as easily be painting a picture of the other. They are men cut from the same cloth, and it is hardly surprising that theirs was a friendship that blossomed.

They would meet most weeks, more often than not convening in their favourite Italian restaurant to chew the fat and talk of life, the universe and everything. Inevitably, conversation around the dinner table would revert to football, the subject Souness knew best.

For months on end, he regaled his close friend with tales of Ibrox life and the challenges he faced along the M8 on the west coast. The drama and the theatre of the rapidly developing Rangers story were all heartily endorsed by the enthusiastic young manager. All the time, the seeds were being sown for Murray to negotiate his way into a part in the same play.

As their friendship developed, Souness became a confidant as Murray revealed his ambition to establish a foothold in football. He provided counsel during the abortive effort to buy Ayr United, despite remaining unconvinced that the lower-league outfit was a club able to match his friend's burning ambition for success.

It was at around the same time that the Gers boss began to tap into a vibe that suggested his superiors at Ibrox were ready to hand over to a new regime. According to Souness, chairman Holmes was beginning to give the impression of being distracted, and when he gently sounded out the possibility of a change in ownership, there was a surprisingly positive response.

Marlborough and Holmes were ready to work on an exit strategy, and Murray was knocking at football's door looking for an entrance. Souness was quickly able to persuade his sidekick to pursue the opportunity.

Over fine Italian food, Murray's appetite was whetted, and when he finally got the call from Souness to say that the time was right to make his move, he was already well versed in the ins and outs of the revolution being conducted by a manager who had succeeded in landing the title in his first season but had been hauled back down to earth when Celtic got their hands on the league crown in 1987–88.

Between them, they cooked up a structure that would allow Souness to form a coalition with the prospective new owner, albeit as a very junior partner. The manager was ready to plough £500,000 of his own fortune into the takeover effort, and duly earned himself a chunk of shares and a place on the board of directors when the rapidly evolving deal was rubber-stamped late in 1988. The half-million sum was exactly the fee Rangers had had to pay to Sampdoria to secure Souness in the first place, so he had paid his own way.

124

It was not an investment that Murray needed or solicited, more an expression of commitment on behalf of Souness to a project that would consume both men in the years that followed. They were in it together, with a common purpose and shared work ethic.

The Friday night meals that had once been purely pleasure took on a business aspect as the two Ibrox directors continued to meet for their weekly catch-up. The dynamic might have changed, with Murray now the paymaster, but the rock-solid relationship did not falter. Whereas other clubs were divided, there was an incredible, unique sense of unity at Rangers that washed through Ibrox and manifested itself in a wonderful one-for-all spirit among the staff. The real test, of course, would come on the field.

Would the relationship between the two top men show the strains of their considerable responsibility? They might have started the working relationship as close friends, but would that same spirit exist when it ended? That was an intriguing question that was graced with an answer sooner than either man could have anticipated as they sat hatching their plans in the early days.

Souness had been untested as a coach or manager when he had committed himself to the rebuilding task at Ibrox in 1986, persuaded by Holmes to give up his new life on the Continent, where he had led Sampdoria to cup success as a player, in favour of his first crack at Scottish football. He had seen his former Liverpool and Scotland teammate Kenny Dalglish take on a player-manager's role at Anfield and wanted a piece of the action.

By the time he teamed up with the new owner, he had already established his credentials as a trophy-winning boss capable of ruling his club with an iron fist. To have taken on such a mammoth task at such a tender age, just 33 when he joined, was an achievement in itself. To then go on and win a league and League Cup double at his first attempt was all the more remarkable given the lull Rangers had been in prior to his arrival.

Then came the stall, as he ended his second campaign empty-handed. The pressure was on for a man who had arrived amid great fanfare, paraded in public by Holmes with total support – but with the warning in private that failure would result in dismissal for him and his new assistant Walter Smith.

Phil Boersma, a name unknown outside of his homeland of England, was the third member of the new backroom team. Boersma, a Liverpudlian, had been on the books at Anfield and a fringe player for the Reds in the late 1960s and '70s before spells with Wrexham, Middlesbrough, Luton and Swansea. It was at Middlesbrough that he

125

had first worked alongside a young Scot by the name of Souness, who was making his way in the world, and the two became close friends.

Boersma was serving as assistant manager to John Toshack at Swansea City when the call came from his old friend to join him in Glasgow in 1986. He was enlisted at Ibrox as a coach and physio, using skills he had trained in over the years, and went on to follow Souness back to Liverpool and join him at a succession of clubs after that.

There were highs and lows along the way. The loss of the league in 1987–88 was a mere glitch in the scheme of things, as Souness went on to send Rangers on the road to nine in a row, the first of those league wins coinciding with his partnership with Murray in the 1988–89 campaign.

In that first season together, the pair had plenty to toast at their regular dinner dates, with the Premier Division crown and the League Cup landed to add some sparkle to the chairman's maiden season.

The manager's standards always remained high, demanding total commitment to the cause. In his book *A Manager's Diary*, Souness gave an insight into his attitude:

> It is all about being a good professional. You cannot pick your games when you are with a club like Rangers. You cannot go on to the field expecting to take it easy in some matches and then turn it on in others. That won't do. It has to be 100 per cent all the time.

Adjusting to Scottish football did not take long, although Souness was not always impressed with what he saw. He once claimed Motherwell played the type of football that ought to 'get the game stopped'. But he had to find a way to penetrate the type of block defence employed against Rangers at home and away.

There was further league glory to celebrate in 1989–90, and Rangers, roared on by Souness, were confidently on their way to a third consecutive flag in the 1990–91 term, having already lifted the League Cup, when the chairman–manager relationship struck an irreconcilable difference. The third party involved was Liverpool; there was no contest. The midfield general was going back to his first football love.

The bond of the pair's friendship ensured there was no animosity. Souness was sent on his way to England with good grace and the blessing of the Rangers owner – but with a warning ringing in his ears. Murray told his departing manager that he would live to regret his decision, and time has proved him right.

Souness has since travelled the highways and byways of European football as a coach, with his post-Liverpool days taking in the likes of

Benfica, Galatasaray, Torino and less glamorous ports of call including Southampton, Blackburn and Newcastle. Still, blue is the colour for the former Scotland star. Speaking in 2003, he said:

> When I left I had the feeling the grass was greener on the other side, but I realise I made a mistake. I have since been at some big clubs, and had some great times there, but Rangers are the club. You cannot go back and it's hard to say I wish I had never left because I'm married again and happy in my personal life. If I had stayed none of that might have happened.
>
> In football terms there are things I would like to change but I would like to think I did my bit and the club has moved forward in leaps and bounds. I have great memories of Rangers. We flew by the seat of our pants in the early days. There was togetherness and I knew we had a chance of achieving things.

He was right about that, with the team turning from also-rans to thoroughbred winners during his short but eventful tenancy of the Ibrox manager's office. Souness added:

> I would like to mention David Holmes. He was the chairman who brought me to the club. And after that it was David Murray who pushed things to another level. I did my bit but I was helped by great people, most notably Walter Smith, and players like Ray Wilkins, Richard Gough and Terry Butcher.

Souness can look back with satisfaction at what he and Murray achieved during their time together at Ibrox. At the time, he admitted, he had doubts about Murray's understanding of the project he was taking on. *A Manager's Diary* charts the tumultuous 1988–89 season and the takeover drama. In the days leading up to the completion of the deal, he wrote:

> Maybe I have got David into something so big that he does not quite realise it – but I know he will enjoy it. I have told him how big Rangers are and I have told his wife too, that this will start to take over their lives. You don't get much of a chance to walk away from the limelight when Rangers are involved. Anything you do is news. You learn to live with that. David says it won't affect him but it will. We will wait and see how that one goes, but I have seen the picture.
>
> This club becomes an all-consuming passion for anyone who

gets involved. You cannot help yourself. I used to think that Liverpool was mad about its football – it doesn't reach the same passion which is produced by the people who follow, follow Rangers. I have seen it all for myself and David is going to learn about it from the inside. He will be a part of the club and I know he will be an active part because he is a 'hands-on' kind of guy. He buys something, be it another business or a football club, and he wants to know what is going on there. He won't be making this kind of major investment to sit back and relax. He will get himself involved and then he will learn what we have all learned – that Rangers takes over your very life.

Souness said he doubted whether his chairman-in-waiting had any limit to his ambitions and noted that his excitement was palpable as he counted down the days until they were united together at Ibrox. The manager viewed the potential of the club as 'limitless' and, with his new employer's drive and clout, he was confident that progress domestically and in Europe was just around the corner.

Within months of the takeover being completed, the dynamic of the relationship between Murray and Souness began to change. They had gone from friends to business partners, albeit in a partnership skewed in the chairman's direction, given the size of his stake. By the start of 1989, *A Manager's Diary* reveals, Souness was noting:

> There is a change in David now. More and more he is becoming steeped in the club and what we want to do. And he is not afraid to tell me what he wants – friend or not. That is the way it should be. It has to be that kind of relationship because I don't reckon it would work any other way. I may be a director and I may be the second largest shareholder – but I am also still the manager and I remain answerable to the board of Rangers Football Club as far as the on-field results are concerned. I still know that I can be sacked. If the results don't come then I would be off. It is as simple as that and I would not have it any other way because no other way would it all work.

The big-money signings had already begun to flood in to Ibrox before the Murray takeover was complete. Terry Butcher, Chris Woods, Mark Walters, Richard Gough, Gary Stevens and Ray Wilkins all arrived under David Holmes' watch.

Indeed, the first new face after Murray took office was hardly a superstar; Mel Sterland arrived from Sheffield Wednesday in a £750,000 deal. Sterland stayed long enough to help the club to the title before being sent south again to join Leeds United.

The recruitment of England international Trevor Steven from Everton, a £1.5-million man, was next on the agenda, and he was more the type of big-name recruit that the supporters were developing a taste for. It was a signing befitting the new Souness–Murray partnership.

According to Souness, when he had travelled from Genoa to Glasgow to take on his first managerial challenge, he could have signed any of 200 players who would have been an improvement on the standard of player he inherited. Within three years, he reckoned there were only 20 players in the game he would have put ahead of those already on the staff. It had been a fast, consistent and well-organised period of improvement as a new team was assembled.

While much was made of the open-cheque-book policy as a string of England internationals arrived on big money, there were other, lower-profile signings that gave the manager just as much pleasure.

The less glamorous leagues of Scotland were trawled for young talent, with the likes of Davie Kirkwood from East Fife and Clyde defender Tom Cowan recruited to bolster the reserves and build for the future. While the scouting team would identify the talent, Souness liked to personally cast an eye over prospective recruits, even those coming in beneath first-team level, and took pleasure in unearthing a rough diamond to take back to Ibrox and polish.

Cowan, who cost £100,000 in the face of competition from Nottingham Forest and Coventry City, was a case in point. Impressed by his attitude, Souness quickly propelled the young defender into the first team as he groomed him for a role in the success that was to come in the years ahead.

At that stage, the manager spoke of seeing out his career at Ibrox, safeguarding the considerable investment he had made in shares and passing his stake in the club to his sons as a legacy. Even in the months leading up to his departure, Souness reiterated his intention to rebuff any approach from Liverpool in favour of remaining in Glasgow.

But the English giants were persistent and eventually got their man in April 1991. At the time, the firebrand coach was serving his latest touchline ban after another run-in with disciplinary chiefs at the SFA. His consistent issues with the governing body were cited as one reason for his decision to reverse his earlier intention to remain north of the border. Attempts to persuade him to remain in Scotland fell on deaf ears. His mind was made up.

His Liverpool homecoming was not all that he had dreamt of, with league success elusive. Speaking to *The Independent* in 1999, he said:

Liverpool were always the only club I would leave Rangers for. Whether I would have ever got another chance at it if I turned it down then, who knows? I was at the right place at the wrong time. What's happened since has gone to prove that I wasn't to blame for all the ills. The place was in decline long before I went there.

My problem was that I tried to change it too quickly. It's interesting now that they're about fifth in the table and everything's said to be rosy in the garden. Well, when I was there they were about fifth or sixth and it was all doom and gloom. At least that was how it's been portrayed to the public. But I was naive. Communication is everything and it's how it comes across that's important.

I've got a far better football knowledge now than I would have had if I'd have stayed at Rangers. I've worked abroad. I've worked with different people, with different attitudes to the game. That's broadened my horizons and increased my knowledge. I'm far better qualified now, more knowledgeable, than I've ever been. Yes, you make mistakes, but you learn from them . . .

. . . The PR image is far more important now than it has ever been. People who go straight into management from playing have got no training for that. Some find it difficult. I found it difficult. I was falling out with everyone and anyone when I was at Liverpool and Rangers.

He matured as a manager while on Merseyside, and in subsequent posts, but never lost the fiery streak so familiar to Rangers supporters. Even heart problems failed to curb his passion. Speaking to *The Observer* as he prepared to take his Blackburn Rovers side north to face Celtic in the UEFA Cup in 2002, Souness admitted:

Experience changes you. You're an absolute fool if you don't learn from your mistakes. People make a big deal about the medication I'm on and, physically, I suppose, I operate at a few levels down because of it. But mentally? Well . . . I've just been fined 15 grand. I'm still very passionate.

Anyone who remembers me at Rangers will recall that I was extremely confrontational. I realise now that it was the wrong attitude to have, but as a young man you won't be told anything. You think you've got all the answers, you're the bee's knees. Then things happen to you along the way that make you realise that you're not. But I have changed. My relationship with players is very different now.

The friendship between Murray and Souness survived the split. There may have been distance between them, but the two men remained in contact and there were repeated suggestions that Souness might one day return to the Ibrox manager's chair.

Those were strongest towards the end of 2005, when manager Alex McLeish was toiling and his predecessor Dick Advocaat was preparing to vacate his advisory role. Souness, himself struggling to turn around the fortunes of Newcastle United, was touted as the candidate of choice for the director-of-football role vacated by the Dutchman. It merited a response from Souness, who insisted: 'I have fondness for Rangers, but I have no interest in returning to the club.'

Instead, he watched from afar, no doubt hurt by the way in which the club began to unravel in the closing years of his friend's ownership. In an interview with the *Daily Mail* in 2009, after Murray stepped down from the chairman's role, Souness said:

> I think Sir David will be remembered as the greatest chairman Rangers ever had – and one of the most significant figures in the club's long history. How many league titles were won during his tenure? Or the number of trophies overall? If that's how you measure success, then he has been the greatest and presided over a huge era. Count the silverware and it tells its own story. I think it is a classic case that he will be more appreciated in later years once he has left Ibrox.

Souness claimed the exit strategy was no secret and no surprise, adding:

> I have known about this for some time and he feels the time is right. He has been involved for more than 20 years and everyone is entitled to weary a little of that. It's a fact that, right now, history is being unkind to Scottish football and David has felt the frustration of that for a while.
>
> He is a Rangers fan but every Old Firm supporter is feeling it right now as English Premier League clubs beat them to players. When you see the money around in England, then players will go to Burnley, Hull or West Brom before they sign for Rangers or Celtic – despite the fact the Old Firm are massive clubs.
>
> It is the same in the Champions League. There might be one or two shock results in the first group stages but, after Christmas, we will pretty much see the same line-up of super powers for the last sixteen or the last eight. David wanted to take Rangers to the latter stages of the Champions League – just like any fan. But the finances

of Scottish football make that an impossible dream.

Time will tell if he can let really go [*sic*]. I've known him a long time and he has enjoyed running Rangers – I think that is pretty obvious. He always had his finger on the pulse of the club. We will have to wait and see what happens. I don't know, because Rangers get under your skin and he has been there a long time.

He was young and keen when he arrived at 36 and I introduced him to the right people to buy the club. He didn't have any football experience. But, of course, he was a clever businessman. Let's just say he was a quick learner.

Murray did let go, albeit after protracted negotiations, and joined his one-time sidekick Souness among the ranks of former Rangers servants. But, as Souness will testify, once a Ranger, always a Ranger.

CHAPTER 12

'We're not denying we've got a problem but some people seem to put all the ills of Scottish society on Rangers.'

David Murray, 2008

THE WORLD MOVED on immeasurably during the two decades and more after David Murray swept into power at Ibrox. The Berlin Wall tumbled, apartheid ended and America elected its first black president. Some tremendous developments took place, but, on Scottish soil, the solution to ridding society and sport of sectarianism has proved a mountain too tall to scale. Initiatives, publicity drives, directives, government intervention, pleas, demands, punishments: all have been tried; none has succeeded.

The issue, so long centred on the Old Firm and Glasgow, has become a favourite in the debating chambers of the Edinburgh institution that is Holyrood. To employ an apt pun, sectarianism has become a political football for all the major parties to kick between them. The problem is that the end goal appears to be forever simply a dot on the horizon, never moving any closer.

In 2011, the politicking reached fever pitch. The now infamous touchline spat between Neil Lennon and Ally McCoist, the type of confrontation you could see on any Saturday afternoon up and down the land in public parks hosting amateur football, brought it to a head. But the pitch-side shenanigans did not happen in isolation; they came in the context of threats against Lennon in the shape of parcel bombs and of an infamous attack on the Celtic manager by a Hearts supporter at Tynecastle.

The result was a hastily convened summit involving police, football clubs, elected representatives and the game's governing body. The outcome was an announcement from the First Minister that new

133

legislation specifically designed to tackle sectarianism would be pushed through the parliament.

Among the measures planned by Alex Salmond was an increase in the maximum jail term for sectarian hate crime from six months to five years. Online bigotry and bile, such as death threats posted on the Internet, would become an offence and sectarian displays during football matches would be outlawed.

All sensible suggestions, even if they posed as many questions as answers. The main one being, why were these measures not already in place? Surely common sense would dictate that any form of death threat was already illegal? Never mind that. The aim was to press ahead with measures that were being heralded as somehow innovative.

Salmond said at the time: 'We've got a particular problem attaching itself like a parasite to our great game of football and that is now going to be eradicated. It's over. It's finished.' Laudable as the sentiment is, those were bold claims. Could Salmond and his government triumph where generations had met with failure in similar efforts to combat what any civilised person would identify as an obvious blight on the national game?

To dip back into football parlance, the First Minister's plans came unstuck even before a ball had been kicked. When the grand plan was first unveiled against a backdrop of what at times appeared to be public hysteria surrounding the issue, the intention was to have legislation in place for the start of the 2011–12 football season. After everyone paused for breath, it soon became clear that the consensus was that rushing new laws through the parliamentary process would be a recipe for disaster. Instead, in June 2011, a six-month delay was confirmed, allowing further discussion and consultation. A litany of concerns had been raised in the interim, not least the fact that singing national anthems including 'God Save the Queen' and 'Flower of Scotland' could be construed as offences under the draft legislation. The SNP moved quickly to dispel those particular fears but did have to admit that more time and diligence were required.

What must David Murray have made of it all as he watched from the sidelines? For the first time in almost a quarter of a century, he was a bystander rather than a participant. The issue had become Craig Whyte's to address; his was the new face representing Rangers in the discussions.

It is safe to assume that the perpetual sectarianism debate is one that Murray will not miss. Having spent years making great advances, he often found himself pushed back during his tenure as chairman and owner as individual incidents threatened to undo the good work being done at Ibrox.

During his stewardship, however, the greatest barriers to eradicating sectarianism were broken down. In fact, not just broken down – they were well and truly demolished and turned to dust.

From the moment Maurice Johnston was paraded in front of a shell-shocked media scrum in 1989, Murray signalled his intentions of ripping up the signing policy from a bygone era. His stewardship saw the first Catholic Rangers captain and the first Catholic Rangers manager. The progress made between 1988 and 2011 was huge.

The Johnston signing was brave and it was bold. He blazed a trail for a succession of Catholic players, and in time religion became an irrelevance. It was just as Murray and Graeme Souness had wanted: football ability became the criterion on which potential recruits were judged.

Arguably, it was the elevation of Lorenzo Amoruso to the role of skipper that completed the process. Walter Smith's decision to hand the armband to the larger-than-life Italian was part of the equation, with the adulation heaped upon the Continental defender by the Ibrox loyal the other important factor. He was accepted as a man, as a player and as a captain. Indeed, he still is.

Amoruso, his English still sharp years after perfecting the language in Glasgow, told me: 'You don't realise how important something is when you are in the middle of it. It is when you are older, as I am now, that you really appreciate those good times and the success we had.

'When I am in Glasgow now, I meet people who still go crazy. It is fantastic to see. I tried my best every time I pulled on a Rangers jersey and the fans respected that, as I respected them. To have brought some joy to those supporters makes me happy, whether it was with performances on the pitch or by stopping to sign autographs and talk to people in the street.'

When first approached to join the club in 1997, Amoruso was blissfully unaware of the sectarian background to the Scottish game. Still, he was quickly educated on the darker side of football in the country that would become his home and found out that his Catholic faith could potentially become a thorn in his side. A letter from somebody purporting to be a Celtic fan, telling him he had betrayed the Catholic religion by signing for Rangers, reinforced the strong opinions he would encounter.

He continued: 'I realised that almost as soon as I put my first foot in Glasgow. I knew it could be tough, especially as my first season was a nightmare. I was out injured for a long period and when I eventually came back I did not play well for the first few months. It was a nightmare.

'Expectations were very high and I wasn't living up to those, but I knew if I kept working hard then the real Lorenzo would shine through. That is what happened in the end.

'Some people tried to bring religion into it. It was stupid stuff. I felt some of the press did not like the fact that I was there in the Rangers team and seemed to blame the issue of my religion for some of those early performances. That made me even stronger and more determined to prove people wrong.

'David Murray has been a fantastic ambassador for the changes he made at the club. He was prepared to do whatever it took to make Rangers bigger and better in every way. It could not have been easy as a new chairman to come in and change the rules, even if those rules were never written in black and white. But he did, because he wanted to make the team and the club stronger.

'He made such a big impact and the success he enjoyed, not least with nine in a row, shows that he made the right decisions at the right times. He knew that if he could show what he was doing was right for the club, the fans would back him.'

Amoruso's appreciation of Murray stemmed from the pair's very first meeting, as plans for his £4-million-plus move from Fiorentina to Rangers gathered pace. He was flown to Glasgow for talks, and, after his very first meeting with the club's key men, he was sold on a switch to Scotland.

He told me: 'On the night I arrived in Glasgow, I met with David Murray and Walter Smith. We went and watched the Champions League final on the television, when Juventus were beaten 3–1 by Borussia Dortmund.

'From that first meeting, I knew all about their passion for Rangers and ambitions for the club. The next day, when I went to Ibrox, my mind was already made up about where my future would be.

'David Murray is a very charming person. He had been successful in life even before he was involved with Rangers, but he took the football club to a whole new level and had many important achievements.

'Of course I already knew about Rangers and about Celtic, that they were the biggest clubs in Scotland, but I did not realise just how huge Rangers was as a club or how passionate the supporters are until I had visited the city.

'It was special for me when the chairman and the manager talked to me about their plans for the future, the type of players they wanted to attract, and that they wanted me to be part of that. That was the major attraction for me and other players like me who came in from overseas – far more than simply money. There was great ambition.

'There was the opportunity to play in the Champions League and to win honours in Scotland, but it was more than that. The chairman's dream was to make Rangers stronger in Europe and to compete with the very best by investing in the team. He achieved that in performances, but unfortunately I do not think the results always reflected those performances. As a player you realise that results are always first in the mind of people looking in from across the world – but I always felt the team did not get the credit that was deserved at times in Europe.

'We beat the likes of Parma and other strong teams. We were one penalty and several missed chances away from beating Bayern Munich. I wish we could have progressed further in the Champions League, but it didn't happen for us.

'When you think about the people we had in the squad, and the size and depth of the quality in that squad, you realise it was a very good time. Not many teams in the world have a group like the one we had. There were some very special players and very powerful characters.

'We developed a different attitude over time, a more European approach. We became more confident about our strength and our ability to go face to face with any team we faced. I'm disappointed we didn't get the credit or the reward for that. As captain, I could see my team getting stronger and stronger every year.

'It was a very special moment for me when I was asked to become captain. As a foreigner coming into any league, it would not be common to become captain. Had it not been for a stupid decision by Dick Advocaat to take the armband away from me, I would have been captain for far longer – but even after he made that decision I continued to act and serve in the same way and I always had the respect of the rest of the players on the pitch and in the dressing-room.

'At Bari and Fiorentina, I had not been captain, but I had approached my work as though I was. I was always outspoken and a dominant character, because I believed it was the right thing to do. That was the same at Rangers, even if Advocaat disagreed. In the end, I stayed longer than he did and went on to enjoy great moments.'

Life was many things with Amoruso in the team, but it was never dull. His dashing raids forward, his penchant for potshots from free kicks from any range or angle and his heart-on-sleeve performances all livened up life at Ibrox. He played more like a Scot than an Italian, an all-action performer, and that stemmed from his swift introduction to the values and traditions of the Rangers Football Club.

He recalled: 'The attitude of the chairman, and others behind the scenes such as Sandy Jardine and John Greig, meant we knew exactly what Rangers stood for. We knew what it meant to play for the club, to play for the jersey. That was the message from David Murray. He wanted us to learn quickly and to be proud of our team.

'Jörg Albertz and I, as well as a few of the other foreign players, understood that, and I think it showed in our attitude and performances. When I watch English football, it is clear to me that there are not many of the overseas players who have that passion for their club or understanding of what it means to the supporters.'

Rangers supporters had seen the fabric of their side change dramatically in a relatively short period of time, not least with the way in which Murray, Souness and successive managers had banished the religious considerations of previous regimes.

But the internal changes were not enough. The demand was for the chairman and his club to mastermind a complete reversal of centuries-old attitudes in the west of Scotland and the abandonment of traditions that for tens of thousands on both sides of the Old Firm wall were part of the fabric of their family lives.

Towards the end of Murray's time in charge, the weariness was becoming apparent. In an interview with *The Times* in 2008, he said:

> Years ago we signed Maurice Johnston as a football player first, but also to break the tradition of this club not signing a Roman Catholic – that had been wrong, we did the right thing, and that situation has improved beyond all measure.
>
> But there is still a rump of our fans whose behaviour is totally unacceptable. In Manchester there was no excuse for what happened, you can't defend the behaviour of some of our fans. In some ways it was unfortunate that the UEFA final was in Manchester – it was too easy to get there. We were happy to be in the final, but Manchester wasn't ready for the party, and a minority spoilt it for us.
>
> You can talk about good PR but it's quite hard to stick up for people behaving like that. We have an element in our support whose behaviour is totally unacceptable, but there are only so many times you can say, 'It's unacceptable, it's unacceptable.' Having said that, there are more important things going on in society than bigotry. I hope there's no one in Scotland dying because of sectarianism, but there are certainly people dying today because of drug abuse and obesity.
>
> I do think Rangers have become a soft touch for many of the politicians. We're not denying we've got a problem but some people seem to put all the ills of Scottish society on Rangers. Get off our backs and let us play football.

And that was before Salmond's hastily constructed bill had been put together, before parliamentary summits or anything of the like. In so many ways, Murray's actions spoke louder than words ever could.

The Mo Johnston signing was a seminal moment for the club, its manager and its chairman. Today, most supporters would be hard pushed to pinpoint the religion of each and every member of the Ibrox squad. In the 1980s, there was no such difficulty.

It is easy to forget how huge that acquisition was. Granted, it wasn't simply a case of signing a Catholic player – he was, after all, no 'ordinary' Catholic player. It is also easy to forget how high tensions ran at that time, the gauntlet that Murray, Souness and Johnston all ran together. Scarves were burned in the street, season-ticket books ripped up in protest. The row rumbled on for days, weeks and months as views on the finer points of the landmark decision were aired with varying degrees of restraint.

I can remember making a visit to Ibrox one weekday early in Johnston's time on the staff. From the outside, all appeared calm, everything was normal. On the inside, there was a subtle reminder that Glasgow was a powder keg waiting to ignite – it was metallic dark grey, wore the three-pointed Mercedes star on its bonnet and was parked snugly alongside the pitch. Johnston's car could not be left in the street; instead, it had to be carefully manoeuvred into the safe confines of the stadium each morning to guard against the more sinister elements of the city's football followers while he went about his business at training.

Johnston had been the subject of death threats and the security surrounding his wheels was matched by the precautions taken to protect the player, a far more valuable asset than his German sports car. A 24-hour bodyguard was employed, even after the Glaswegian had opted to base himself in Edinburgh in a further attempt to put distance between him and the unsavoury elements back home.

It must have been an incredible strain for any individual to live under, although performances on the park did not suffer as Johnston set about doing what he did best. At least for 90 minutes on a Saturday he could leave the troubles behind and focus on football.

Of course, he could easily have saved himself the inconvenience by refusing to sign for Rangers; Souness and Murray could have rejected the idea too, if they had thought differently about the prospect of recruiting such a controversial figure. But they didn't. They chose to confront the elephant in the room and try to reset the Old Firm psyche.

Rangers fan Bill McMurdo, Johnston's agent at the time, had as big a part to play as anybody. He was said to have been frustrated that his player had spoken to Celtic without his knowledge, hoping to engineer

139

a return to Parkhead. When McMurdo flagged up to Graeme Souness that the deal was not complete, the seed was sown.

There was no doubting that Souness had the courage to go through with the most controversial transfer Scottish football has ever seen. Would his chairman share that bravery and throw caution to the wind. The answer? A resounding yes.

Souness later reflected:

> It was a complicated matter signing Maurice and we knew it would create special problems for the club and ourselves – but we agreed that a Catholic had to be signed at some stage and it was never going to be a token transfer, it needed to be someone we wanted for his football ability. Mo fitted that description.

Murray, addressing the decision to sign a Catholic player and buck the trend of decades, remarked in a 2002 interview with the BBC:

> I thought we had the social responsibility to take away this tarnish from the club. It was the ultimate signing – but we thought it was the right thing to do football-wise. He was a brave little bugger at the time.

That courage was shared by Murray, and if he is remembered for nothing else, he should go down as the chairman who had the guts to break with tradition and follow his principles. He stuck to them too, even in the most testing of circumstances.

In 1999, the furore surrounding then vice chairman Donald Findlay's renditions of the 'The Sash' and a sectarian version of 'Follow Follow', exposed in newspaper reports, put the club back in the glare of the nation's media for the wrong reasons.

The exposé came during one of the many anti-sectarianism drives led by Murray, and Findlay's departure was deemed the only course of action. His resignation from the board was accepted. The vice chairman penned an open letter to announce his departure, stating:

> The events of Saturday night were a serious misjudgement on my part. It was a private function to celebrate a successful season. It is disappointing that someone attending should have felt it necessary to go to the press. However, even at such a function my conduct was not acceptable and I ought to have realised this. I regret any harm done to the club I care about deeply. I apologise unreservedly for the offence caused to anyone. I will continue to be the Rangers supporter I am.

The issue continued to rear its head in various guises, with Murray leaping to the defence of John Greig when the Gers director was the subject of a mischief-making report illustrated with a nine-year-old image of him apparently miming the action of a flute player.

Those incidents, and the similarly high-profile furore stoked up by Paul Gascoigne's impromptu flute routine on the pitch during an Old Firm match, proved to be rare blips during a period of concerted efforts to stamp out sectarianism.

Various initiatives were introduced over the years and the results were tangible, leading to frustration on the part of Murray on occasions when the good work was ignored by outsiders. In time, he became more and more defensive about the club's record of tackling the issue of sectarianism.

In 2004, it was Celtic and, in particular Martin O'Neill, who incurred the wrath of the Rangers owner. O'Neill claimed that 'racial and sectarian' abuse had been directed at Neil Lennon during an Old Firm encounter. Murray took the bull by the horns, claiming:

> We should, without doubt, guard against broad generalisations by individuals that endeavour to blacken the name of Rangers FC and stereotype our fans as racist bigots. This is not acceptable. The vast majority of those that support and follow our club are decent, respectable people and it would be wrong for me just to sit back and allow them to be condemned in this way. Collectively we should remind ourselves that there remains a minimum of two Old Firm games still to be played this season and both clubs should appreciate their responsibility in ensuring safety and fair play, irrespective of the result.

He went head to head with First Minister Jack McConnell in the months that followed. McConnell had labelled religious bigotry as 'Scotland's shame' and Murray labelled that outburst as 'disrespectful' to both Rangers and Celtic. He said: 'I don't think he took on board all the work that has been going on behind the scenes. His statement was made without having all the relevant facts in front of him.'

That work included the issuing of codes of conduct for employees and supporters of the club. A *Panorama* investigation into the issue in 2005 did not portray the club in a good light, however. Murray again came out fighting, insisting:

> There is simply no place for the FTP brigade and those who would have us wading through Fenian blood. We have tried to be pro-

active in terms of the Ibrox atmosphere by encouraging fans to sing traditional club songs without additional sectarian lyrics. These things take time but at least we are trying through a variety of platforms – most importantly by educating the next generation.

In 2005, both sides of the Old Firm joined forces with Communities Scotland in a £450,000 pilot scheme designed to build bridges between the rivals through programmes in 140 primary schools throughout Glasgow. Rangers and Celtic coaches worked in schools to train youngsters while delivering an anti-sectarian message. In the same year, two ten-point plans were introduced to further focus the minds of club officials and supporters.

It prompted Murray to remark:

> I think the bigotry problem has improved dramatically at Ibrox in my tenure. Behaviour has improved dramatically. It's improving but we've a bit to go.
>
> In my first season here, we averaged 120 to 130 arrests at a Rangers–Celtic game. On many occasions, you can actually get more arrests at a Hibernian or Aberdeen game for a variety of reasons.
>
> The vast majority of fans have improved dramatically. Every football club has them, there are still a few people who don't behave correctly and we are aiming that [the initiatives] at them. But Rangers fans should be applauded.

The action plans were just part of a string of educational programmes pioneered over the course of two decades. Success was difficult to measure, whereas negative incidents were easy to highlight.

In 2006, Rangers were fined £9,000 for an attack by fans on the Villareal team bus before a Champions League match in Spain and subsequent damage to the host team's stadium. But, crucially, the club and its supporters were cleared of allegations of sectarian behaviour. For Murray, it was vindication for the efforts being made to rid the club of its reputation for prejudice, and he commented:

> We were confident throughout that the tremendous efforts made by the club to tackle sectarianism, racism and all other forms of inappropriate behaviour over a protracted period would be recognised and acknowledged by UEFA. Few clubs in Europe can match the sustained effort we've made in this respect over the past five years and even less would have been able, within the tight

deadlines imposed by UEFA, to produce such comprehensive material to support this.

Murray did strike a word of caution when he said:

> None of this, however, should mask the fact that sectarianism remains a very serious problem within Scottish society and it now has to stop. Nothing in our submission to UEFA denied this fact. A minority of our supporters are going to have to realise, and realise very quickly, that the controlling authorities in football, whether FIFA, UEFA, the SFA and SPL or the SFL, are going to be obliged almost immediately to impose the heaviest possible sanctions for discriminatory behaviour.
>
> This, of course, could involve matches being played behind closed doors, a particular stand or stands being closed down, percentage reductions in authorised capacities, points deducted or, in the worst-case scenario, suspension altogether from competitions. It's time for the 90-minute bigots to remain silent; for others to speak out, exerting a peer pressure on those that disgrace their clubs; and for the promotion of decent football songs and chants, of which there are many.
>
> There is nothing wrong with intense rivalry, but it has to exist within a respectable environment where everyone, no matter their religion, colour, age, sex or background, feels completely comfortable. This is what Rangers FC has sought to achieve with the establishment of an in-house sectarian and racism monitoring committee. These fans now have to be totally committed as we move forward or the social, and perhaps financial, implications for Rangers could be severe.

The negative publicity generated by the sectarianism allegations was as much of a concern for Murray and his executive team as any of the fiscal penalties open to the game's rulers. Time after time, he saw own goals scored by fans, with the advent of the Internet only serving to intensify the risks. Speaking at the annual meeting in 2008, the owner said:

> We have people involved with this club who put bile – that's the word for it – on websites every day. All we are doing is playing into the hands of the media.
>
> I've repeatedly said that Scotland's shame is not sectarianism – it's drugs and obesity. In the 20 years I've been at this club, there

has been a vast, vast improvement on the behaviour of sectarianism at the club. Then we don't help ourselves by giving people stuff on a daily basis.

But all the problems with Scottish sectarianism should not be just put at the feet of Rangers Football Club. Some people who are supposedly supporters need to have a hard look at themselves. Not all of our supporters are pulling in the right direction and they give the media it on a plate.

During the 2006–07 season, plans to play long-forgotten Rangers songs over the tannoy at Ibrox, complete with lyric sheets for supporters, were announced. The idea had first been floated during meetings between supporters' groups and Murray over the summer. Anti-sectarian videos were also used on coaches transporting fans to European ties. During the same campaign, a fans' charter was drawn up to put the ideas in black and white, following on from the successful Pride Over Prejudice campaign that had run for two years up to that point.

The chairman, speaking after UEFA overturned its earlier decision and fined the club for 'discriminatory chanting' by its fans, told Rangers TV:

> The supporters need to show a certain level of integrity and behaviour in the grounds. But, if they don't, be prepared for the consequences.
>
> We are creating initiatives for match days, we've been meeting supporters' groups, we've been meeting editors of newspapers, we have been pleading with the fans to show respect.
>
> There is only so much the club can do. We can only reiterate it before every match. But, if we have a small group of fans who want to continue to behave in such a manner, they're doing no service to this club whatsoever and I am sorry to say it, but in the modern world we live in, that behaviour is totally unacceptable.
>
> You can only receive so many warnings and we will receive a stiffer penalty of which every decent ordinary Rangers fan will suffer, so I just ask those people who wish to continue to sing such songs to please stop. You are jeopardising the future of our club.

It was an impassioned plea from an increasingly desperate man. Every fine and every threat from the game's governing bodies was sapping vital funds from the club but also draining the man at the top as his best efforts met with resistance from a small minority.

EMPIRE: David Murray built his business into a global enterprise, working from his offices in Edinburgh.

HISTORY: The grand façade at Ibrox has remained untouched, but the Main Stand was developed with the addition of the top deck to boost capacity and earning potential.

GROUNDBREAKING: Mo Johnston, led by Graeme Souness as the chairman looks on, is introduced to the media as a Rangers player.

PROFILE: David Murray, pictured with VIP guest Sean Connery at Ibrox, became one of Scotland's most prominent figures through his business and football achievements.

SPORTSMAN: Rugby was David Murray's passion as a keen player with Dalkeith, before a serious road accident ended his days on the field. Murray is pictured (back row, second from left) with his teammates at the east coast club. (copyright unknown)

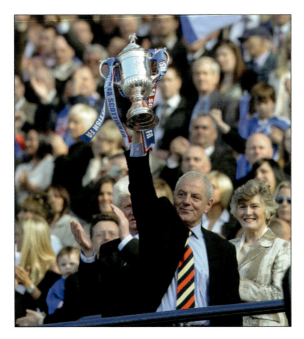

LEGEND: Walter Smith holds aloft the Scottish Cup, just one of the many honours the veteran coach won during his two stints as Ibrox boss.

STAR: The Great Dane, Brian Laudrup, was one of the best-value big-money buys ever made by Rangers.

TALISMAN: Paul Gascoigne, pictured celebrating eight in a row, was a driving force during vital seasons at Ibrox.

UNVEILING: Manager Dick Advocaat reveals the choice of name for the new Rangers training complex in 2001.

LEGACY: The Murray Park complex is one of the tangible assets from the Murray years, bearing the then owner's name in testament to his vision for the training base.

RECRUIT: Tore André Flo, the record-breaking £12-million man, celebrates a rare Rangers goal during his unremarkable Ibrox stint.

PRIDE: Alex McLeish was drafted in to provide pragmatism and good old-fashioned Scottish passion at Ibrox.

FLOP: Frenchman Paul Le Guen's appointment proved to be David Murray's only mistake when it came to choosing Rangers managers.

SUCCESSOR: Craig Whyte, pictured settling into his new surroundings at Ibrox, found himself in the limelight when he arrived as chairman after replacing David Murray as owner.

CONCERN: Craig Whyte takes his seat in the Ibrox directors' box alongside former chairman John McClelland (left), who was one of those to express grave concerns about the new owner's suitability.

CASUALTY: Gordon Smith (right) was employed by Craig Whyte, but became the first to lose his job when the administrators moved in.

He once admitted:

> I have found myself watching games on Sky and sometimes I cringe
> . . . It's unacceptable and I am asking our fans to think twice about
> singing songs like this. You can't change a club in a year or so, it
> takes an era. But I think fewer fans are singing sectarian songs now
> and I won't be happy until they are wiped out altogether.

Murray even went so far as to consider not accepting tickets for away
ties in Europe, such was the concern at board level about the prospect
of further sanctions.

Meanwhile, novel steps were being taken to further address the issue.
In 2007, an Old Firm encounter at Ibrox had a twist to it as leaders
from the Church of Scotland and the Catholic Church joined
counterparts from the Muslim, Hindu and Sikh faiths. A similar fact-
finding mission to Parkhead had taken place earlier in the year. It was
just another indication of the strenuous efforts being made to create an
inclusive atmosphere in Old Firm football.

All the time, however, the criticism continued to flow. Murray was
consistently irked by the 'Scotland's shame' tag attached to the sectarian
issues. The Rangers chairman argued that the lack of opportunities for
children in sport would be more deserving of that title. Commenting in
October 2008, he said:

> You would not think that Scotland has even emerged from the dark
> ages in terms of racism and sectarianism when you see the endless
> obsession there is with these issues that now involves clubs,
> supporters, the media and politicians.
>
> The reality is that sectarianism and racism are not the problems
> they once were in this country. It would be absurd to suggest these
> problems do not exist, but we need to put them in perspective.

Perspective: not a word that has often been applied to the very real
issues of bigotry and sectarianism in football.

To put the issue in some form of perspective, think back to 1988. It
was a time when a high-profile Catholic had never played for Rangers
Football Club. It was a time when it was unthinkable for a prominent
Catholic to pull on the blue jersey, never mind captain the team with
the spirit, bravado and pomp that Lorenzo Amoruso did.

The extent of the change at Ibrox, led by the man at the very top,
cannot be overstated. Perhaps in time David Murray will get credit for
playing his part in making Scottish football a better and more tolerant

place. Unfortunately, no matter how much progress is made, as long as sectarianism remains a part, no matter how small, of our game, the good work will never be deemed to have been a success in the eyes of those looking in from the outside.

CHAPTER 13

'The chairman's abiding legacy will be the success Rangers enjoyed under his stewardship. At this club, working in our unique environment, trophies are your only currency.'

Walter Smith, 2009

IT COULD HAVE been an agonising decision. Replacing the extrovert, world-renowned and über-confident Graeme Souness should have been a demanding task for a chairman set to make his first managerial appointment. But it wasn't. Within moments of Souness tendering his resignation in 1991, the single-minded David Murray had decided exactly who would be taking the place of the former Scotland skipper in the Ibrox dugout.

Walter Smith was not a glamorous choice and nor was he a safe choice. He was, after all, completely untested as a manager in his own right. He had a solid playing background with provincial teams but none of the accolades that Souness could boast. He had a steely will to win but not the overbearing character of the man he had assisted for the previous five years. Nor did he have the public profile of some of the established managers vying for the coveted role.

Yet, for Murray, there was only one man for the job. The chairman declared: 'There was never any doubt Walter would be the next manager. He has a wonderful pedigree and has been waiting for his chance. He was appointed within minutes of Graeme Souness deciding to leave for Liverpool.'

Souness would dearly have loved to have taken his loyal assistant with him on his Anfield adventure but had to accept there was no contest between a second-in-command role and the opportunity to manage the team that Smith had cheered from the terraces as a boy. It was a humbling experience for a man who had never lost sight of his roots and who had worked tirelessly for more than a decade to put himself in a position to take on one of the biggest jobs in British, and European, club football.

Reflecting on his big break, Smith, in a round of press interviews in 2009, said:

> When Graeme Souness left, the environment was different to now and the chairman could have gone anywhere to get a new manager. I had no track record as a manager and he could have gone for someone with a track record behind them. He took a chance on me, gave me an opportunity to get into management, the opportunity I wanted, which could not have been an easy decision to make. I will always be grateful to him for that.
>
> It is difficult to know what would have happened if he had chosen someone else. Graeme also gave me the opportunity to go with him but there were too many people at Liverpool at that stage. I didn't want to go. There was no guarantee of a job here at that stage. Maybe I would be back in my old job at Dalmarnock power station now, I don't know.

There was never any danger that Smith would find himself back working in his pre-football trade as an electrician, but the sentiment was genuine. Smith will forever be grateful for the opportunities presented to him and that attitude is what sets him apart from so many in football. Through all the success and the adulation, he never forgot those who had helped him along the way or those around him who played a part, no matter how big or small, in his triumphs.

He served his apprenticeship the hard way, working his way up through the system as a coach under Jim McLean at Dundee United before becoming assistant manager at Tannadice and then being lured back to the west coast by Rangers to lend valuable knowledge of the Scottish game to the incoming Souness.

When he accepted that post in 1986, he could not have envisaged what lay in store as he set off on an incredible and exhilarating career journey. Rangers manager, Everton manager, Scotland manager and an Ibrox return – the tools of the electrical trade remained firmly in their box as the inexperienced manager Murray had put his faith in carved out a reputation as the godfather of coaching north of the border.

He may not have had the benefit of the pre-football relationship that Souness and Murray had enjoyed, but in time the links between Smith and his chairman grew just as strong. He was Murray's right-hand man, far more than simply a football manager, and the two had a mutual respect.

That type of kinship has been a common theme through all of Murray's managerial appointments and close working relationships have also been key to his business life. He puts his utmost trust in senior management and expects loyalty in return. From Smith, he certainly got that. The former Ibrox boss has said:

> The chairman always had a great relationship with his managers. You can see that when the club has get-togethers. There are not many clubs where the managers who have been there are happy to come back. But every one of the boys who have had Sir David as chairman are always ready and willing to come to any function. That says a lot.

Murray in turn had great respect for the manager, born of Smith's long and carefully cultivated coaching CV, which won him admirers throughout Scottish football and beyond.

He served for nine years through the latter part of the 1960s and first half of the '70s as a dependable player for Dundee United, joining Dumbarton in 1975 for a two-year stint with the Sons. Jim McLean lured him back to Tayside within two years with the promise of a player-coach role. Smith quickly became hot property. Alex Ferguson, newly installed at Aberdeen, had wanted him to head up the A90 and become his assistant manager at Pittodrie, but McLean beat off the competition. In 1982, he promoted Smith to the assistant's role at Tannadice at the tender age of 34.

Within a year, St Mirren had tested the water with an approach when they were seeking a new manager at Love Street, but Smith's loyalty was to McLean and Dundee United. His reward, in 1986, was a place on the board at Tannadice and what looked to be a certain career path as successor to his mentor.

But soon the lure of Ibrox would put that plan to the test, and Rangers won the day, with Smith joining the cause at the end of the 1985–86 season to take temporary charge of the side while he and the rest of the club awaited the arrival of new gaffer Souness as he fulfilled his commitments with Sampdoria.

Smith's intimate knowledge of the Scottish Premier Division would be heavily relied upon by the new manager and they worked in tandem to build a team capable of beating the best in the land, including the New Firm duo of Dundee United and Aberdeen, which had caused such a headache for the Old Firm over the course of a decade. Smith had played a part in that during his role at United, and he proved he knew how to turn the tables on the young upstarts of the Dons and

Arabs when he moved to the other side of the fence.

By the time Souness departed five years later, there was even more depth to Smith's CV, which already included working with Scotland's Under-21 side during Jock Stein's tenure and serving as assistant to Alex Ferguson at the 1986 World Cup finals.

Crucially, Smith had the total respect of the squad of stars he was set to inherit. It was an appointment that made perfect sense and the results spoke volumes.

Archie Knox was brought north from Manchester United to become his right-hand man and the pair delivered the title in the summer of 1991, completing the job Souness had started.

Murray said at the time:

> In the past, we have needed a high-profile manager to get big players to come here. We don't need that any more. If good players become available then there will be money to go and buy them. I don't see any less money being made available to Walter than Graeme had.

Smith guided his team to the championship in each of the following six seasons and completed the nine in a row mission. A hat-trick of Scottish Cup successes and a matching set of League Cup wins, with a domestic treble in 1992–93 into the bargain, only added to his credentials as one of the greatest managers ever to serve at Ibrox.

There was also the highlight of narrowly missing out to Marseille in the race for a place in the 1993 Champions League final, the first of two notable European runs for the manager over two periods in charge.

The first of those chapters ended in 1998 and did so on a low note. Hopes had been high for a historic ten-in-a-row triumph to bow out on, after Smith had announced his decision to step aside earlier in the 1997–98 campaign. But the dream ending was not to be, and the baton was passed to Dick Advocaat.

When the curtain began to fall on Smith's time as manager in the spring of 1998, the club made it clear there was still a place for him at Ibrox. Indeed, the lauded coach was rewarded with a testimonial match against Liverpool in the closing months of his tenure, as a mark of appreciation for his sterling service.

Whether to soften the blow of Smith's imminent replacement by Advocaat or in genuine anticipation of a lasting relationship, directors made public noises about the prospects of Smith extending his connection with the club in a new role.

It was suggested he could become a general manager, following the model adopted by Celtic with the installation of Jock Brown, or perhaps work in a consultancy capacity with a view towards scouting youth and foreign talent. The latter job description was one that Murray was initially believed to have earmarked for Kenny Dalglish, whom he was thought to have been keen to bring in to work in tandem with team boss Smith prior to his decision to step down.

The only word of caution was the admission that the club fully expected Smith to attract interest from English clubs, suggesting the bluster surrounding the likelihood of a long-term role for him in Glasgow shrouded a realisation that their man was destined for front-line duties elsewhere.

As it happened, Smith did remain in place long enough to take on a new job – and the description came straight out of left field. No consultancy role, no lofty boardroom perch. Instead, according to the announcement at the end of the 1997–98 season, he would remain at the coal face, passing on his experience in the more humble capacity of manager of the reserve and youth teams. Described as a sideways step for the veteran coach, the role prevented the scenario, possible if Smith had been handed a more senior role, of Advocaat arriving and having to bow to Smith's superiority.

As anticipated, however, the hugely experienced coach was a man in demand. The English Premier League was calling, and it was Everton who made the move in the face of competition from Sheffield Wednesday, installing Smith as successor to Howard Kendall in 1998.

It was a very different club from the one he had left behind, with financial constraints proving a constant frustration. Rather than chasing honours, he was left to try to keep the sleeping giant alive in the top flight against the odds. When fans' favourite Duncan Ferguson was sold to Newcastle to balance the books early in Smith's stay on Merseyside, the manager's own future at the club was shadowed with doubt as he came to terms with the challenge he faced.

He regrouped, however, and came out fighting, keeping Everton in the promised land of the Premier League throughout his time in England – even calling upon his old talisman Paul Gascoigne during that period. It was not enough for the club's board, who replaced Smith with fellow Scottish coaching product Davie Moyes in the spring of 2002.

But you can't keep a good coach down. When Smith returned to centre stage in 2005 as Scotland manager, he proved that he had lost none of his desire. He hauled the national team from the path of alarming decline charted under Berti Vogts and back on the road to respectable performances. A 1–1 World Cup qualifying draw with Italy and the memorable 1–0 victory over France at Hampden in the European Championship qualifiers proved that, even with scant playing resources, it was possible to compete with the game's leading lights.

The shock result against the French proved to be Smith's penultimate match in charge, with the call from David Murray seeing him resign from the Scotland job to make an emotional return to Ibrox in January 2007. Smith admitted that it had been a torturous decision, but in the end club won over country. When Murray left Rangers, Smith said:

> Sir David is one of the big reasons I came back to Rangers from the job I had with Scotland. That was a job I didn't think I'd leave. It was not an easy decision. The lure of returning to Ibrox was huge, as was working with him. First and foremost, and even he would say it, the lure of Rangers is the main thing. But had it been any other chairman, it would have been an even harder decision.

The move provoked a storm of controversy among the Tartan Army, or at least those without Rangers leanings.

Paul Le Guen had quit Ibrox on 4 January. Within a day, reports of a meeting between Murray and Scotland duo Smith and Ally McCoist emerged. In his hour of need, Murray had turned to his trusted ally.

Smith, however, had 18 months remaining on his contract. He had steered Scotland to a stunning start to the Euro 2008 qualifying campaign, with the national team perched at the top of Group B, ahead of both Italy and France, and the SFA were intent on holding out for substantial compensation. The issue rumbled on for days as offer and counter-offer were batted back and forth between Hampden and Ibrox.

Smith took matters into his own hands when he quit and accepted a three-year contract with Rangers, taking Scotland coach McCoist with him as assistant manager. He offered the olive branch of retaining his Scotland duties on a part-time basis but was not taken up on the idea.

Murray stood accused of jeopardising the national team's chances of qualification for Euro 2008 for his own self-interest. Guilty as charged, Murray said: 'I'm not involved in the SFA. I must do the best for Rangers. This is the best for Rangers.'

The old partnership had been restored and the big question was whether they could return to the winning ways that had been a hallmark of their working relationship previously. Smith answered in resounding fashion, overcoming an ever-diminishing budget for transfers and wages to restore the Light Blues to their place at the top of the Scottish football tree.

Smith's decision to take McCoist with him, giving the Ibrox legend his first coaching role at the club, was no surprise. Even when Super Ally was a player, Murray had hinted that he had plans for the striker. As the veteran forward wound down his career in the late 1990s, the chairman had made noises about getting him involved in Dick Advocaat's coaching team. That never did come to fruition, with McCoist instead choosing to extend his playing career with Kilmarnock, but clearly the seed had been planted more than a decade before Murray eventually elevated the former striker to the manager's chair.

In November 2008, as Murray celebrated his 20th anniversary as Rangers owner, there was the first confirmation of the succession plan that everyone took for granted: Super Ally would become Gaffer Ally. Murray said:

> I would have thought, all things being equal, that he will become manager. Walter and I discussed it when he came back, that McCoist would come in, hopefully we would get back to a successful period and then he would get the chance. It will be success driven. If we are successful, if Walter is successful, then the natural successor would be McCoist. But if we go another two or three years without winning the league then we will all be under pressure. You wouldn't have thought of him as a manager 20 years ago, would you?

Smith was determined to make it happen and said:

> I hope Alistair does get the opportunity. He finds himself in the same situation I was in with Graeme Souness. I was assistant manager a bit longer than Alistair has been but, once you've been assistant manager for a few years, you want to take the job. He has the opportunity to take over here but he will only get the opportunity if we are successful – and I was the same. If Graeme hadn't had the level of success as manager, I don't think I would have been asked to take over.

League championship wins in 2008, 2009 and 2010 ensured the succession plan did come to fruition. There were also triumphs in the Scottish Cup in 2007–08 and 2008–09 and in the League Cup in 2007–08, 2008–09, 2009–10 and 2010–11.

Sandwiched in between was the UEFA Cup run of 2007–08, when Smith's resilient and plucky troops took the Rangers support on an adventure they had not experienced since the heady days of 1972. It culminated in Manchester with the final against Zenit St Petersburg, proving that Scottish clubs did not have to be also-rans in the race for European honours. An agonising 2–0 defeat against the Russians denied Smith the Continental cup that he and the Rangers owner craved, but that did not detract from the achievement of taking his side to the final or from the fact that he had restored domestic dominance to the Ibrox agenda.

The second batch of trophies was won in a very different manner from Smith's array of honours during his first spell in charge. The days of multimillion-pound superstar recruits were long gone, and for large swathes of his second spell in charge, it proved impossible to recruit players at all.

Still, Smith remained defiant in his support for his embattled chairman. When Murray announced his intention to step down from the top job in 2009, it was the manager who led the tributes. He said:

> There have been chairmen of Rangers and owners of Rangers. But, until David, no one had ever been chairman and owner. When I think about the pressures of my job I remember the chairman was in his own highly pressurised zone for over two decades and that's a remarkable achievement considering the changes which took place within football at that time.
>
> That's why it's been a strange week for me. I'm trying to come to terms with the fact that the man I've worked with since the '80s, and who was instrumental in me becoming Rangers manager, isn't at the club any more. It's taking a bit of getting used to for me, I can tell you.
>
> The chairman's abiding legacy will be the success Rangers enjoyed under his stewardship. At this club, working in our unique environment, trophies are your only currency.
>
> But there were occasions when I realised you can never do enough for some people. The chairman had been a big part of it when we reached the UEFA Cup final. At the start of the following season he came out into the directors' box and I went to the dugout to see a banner saying 'We Deserve Better'.

Nobody had a better insight into the stresses and strains endured by Murray than Smith, a man who had worked with him for longer than any other manager. The coach had his own problems to contend with during his times in charge but insisted that those paled into insignificance in comparison with the burden shouldered by his employer. He said:

> I'm four years older than the chairman but haven't had twenty years

of sustained pressure to deal with at Rangers. I think for somebody to handle the post of Rangers chairman as Sir David did for 20 years was nothing short of remarkable. Since football became a more financially based game he has been the person who has had to bear the brunt of finding the finance to keep his club at the forefront.

I think he has done an incredible job and the testimony is the number of trophies he has won. I don't think there is anyone who could have handled the situation as well as he has done. Just look at the success and the trophies that have come to Rangers during his time as chairman.

Longevity is not so common in football these days and over the last ten years football has become really financially orientated. At the moment there are very few clubs successful on a budget, so to speak. Therefore, you have to try as best you can to keep up and Sir David handled that side of things extremely well.

Of course, there were strong personal reasons for Smith's unstinting loyalty to Murray. He was the man who made a dream come true by appointing him manager in 1991. He was the man who had given Smith an unexpected second crack at the Ibrox job.

Ever the realist, Smith believed that second approach in 2007 could have been the move that extended his career beyond its natural life. He added:

Who knows if I'd still be in football at all by now if that call hadn't come? International managers appear not to get a lot of time if anything goes wrong. What I do know is the man who brought me back to Rangers will be a hard act to follow.

He could not pin down a highlight of the pair's working relationship, insisting: 'I don't think you can take things in isolation. Too many years have passed for that. The biggest indication of Sir David's work is, as I have said, the trophies and his relationships with people.'

Tellingly, Murray's stepping down and handing the chairmanship to Alastair Johnston marked the end of Smith's tenure at the club. He confirmed he would not be seeking a new contract as manager and that the wheels had been set in motion for Ally McCoist to take over, following the succession plan laid down by the departing chairman and owner.

It had been an honour to serve Rangers, but the appetite to continue under a new and unknown owner was not there. For decades, David Murray had been entwined with Ibrox life, and Smith had been part of that story.

Now, as one prepared to move on, the other laid his own exit plans. Smith said: 'He gave me my biggest opportunity and, when he asked me to come back, it was obvious to repay him. I hope, by what we've achieved in the last couple of years, that I've done a bit of that.'

As Smith prepared to leave, he did so with a word of caution for the prospective new owners who were circling around Rangers at that time. Quite simply, he felt repeating the achievements of the Murray years would be an impossibility:

> When you've been chairman of a club for 20 years, you always look at what has been achieved on the pitch. In football, that's the most important area of a club. Rangers have been extremely successful under his ownership over those 20 years. It's possibly not been enough for a lot of people, but I don't think anybody will ever achieve that at Rangers. Over the last 20 years, he has been the person who has led from the front and Rangers have had an extremely successful period while he has been the chairman. That's what he should be remembered for.

CHAPTER 14

'Of course I'd take satisfaction out of nine in a row
– I'd love to see nineteen in a row – but it's
becoming a real strain on us.'

David Murray, 1996

ON 7 MAY 1997, it happened. Nine in a row, the ambition that had been a distant dream when David Murray had swept into power at Rangers in 1988, was realised. The blue half of Glasgow partied, Gers fans across the world rejoiced. The players had become legends, the manager an immortal, and the chairman had put his indelible mark on the history of the institution of which he served as custodian.

Of all the playing successes during the past quarter of a century, the ninth league crown is the one that gave the most satisfaction to the Bear on the street. There had been highs and lows along the way, but mainly highs. The run had teetered on the brink of failure at times but was always pulled back to ensure the juggernaut thundered on, with Murray and Walter Smith at the helm.

The win-or-bust match against Aberdeen in 1991 was one of those nerve-shredding, fingernail-chewing moments. One Mark Hateley double later and the doubts were cast aside; the joy of nine was back on the agenda. That match, when the Dons had to be defeated at Ibrox to prevent them snatching the Premier Division crown from Rangers' hands, has been cited by Murray as one of the defining memories of his chairmanship. It was a never-say-die display that typified all that was good about his tenure. Because of the nine-in-a-row incentive, it was a match that meant more than simply winning the title. It was about keeping the dream alive.

The tension of those years took their toll on Murray, as he himself admitted. Speaking to the *Daily Record* in the autumn of 1996, when the embers of another European campaign flickered and threatened to die, he said:

Nine in a row is having a negative effect . . . Rangers will stand still until it disappears. It's like a monkey on our backs. Of course I'd take satisfaction out of nine in a row – I'd love to see nineteen in a row – but it's becoming a real strain on us.

Celtic are also suffering. I noticed Tommy Burns and the Celtic captain both talking about nine in a row. I can understand why it means so much to so many. They lived through it when Celtic did it. I didn't live through it and I don't agree that it is so vital now. Frankly, I'm becoming tired by it – I'm fed up reading about it.

There isn't another country where this would be an issue. In any other country it is honourable to come second in the league. For Rangers and Celtic second place has become failure. English clubs start the season looking to win a place in Europe. That is judged as success – but not here.

Even at the height of nine-in-a-row fever, the chairman was frustrated by those who lined up to take shots across the bow of his club. The league domination, without European success to match, did not always earn the plaudits those within Ibrox believed it deserved. Murray added:

We're so downbeat about our game. I've stopped listening to the radio on Saturdays because it's getting me depressed! . . . A minority of Rangers fans are far too critical. When this successful period is over they'll realise what a great era it has been.

When it all ended, the pain was palpable. Just as Smith would have loved to have been the manager to make it to the magic ten consecutive championships, so too would Murray have loved to have been the chairman to have reached the milestone. Reflecting on the meek end to the ten-in-a-row effort, compounded by defeat against Hearts in the Scottish Cup final, he said:

Everyone at Rangers is very disappointed about the past week and I congratulate Celtic and Hearts – but they will be playing under a different pressure next year that we have had for the past nine years. Walter Smith said this is as bad as it gets for Rangers and we have had to take one step back to take two forward.

Skip forward a decade or so, to the summer of 2009, and the owner was able to look back with satisfaction on a period in time when Rangers ruled the roost for longer than anyone could have anticipated after Graeme Souness laid the foundation with the first title of the sequence in 1988. Speaking as he stepped down from the role of chairman, Murray said:

> It has been an emotional roller-coaster but I consider it to have been mainly successful. My legacy in my eyes is nine in a row, the UEFA Cup final and the new training complex at Murray Park. Those are the highest points.

He then quipped: 'My major regret? Not winning ten in a row!' It was said at least partly in jest, but at the time the pressure was very real. There was a greed about the pursuit of title after title, fostering an atmosphere that demanded excellence – even if at times the chairman felt it clouded the focus of the club, with his European ambitions too often pushed to one side during the relentless quest to match Celtic's earlier achievements in the league.

What the successful chase did do was ensure he had something to call his own, a unique selling point, if you like. Murray was the man who brought an end to Celtic's decades-old bragging rights, and for that a club and its support will forever be grateful.

Yes, the twin-pronged management of Graeme Souness and Walter Smith had their hands on the tiller, but they could not have succeeded without the support of the owner and his willingness to sanction the finances required to keep the team on top. That was the key to nine in a row. To win the championship once was relatively easy. To keep doing it year after year, leaving the likes of Aberdeen and Celtic suffering from severely wounded pride, required persistence, and that is a quality that Murray has demonstrated not only in football but also in life and business. When the Dons and the Hoops came back stronger, they found Rangers were ready to match them and more.

In 2009, Mark Hateley, in his *Daily Record* blog, gave an intimate insight into the role the chairman had played in the most memorable of years and the regard in which he was held by the players he employed. Admittedly, they benefited financially by the chairman's generosity, but it was his spirit as much as his cheque book that endeared the man to the players on the staff. Hateley wrote:

> When Rangers fans look back on the chairmanship of Sir David Murray one fact should stand alone – without him there would

have been no nine-in-a-row glory. There will be those who have their own memories, their own highs and lows and feelings about what was achieved. But for me that world-record-equalling achievement will be the main legacy.

Without a man of Sir David's vision, drive and determination at the helm, that feat would never have been achieved. Rangers would never have had the managers or the players he brought in to take the club to the peak of its history.

It was his vision – and financial backing – that brought the whole thing together. Sir David was a man who shared the same drive as characters such as Graeme Souness, Walter Smith, Ally McCoist and Andy Goram.

He plunged his life into the club and today every Rangers fan should be thankful to him. He is part of the history at Rangers and has been highly successful during his 20 years. In my opinion, he must go down as one of the greatest custodians of the club. I think it is safe to say he has taken the club further forward than anyone else. Had he not arrived when he did, who knows what would have happened? It wouldn't have enjoyed the success it has over the past two decades, I'm sure.

And nine in a row will forever be a major part of his legacy. Yet, ironically, the greatest achievement of his time as chairman was the one that took the greatest toll. As the supporters basked in the reflected glory of the groundbreaking success, their leader had other thoughts.

When the annual accounts were published in the aftermath of the 1996–97 season, Murray stated:

> Last season was a landmark for the club and achieving the record was a source of great pride for everyone associated with Rangers. But I believe it was the focal point for everything we were trying to do last year and it became unbearable. I think the media created the hype – you saw stories every day about 'nine in a row' – and in the end it got too much.

The hangover was evident at home and abroad. Just as Walter Smith's ageing side toiled in vain to make it ten in a row as the season wore on, in Europe too there was disappointment. The club crashed out of the Champions League, against IFK Gothenburg, and then the UEFA Cup, after losing to Strasbourg over two legs. Again the desire for European success, and the frustration of repeated failure to achieve it, bubbled to the surface. Murray's statement to shareholders continued:

160

We have no divine right to do well in Europe and domestically everybody treats playing Rangers as a cup final. You look at teams like Milan and Borussia Dortmund, who are not finding it easy to make an impression on their own leagues this year, whereas we are the only undefeated team in Scotland. No one's criticising Arsenal, who also went out of Europe last week, and they have spent as much money recently as we have.

Spending money on players and, just as importantly, raising money by selling them was about to become an outdated concept as the Bosman ruling came into force. In time, it would lead to a rethink about the way contracts were managed at Ibrox, with longer-term deals on the agenda and greater urgency about securing valuable assets to those contracts. What Bosman also did was lead to the club altering its balance-sheet, with players no longer the cast-iron assets they had once been. Murray stated: 'I believe the Bosman rule is going to dig into clubs like ourselves bigger than people realise.'

Not that Rangers success in the nine-in-a-row pursuit was based on selling players – traffic inwards was far more frequent than that heading out of the door.

Richard Gough, captain for large swathes of that winning run, has admitted that the disparity between the Old Firm rivals on and off the park was at the time embarrassing. The house that Murray built had put Celtic well and truly in the shade. In a 2009 interview with *The Sun*, Gough said:

> We were stronger financially than Celtic in my era and, by the time we won a fourth title, we were well ahead.
>
> Celtic had a barren two or three years at that time and were forced to buy players they shouldn't have had. I can remember going to Parkhead and being 3–0 up after fifteen minutes in one game. Even Oleg Kuznetsov scored – that's how bad it was.
>
> During that period I used to socialise with Paul McStay, who was Celtic's best player. I felt sorry for him because I was playing with the best of British and he wasn't. Even in the tunnel before derbies, I'd look at him and think, 'You've no chance, pal.' It was just because Rangers could afford quality at that time and Celtic couldn't.
>
> It was three or four years before they could recover and afford real quality players again. They brought in the likes of Pierre van Hooijdonk, Jorge Cadete and Paolo di Canio. I had to wake myself up because I had a game on again.

And Rangers did indeed have a game on. When Celtic came through in 1998 to win the championship and halt the ten-in-a-row dream dead in its tracks, it marked a new era in the Scottish game. Single-team dominance was cast aside as the tit-for-tat years loomed.

For years, it had been conventional wisdom that if any team was going to wrest the Premier Division prize from Rangers' collective grasp, it would be Aberdeen. While Celtic had fumbled around in the dark, the Dons had been purposeful in their rivalry with the established kings of the domestic scene. They had run Rangers close more than once and had looked like the only contenders for some time.

Yet it was Celtic who eventually came through and got themselves back on track, something that rubbed salt into the wounds. Breaking the winning sequence was one thing – but having it broken by that particular team was quite another.

It was a strain on everyone connected with Rangers, not least the manager. When Walter Smith parted company with the club in 1998, it prompted a rethink on the structure and the strength of the coaching and support staff. Speaking on Radio Scotland before Dick Advocaat and his entourage were appointed, Murray admitted:

> Walter has had far too much to do. It was unrealistic. The guy badly needs a break. What's more, the day of the football manager as we have come to know it, doing everything, are gone. We are looking for a coach as opposed to a manager. There is a football side to the job and there is a business side to the job, so we will do exactly that. The coach's job is a massive job in itself. I don't think people in Scotland seriously realise or appreciate exactly how difficult it is to win championships.
>
> I have read with interest newspaper stories linking the likes of Dalglish, Graham and Robson with the Rangers job. Now that gets those names out of the way, and we can get on with things. We need a top-class first-team coach, someone who has a proven track record in Europe, someone who has done it. We are probably talking about someone from northern mainland Europe, as we want to try and avoid any language barriers.
>
> But you can be assured we will have the new coach well in place by the end of the season to give him and Walter as long as possible together before the new coach takes over completely. Walter will be involved very much in the process of finding the new coach.
>
> We need continuity with the coaching. Walter was recently away for a couple of days looking for players. That's two days away from the players and the coaching. We can't have that. We want the

coach to identify the players he wants and then it will be up to a chief executive or myself to take that forward.

And so it came to pass. Smith exited stage left, with the lead role taken over by Advocaat. It was the dawn of a bold new era as far as the chairman was concerned – and there was no room for sentimentality.

The departure of Smith from the dugout removed the keystone from the nine-in-a-row pyramid and paved the way for the new man to dismantle it piece by piece. According to some of those within the dressing-room, it was in fact more of a sledgehammer approach.

Andy Goram, in his 2009 book *The Goalie*, remembered:

I have never . . . spoken to [Dick Advocaat] in my life. I was simply told by the club he didn't want me. Advocaat's treatment of the team who won nine in a row left a sour taste in my mouth . . .

In the wake of his decision to jettison us all, I was on the next table to him at Rangers dinners three times, and he couldn't even look at me. We never exchanged a word. That sums the man up for me. After all we had done for the club, we deserved to be told in person by the next manager that we were out. He chose not to do that.

Listen, forget about me. There were players amongst those he dumped who could easily have given him another season or two. He wanted his own team, and that's fine, but if you're going to ditch legends – and that's what we had become – then do it the right way . . .

. . . I think when you've earned respect in football, you should be given it. We'd earned it, and he didn't show us a shred of it. He should have pulled us into the office and told us why he was letting us go. Instead, he simply told David Murray, 'I want rid of Goram and Gascoigne, and I want money for Laudrup.'

Well, he got his way with me and Gazza, but he didn't realise that the chairman had an agreement with Brian that he could leave for nothing after our bid for ten. Lauders was on his way to Chelsea . . . but Advocaat was grasping away, trying to get money for him. Fair play to David Murray. He stuck to his guns and told the manager the deal had been done as a mark of gratitude for what Brian had given to the Gers.

That shabby attempt to cash in on Laudrup gnawed at me, though, as did Advocaat's disregard for what we had achieved. I understood that he felt if he was going to fail, it would be with his own players. But he came in and surrounded himself with Dutch coaches and Dutch players.

History will show that going Dutch had mixed results. There were memorable highs, not least the first season under Advocaat's rule, but there were also frustrations connected to the big-money, high-risk strategy adopted during that period in the club's history. The close relationship that the chairman had with players during the halcyon years became more detached as the revolving door brought a succession of figures into Ibrox.

When Murray was asked by Rangers TV to pick his all-time Rangers XI in 2008, the relatively modestly rewarded heroes of nine in a row featured far more heavily than the high earners who arrived by the planeload during the Advocaat years.

Murray's team selection read: Andy Goram, Sandy Jardine, John Brown, John Greig, Richard Gough, Jim Baxter, Willie Henderson, Graeme Souness, Derek Johnstone, Ally McCoist, Davie Cooper.

It would be a fearsome prospect for any opposition team, and it was a side made up entirely of home-reared talent. No de Boer, no Flo . . . no Advocaat influence at all in the owner's dream team. Instead, there was room for the nine-in-a-row heroes Goram, Brown, Gough, Souness and McCoist.

Murray said:

> I felt it was important to go for people I've had an involvement with, who are Scottish and who gave long-term value to the club. It's easy to put in Brian Laudrup, Paul Gascoigne and Mark Hateley, but I have looked at it from a different angle. I've gone for those who know what Rangers are about, and if they had all been playing at the same time, what a great team it would have been.
>
> I was involved in the signing of Andy Goram. He was a great character and there were so many games where he had very little to do and would make one or two exceptional saves and we'd win. He was a great servant to Rangers Football Club and is the best we've seen in our time.
>
> Richard Gough was a great captain with a never-say-die attitude. His bravery was unquestionable and he was a catalyst for the success we saw in nine in a row. He played with passion and commitment and gave the team great stability.
>
> John Brown is another who'd have died for the cause. He wanted to play for Rangers. He'd almost gone to Hearts but failed a medical and I remember Wallace Mercer telling me how much he regretted not signing him. He was a great servant.
>
> Graeme Souness would be on the phone if I didn't pick him but he'd be in any Scottish team. You need that bit of grit in there and

sometimes people need sorted out. Graeme brought me to Rangers and he helped turn round the club's fortunes.

Man and boy, I don't think there's been a better striker for Rangers or in Scottish football than Ally McCoist. He was just a reliable source of scoring goals and he won many games for us.

With a few nods to the past intertwined with those more familiar to Murray, the dream-team selection left nobody in any doubt about the fondness with which he looked back on the earliest years of more than two decades at the head of the boardroom table.

And the manager for the team of all stars? There was only one candidate for the job as far as the chairman was concerned, the man he'd turned to more than once in an hour of need: 'Walter Smith – he'd have won a few games with that team. We have a great working relationship but also a great personal relationship.'

CHAPTER 15

'When I started, we could buy the biggest players in England – the equivalent of the John Terrys and Frank Lampards of this world. That has gone from us now, which is frustrating.'

David Murray, 2008

ONE WAS A dedicated, flawless and athletic star. A European Championship winner who married impeccable technical skill with the ability to turn a game on its head. The other was a restless soul, flawed and haunted by injuries, a tortured World Cup nearly man who mated mesmerising ball mastery with an infuriating propensity for self-destruction. Together, Brian Laudrup and Paul Gascoigne made hearts sing and pulses race during the heady days when the transfer ambitions of Rangers knew no bounds.

Serie A clubs quivered with fear when David Murray came calling. The English elite knew a bidding war would end with only one winner. Ibrox was the destination of choice for players who could have their pick of Europe's leading lights. Those were happy, happy days for loyal Bears, who thought all of their Christmases had come at once.

With the Great Dane on the wing and Gazza pulling the strings in midfield, the Rangers team of the late 1990s in full flight truly was a sight to behold: two world-class stars in one Ibrox team thrilling tens of thousands on a weekly basis. Life was good.

It was an era in which each summer brought a gift from the chairman to the loyal season-ticket holders. Packaged with a bow, a mouth-watering treat was delivered with almost monotonous regularity to keep the blue order enthralled and enthused.

Laudrup and Gascoigne were a good old-fashioned one-two, with the Dane landing in Scotland in the summer of 1994 and the English entertainer checking in a year later as the star count grew and grew.

So how did Rangers land such a prize pair? On paper, it was all rather easy – but the ambition and courage required cannot be overestimated.

Laudrup proved to be the bargain of the century. At 25 years old, he had his best years ahead of him, yet he already had a considerable pedigree as a former Danish Player of the Year and member of his nation's squad for the against-all-odds win in the 1992 European Championships. His efforts in that tournament earned him a nomination in the World Player of the Year awards – and at club level a passage to Serie A with Fiorentina. AC Milan moved to take him on loan to the San Siro, but it was against the backdrop of the abandoned shipyards of the Clyde, rather than the boutiques of the fashion capital of Italy, that Laudrup's future lay.

For the princely sum of £2.3 million, the services of Laudrup were secured. Most at Ibrox, including the manager, had major doubts about the chances of completing the deal, but the ever-confident David Murray was adamant he would get his man. And he did.

By the time his first game was over, the Scandinavian had demonstrated his worth, setting up two goals with the type of delicious deliveries that became his trademark. At no stage did Laudrup ever threaten to fail to live up to his considerable reputation.

The same could be argued of Gascoigne, even if his reputation was not quite as clean-cut as that of his teammate. Gazza had a history of controversy and brilliance in equal measure, and the Rangers years proved to be very much par for the course for the wayward hero.

Gazza was the more expensive of the duo, appearing on the Ibrox cheque-book stub at £4.3 million. He had a catalogue of surgical procedures on his record, and the deal in the build-up to the 1995–96 season was a huge risk. Interest from Manchester United and Chelsea, among others, suggested it was one worth taking, however, and Murray and Smith jumped in at the deep end.

It was solicitor Mel Stein who acted as broker in the deal, having served as Gascoigne's agent for the bulk of the midfield star's career. Stein told me: 'Lazio had pretty much run out of steam with Paul after his problems with injuries in Italy. There had also been a change of ownership at the club – the president, who absolutely adored Paul, had gone and the new man was not so in love with the cheeky-chappy persona.

'We found out that Walter was interested and he came across to Rome for talks. In turn, I went to Edinburgh and met with David Murray. We got on really well and it turned out to be probably the simplest transfer I was ever involved with while representing Paul.

'David Murray really wanted him at Rangers and had an extraordinary empathy with him. In some ways, they were like soulmates. Paul had always gone to clubs that loved him. He had that at Tottenham with Irving Scholar and Terry Venables, then again at Lazio when he joined, and later it was the same at Everton with Bill Kenwright. He had that at Rangers too, with Walter Smith and David. The biggest selling point with Rangers was the relationship he built with the chairman and manager in a short period of time.'

There was competition from England for Gascoigne's services, with the player still one of the most instantly recognisable in world football at that stage. Murray and Rangers were not overawed and had every reason to be confident.

Stein added: 'Rangers and Celtic at that time could still compete with the biggest clubs in Europe, but it was not purely a financial decision. I think Paul was homesick in Italy. His relationship with Sheryl was going through a rocky patch and he felt being back in the UK would provide a better chance of reconciliation. Glasgow was also closer to his friends and family in Newcastle, so it was ideal in many ways. There was no persuasion necessary.'

Initially, it went swimmingly. Just as Laudrup had done in his first season and subsequent campaigns, Gascoigne quickly established himself as a major player in the championship-winning Rangers team.

After arriving to sign from Lazio, the player was swamped by Gers fans eager to catch a glimpse of the new recruit and wish him well as he embarked on the Scottish leg of his career journey. What followed was a season of incredible individual performances, of passion and of desire. The midfielder, who had been on the brink of superstardom before his injury curse struck, was back in the game and at his best, terrorising the opposition with every swivel of the hips and dip of the shoulder.

John Hughes tells a wonderful anecdote about Tommy Burns, as Celtic manager, and his approach to thwarting Gazza. Instructing Peter Grant to man-mark the enigmatic England star during one Old Firm encounter, Burns ordered his man to take it to the absolute limit. Burns reasoned: 'If you both get sent off, they'll miss him more than we'll miss you.'

Laudrup, too, was flying, striking fear into defences up and down the country with his incisive displays.

Both offered skills reminiscent of the days of Jim Baxter, Willie Henderson and the other entertainers from glory days gone by. But there was more to the dangerous duo than individual flair and artistic licence; they slotted in to Walter Smith's team and adopted the famous collective ethic that the nine-in-a-row success had been built upon.

Confidence was never in short supply, but egos were kept in check. Even when Gazza was at his arrogant best, he showed a willingness to dig in and do the dirty work in the trenches with the rest of his comrades.

A major part of the success was the warmth he felt off the park, quickly settling into his role with the club thanks to the efforts of the Ibrox top brass. Mel Stein added: 'Paul was looked after sensationally by Rangers. I remember he was staying down at Cameron House when Walter realised he was alone and invited him back to his house to save him from being lonely. David Murray would invite him to his house and they would sit and talk and talk.

'David Murray is a great human being, a wonderful man. He has come through terrible tragedy and battled on to enjoy success. He is an extraordinary personality, and Rangers through and through. There is no doubt in my mind that Ibrox is a poorer place without him.'

The results were impressive and the part played by each of the fans' favourites was clear. It was Gazza who clinched eight in a row with his match-winning hat-trick against Aberdeen in the second-last game of the 1995–96 campaign. It was Laudrup who secured nine in a row with his decisive header against Dundee United at the climax of the 1996–97 term. Money well spent.

But the cheque book was not closed, even in the face of what could be considered an embarrassment of attacking riches. No club was out of bounds, not even the undisputed kings of Europe.

Murray has revealed in recent years that he came within an ace of cherry-picking from Juventus in all their pomp when he went after Gianluca Vialli at the height of the nine-in-a-row chase. He remembered:

> I flew to Turin with Walter Smith after Juventus had won the Champions League in 1996 and offered him a contract. He was available for nothing and considered what we put on the table, but eventually signed for Chelsea. Some time later I got a letter from him, which I still have, saying he had made a mistake in not joining us. However, most of those big names we truly went for at that time did sign for us.

To be able to go to Europe's finest and not feel intimidated, to do so with full expectation of landing one of their most influential players, was what the era was all about. 'Inferiority' was not a word in Murray's vocabulary, and that spirit permeated Ibrox.

What Murray soon discovered was that getting hold of talent was only part of the battle. Harnessing that talent, in the case of Gascoigne, was an even tougher fight. It was not long before the demons began to surface.

As the star's personal problems engulfed him, he found typical loyalty from the club and its owner. Behind the scenes, there must have been deep soul-searching, but Murray presented a united front in public.

The circus surrounding Gazza was far removed from the tradition and virtues extolled by Bill Struth in the formative years of the club, but at no stage was the player hung out to dry by his supportive club. Too supportive, it could be argued, but that was what being part of the Rangers family was all about during a period in which the one-for-all-and-all-for-one attitude was demanded of players and reciprocated by the senior management.

Murray, when asked if the player's behaviour and off-field antics were damaging the good name of Rangers, claimed: 'I don't think too deeply about that. But I will say, in footballing terms, he's delivered. No one could tell me that he's failed on the field.' The chairman refused to be drawn on whether the antics off the field would lead to a premature end to Gazza's Ibrox career, adding, 'It's up to Walter Smith what happens in the future.'

There was a certain degree of sympathy emanating from the club when all on the outside were lining up to attack the wayward player. Perhaps, with the full extent of Gascoigne's problems surfacing, those closest to him had a greater appreciation of the turmoil his life was in and the daily battle he had to keep his career on as close to an even keel as was possible in the circumstances.

Murray, speaking in spring 1997, said:

> Paul's personal life is his own, I cannot comment. He has brought much of it upon himself. I will not argue with that. He lives under tremendous pressure. Go to his house. The gates are locked, but there will still be somebody sitting outside waiting for him. No one else I know lives with that kind of attention.

The player himself concurred with that line of thought and let his guard slip often enough to demonstrate the difficulties in his life. In 1997, Gascoigne admitted:

> A lot of footballers do a lot of things outside of football but I am always hassled. I can't win, every game I play now I get hammered. Too fat, too thin – not beating five players, should beat five players. It's the same old story.
>
> If I keep getting hammered the way I am, then I'll play as long as

I think I'm happy. Then if I think I've had enough, I'll do what's best for me.

I accept that comes with the job but I feel like saying, 'I've had enough, I've had enough.' I've enjoyed my career, if someone said I could turn the clock back ten years, I'd say, 'No, definitely not.' I've enjoyed all my career so far and I want to continue to enjoy it. I wouldn't turn the clock back on anything.

This was the start of a period during which Gascoigne's off-field troubles would begin to build, although he managed to maintain a consistency in his play in the face of those difficulties.

Mel Stein told me: 'It is clear there were problems at that time – and I would say Glasgow is not necessarily the best place to be if you have an issue with drink. I don't think there was ever a chance of David or Walter sacking Paul. It never got to that stage. Rangers got very good value from Paul. He actually played some of the best football of his life while he was with Rangers. Of course, he scored that wonder goal against Scotland during that time too.'

For Stein, his memories of Gascoigne are mixed. For all the good times, there were also difficult spells in their professional relationship – a bond that was eventually broken completely. 'I haven't spoken to Paul in five years, since he breached a contract we had set up for a book. I looked after him very well for 15 years and made him a very wealthy young man, but he behaved badly towards me in the end. If I saw him again I would certainly speak to him, but whether he would return that, I don't know.'

But in the 1990s, the pair were very close, savouring the good times at Rangers. The summer of 1997 proved to be a key stage in the attempt to keep the entertainers, Laudrup and Gascoigne, together under one roof. While Gazza was being pulled away from the self-destruct button, there was an equally fierce effort to drag Laudrup away from the lure of suitors in England and the Netherlands, as Manchester United and Ajax appeared on the scene.

Murray responded swiftly and decisively, offering Gazza a new three-year contract and the security that went with it. He then set about determining the long-term future of Laudrup. Job done.

Murray said at the time:

I am absolutely delighted. Brian is staying for another year and after that we hope he will sign a contract to finish his career at Ibrox. Brian is a such a decent chap to deal with. He uses his common sense and I think it told him he should stay. He has seen the changes we are making and the ambition which drives us on. He wants to give it another year to see what we can achieve.

After that we hope he will sign for life but it will depend on how he feels about the new team and the progress made. This is not the time for scaremongering about losing him next year for nothing. It's a time to be happy he's staying. I'm sure the Rangers fans appreciate just how important this is to the club. Yes, he could still leave us next summer for nothing but this was about the future of Rangers – not what kind of profit we could make from his sale.

People will rate it an achievement for us to fend off the likes of United and Ajax but I don't see them signing the quality of players we have this summer.

They were bold claims, but typical of the era, as Rangers took on allcomers in the transfer market. Nothing was out of bounds in the good old days, as the chairman himself lamented in 2008, recalling:

When I started, we could buy the biggest players in England – the equivalent of the John Terrys and Frank Lampards of this world. That has gone from us now, which is frustrating. I wanted to take the club to a higher level but we are restricted to playing in Scotland and competing with Celtic most years for the title.

The monotony of that two-horse race made making money from television revenues and sponsorship a challenge. It also made it more difficult to retain players than it might have been if there had been a bigger stage to play on. The departure of quality players from the top Scottish teams became an annual event as the vultures circled.

The transfer windows of 1998 were a case in point, with both Gascoigne and Laudrup the subject of intense speculation. Prior to the deadline in the spring of that year, rumours about Gascoigne's future with the club reached fever pitch. It was Crystal Palace, under the stewardship of brash owner Mark Goldberg, who showed their hand first, going public with their interest in the player and revealing details of negotiations over a proposed £3-million move to London.

That provoked the ire of Murray – and also sparked enquiries from elsewhere, with Bryan Robson's Middlesbrough entering the fray. What Goldberg perhaps did not realise was that, by crossing Murray, he had ended any hope of pulling off the marquee signing he had set his sights on. Instead, it was Boro who moved to the head of the queue.

Gazza's agent had claimed his client was 'blue through and through' and had no wish to leave the club, but the change in management looming on the horizon, with the Dick Advocaat era imminent, hinted that the playing guard might also be changing. The lure of linking up with old England teammate Robson, as well as returning to his north-east of England stamping-ground, was always going to be too strong to resist. He jumped before he was pushed.

While Gazza was tarnished goods, the desire to retain Laudrup was strong. Chelsea came calling in the summer of 1998 but received no encouragement – despite the player expressing a desire to try his luck in England. He hadn't bargained on the steely determination of Murray, who turned from good cop to bad during the transfer saga as he vowed to fight for compensation despite the player's contract winding down. He said at the time:

> Chelsea are talking to us about compensation and that's encouraging. Brian must respect Rangers' right to look after our interests. We will continue our discussions with Chelsea over a fee because I believe we have a strong legal case for going down that road.
>
> I know he is unhappy and has already gone public to get a few points off his chest and that's fair enough, but as chairman I have a responsibility to act in and protect Rangers' best interests.
>
> When Brian renewed his contract for a further 12 months at the start of the season I told him I had no problem with him going to the Continent or America. What I didn't want was him to go the Premiership because of the fans' reaction – but he changed his mind.

When Ajax flirted with Laudrup in 1997, the Dane discovered just how well honed Murray's powers of persuasion were. The Dutch side, managed by Danish coach Morten Olsen, had wooed the wily Scandinavian star to the point where they were certain he was ready to jump from the Ibrox ship. What they hadn't bargained on was a last-gasp intervention by a club owner who had put in the hours to bring the talismanic attacker to Scotland and was not ready to let him go without a fight. That is, a fight in the Murray way: rather than boxing gloves and spit buckets, think private jets and champagne.

Just as Laudrup was ready to commit his future to his suitors from Amsterdam, he was invited to Jersey for what should have been a farewell meeting with Murray – a chance to chew the fat, to look back over the good old days. The player, his wife Mette and his agent Vincenzo Morabito were flown to the island haven, and by the time they boarded Murray's private jet for the return journey, Laudrup had been talked into snubbing the chance of a switch to the Continent in favour of another tilt at glory in Rangers colours.

Murray commented at the time:

> The negotiations were not difficult. Brian actually told us that Rangers had become the talk of Europe because of the signings we have made already this summer. He knows the extent of our ambition and that was a key factor in his decision.
>
> In all the time he was here we talked about his future for about half an hour. The rest was just general conversation. It wasn't about money. Brian will make no extra money by staying for another year – he's not motivated by money.
>
> And it wasn't about Rangers making a profit from him. It's important to remember that Rangers is a football club not a business and that the bottom line does not win trophies. It was all about keeping a player who has been a key part of the most successful Rangers team and successful Rangers era of all time. Brian Laudrup is a Rangers legend and we did not want to lose him.

The travelling party had intended to make only a fleeting stop in Jersey. Instead, they were wined and dined, spending an impromptu night at Murray's mansion. Morabito later reflected: 'It was all so relaxed it felt as if we were on a picnic. There was no pressure at all.'

By the end of the mini-break, Laudrup's future was settled. He would spend the season in Rangers colours, and Murray could not hide his delight. The chairman said:

> I only ever felt we would lose him if we showed a lack of ambition. I was always hopeful he would stay. I remained silent over the last week because I believe actions speak louder than words. I wanted to speak when I had something positive to say. But it would have been a body blow for everyone at Rangers if we had lost him.
>
> Walter and I were concerned because we had lost players such as Gough and Robertson and others who are nearing the end of their careers from a very successful side. Brian is an integral part of the side and we didn't want him going too.

The decision did nothing to dispel the notion that Laudrup would leave sooner rather than later, with 1997–98 viewed by all parties as likely to be his last season in Scotland. Murray added:

> When talking about his future we had a good, brief debate but it

would not be right for me to go into details about the discussion. What I will say is that the most important thing for him is that he will be playing in a better Rangers team next season. The players we're bringing in are of a quality we have never had at Ibrox before.

It had been an opportunity to cash in on a major asset, but it was one that Murray had passed up. Instead of raking in a transfer fee, he had pledged to spend money to match the ambitions of a player he rated among the finest ever to pull on the light-blue jersey. Murray knew the player would be the big winner, presented with the opportunity to run down the final year of his deal and walk away without a fee the following summer when he was out of contract. Heart had ruled the head, with Rangers ignoring the financial implications in favour of keeping manager, supporters and, undoubtedly, the chairman happy. Murray remarked, 'We should all be delighted that he is staying in Scotland. Brian Laudrup is the man who has brought credibility back to the Scottish game.'

Laudrup did eventually move on, of course, joining Chelsea in the summer of 1998 to bring the curtain down on his Scottish adventure. He had brought entertainment and honours by the bucketload and had undoubtedly provided value for the relatively modest amount of money invested in his transfer fee.

In July 2010, it appeared as though the messiah was heading back to Rangers. Murray had made the approach and found the retired winger receptive to the idea of a second stint in Glasgow, with a role in youth development among the possibilities mentioned in reports. Laudrup was quoted as saying it was only fair that he 'gave something back' to the club. The second coming never did materialise, although the fact that the discussions had taken place hinted at the good relationship between the men; when Laudrup and Murray had eventually parted company, it had been on good terms. What the Dane discovered was that those who won a place in Murray's heart – just as Graeme Souness had done all those years previously, and Walter Smith too – had a friend for life.

While the Laudrup experiment in the 1990s had been a success, in hindsight the owner understood that spending huge sums on individual players did not always make economic or sporting sense. Murray, speaking in the infancy of Advocaat's tenure, remarked: 'Perhaps in the past we relied too much on players like Brian Laudrup and Paul Gascoigne – and when they didn't perform, the team as a whole didn't perform.'

That admission should have signalled the end of the superstar recruits at Ibrox. But it didn't. The arrival of Advocaat brought a renewed sense of vigour to the club and its pursuit of big-name international stars.

The marquee signing of Dutch legend Ronald de Boer in August 2000 was a signal of how serious Murray was about backing his Continental manager. The £4.5-million deal to land the Barcelona star drew crowds to the doors of Ibrox as fans flocked to catch a glimpse of the new man.

Advocaat hailed the arrival as a 'great thing' and claimed a 'player of his quality would not usually come to Rangers'. De Boer's countryman Arthur Numan had played a part in persuading his international colleague to move to Scotland.

Of course, Ronald was just the first of the Dutch masters, with brother Frank joining from Turkish side Galatasaray in 2004 for a brief stint playing to a Scottish audience. They were a calibre of player who by rights should not have been attracted to the SPL, with away trips to rainy Motherwell and windswept Aberdeen on the cards, but they were because of the burning ambition of the man at the very top and the managers he employed to translate that desire on the playing field.

Will we ever see the likes of Gascoigne and Laudrup again, and will Rangers be in a position to plunder the talent pools of Serie A in the years ahead? The answer to both of those questions is no. Those days have gone, a feature of the Murray years that had the Bears singing and the neutrals purring with appreciation. The players have departed, but the memories linger long.

CHAPTER 16

'I believe Advocaat can be the catalyst in us getting a player of a higher standard than we may have done in the past.'

David Murray, 1998

GRAEME SOUNESS HAD been inherited. Walter Smith was the heir to the manager's throne. But where next for Rangers? That was the question facing David Murray as he pondered who should be king in the wake of Smith's decision to abdicate from the seat of power when the curtain fell on his final campaign in the summer of 1998.

It would be the chairman's first independent managerial appointment, in a sense, with both Souness and Smith already on the payroll when he'd moved in at Ibrox nine years earlier. It was, therefore, a crucial one, not only from the perspective of putting the team back on track after the stuttering end to the ten-in-a-row dream but also from the point of view of demonstrating Murray's judgement and ambition.

It was a landmark moment and, when it came, it did not disappoint. The arrival of Dick Advocaat was a clear indication that Murray was not going to take defeat to Celtic in the championship challenge during the 1997–98 campaign lying down. He was ready to come roaring back and would do so with the 'Little General' beside him in the trenches.

Advocaat was a world-class coach with a global reputation and his decision to decamp to Ibrox sent ripples throughout Europe and beyond. His arrival marked a new and exciting chapter for Rangers as a club.

Smith had given his chairman plenty of warning about his intention to step aside, ensuring Murray had the opportunity to take a step back and carefully consider the route forward. The manager had announced his decision to retire during the 1997–98 season, while the chase for ten in a row was very much alive, and a timescale had quickly been set for sourcing a successor. Murray was confident about naming his choice by the time the bells rang in 1998; he had been working away behind the scenes since Smith had come to him in confidence in September 1997 to inform him of his plan to take a back seat.

Although there was no official comment from inside Ibrox, informed sources quickly began to point towards a total shift in emphasis at the club. For the first time in a long and proud history, Rangers were set to appoint a foreign manager. Would it be a Swede in Sven-Göran Eriksson? Or perhaps the wily German operator Ottmar Hitzfeld?

The clearest indication came a few weeks into 1998 when Graeme Souness, by then in charge of Benfica, told reporters that he believed it would be PSV Eindhoven boss Dick Advocaat who would succeed Smith. Souness, who remained a close confidant of both Murray and Smith, proved, not surprisingly, to be bang on the money.

It was on 10 February, more than a fortnight after Souness had made his prediction, that supporters had the first public confirmation of Advocaat's impending arrival. There had been strong speculation that the Dutchman was the chosen one, and finally it had been made official. PSV president Harry van Raaij, whose side was challenging for the title, admitted:

> We have received a fax from Rangers, confirming their interest in Dick, and there's not a lot we can do about it. It doesn't come as a great surprise, but we are disappointed that a club like Rangers have gone about their business this way and that they didn't contact us immediately about the situation.

It would take more than a stinging rebuke to halt Murray in his tracks. He had risen to his prominent place in business and in sport with spirit and single-mindedness, and he had set about his pursuit of his new manager in the same manner.

Similarly, there was no room for sentiment as his Continental revolution took shape. The ambition to go Dutch meant radical change, with proud Scottish firebrand Archie Knox among the most high-profile casualties. While Walter Smith was to be retained in a behind-the-scenes role following his step back from the front line, there was no room at the inn for his assistant Knox.

Smith had recruited the coach in 1991, luring him away from Alex Ferguson and Manchester United, but after six years and a succession of trophy successes, the partnership was to be broken up. Knox would make way for the new man and his own coaching team, if, of course, a deal could be agreed between the Dutchman and his prospective employers.

Advocaat was contracted to PSV until the summer of 1999 but had an early-release clause that enabled him to make the switch to Ibrox. The target did his best to be diplomatic, without ever denying that the move was on the cards. He would only say: 'I will talk next week about Glasgow Rangers, but I'm trying to keep it quiet this week because we have very important games.'

Less than a week later, on 16 February 1998, the deal was concluded. In a short statement, Murray said:

> I'm delighted that Dick Advocaat, one of the game's most respected coaches, has accepted the position of manager of Rangers. Over the past few weeks we have interviewed a number of possible candidates for this position and from this it became quite clear that Dick was our first choice. As already stated, Walter Smith will continue to manage the club until the arrival of Dick from PSV on 1 July.
>
> I promised the supporters that I would tell them as soon into the New Year as possible who would succeed Walter and I am sure they will be as pleased as we are that we have made such a top appointment. The contract details, in terms of duration and remuneration, must remain between myself and Dick for the moment.
>
> What we are trying to do by announcing it at this time is to put to an end to the speculation that was building – we can put the meat on the bones later. I felt some pressure to make the announcement as I said I would reveal our choice near the start of the year and I feel this is the right time.

Advocaat commented: 'I have a very clear vision of the direction I wish to take the club and I look forward to working with everyone at Rangers to ensure that direction brings even more success to this great club.'

Part of the new man's vision was surrounding himself with his own people. It was a plan that Murray had bought into and encouraged, once again digging deep into the club's coffers to enable the recruit to import key coaching personnel.

Bert van Lingen, Advocaat's trusted sidekick, was the first priority. The intention was to install the Dutchman at the centre of the youth-development department in a bid to foster young talent. It was an area that the Ibrox board had had grave misgivings about in the years when the first team was dominating the domestic scene, and van Lingen was the character tasked with righting the perceived wrongs.

He moved to Glasgow from his position as head of youth development for the Dutch FA, having worked under Advocaat during the 1994

World Cup as a scout detailed with compiling dossiers on opposition sides.

There was no place on the staff, however, for PSV assistant manager Rob Baan. He decided that the grass was not necessarily greener in the blue half of Glasgow and opted to stay in his homeland while his compatriots prepared for their new challenge in the rough and tumble of British football.

What was made clear all along was that there would be even greater investment front of house, with money available for the incoming coach to perform root-and-branch surgery on a squad that appeared to be reaching the end of its natural life.

No sooner had the ink dried on the manager's contract than the headlines began to spring up. Red Star Belgrade's Dejan Stankovic, saddled with a £9-million price tag, was among the first of the reputed targets, while French international Stéphane Guivarc'h was another name to crop up.

While Murray denied any concrete interest in Stankovic, there was no hiding his pursuit of the Auxerre striker. He received the full Murray treatment, flown to Glasgow for a VIP tour of Ibrox and then whisked off again by private jet to Jersey for talks with the chairman. The Frenchman, however, declared that he was not interested in playing in Scotland and flew back home to prepare himself for a role in his country's World Cup win that summer.

While that pursuit ended in disappointment, at least for the time being, there were many more successes. Within weeks, the chairman was being swept along on a giant Advocaat-inspired wave, signing the types of cheques that would make accountants wince.

The £5-million splurge on Arthur Numan, completed in May 1998, was the start of what, in hindsight, was a spell of wild abandon. Spending £5 million on a left-back, albeit the captain of PSV Eindhoven and a Dutch international star, was decadent in the extreme, but for Murray it marked a clear indication of the extent to which he was prepared to back his new manager. The chairman said, 'We intend to continue signing players of a certain pedigree. He is one of the best left-backs in Europe and has played to a very high standard.'

The club was criticised in some quarters for spending so heavily on a player not in the first flush of youth, but it was claimed that 'financial value' was not the prime concern. More important to Murray was what a player could do on the park. He added:

> I believe Advocaat can be the catalyst in us getting a player of a
> higher standard than we may have done in the past. In a perfect

world we would have eleven twenty-two-year-old Scots – but Dick has a system and wants players to fit that.

Next on the expensive shopping list was German goalkeeper Stefan Klos, commanding another substantial salary and a £700,000 fee when he moved from Borussia Dortmund. Mind you, Murray had persuaded the shot-stopper to pay a chunk of the transfer fee from his own pocket in exchange for a bumper contract.

Then came deals for Argentine attacker Gabriel Amato and Dutch midfielder Giovanni van Bronckhorst. Amato, with a reputation as an individual talent with crowd-pleasing ability, had a decent pedigree after starring for River Plate in his homeland and Spanish cracks Real Mallorca. He commanded a decent fee too, weighing in at £4.2 million.

The signing of van Bronckhorst was also a demonstration of Advocaat's expensive taste, although his £5-million price tag would in time prove to be well worth the investment. Like Numan, the Feyenoord midfielder had been part of his country's squad for the 1998 World Cup and was recruited during the tournament as the new manager wasted no time in assembling his all-star cast.

Despite the extravagance, there was no open-cheque-book policy. A mooted move for AC Milan star André Cruz broke down when the Brazilian defender was reported to have demanded a weekly wage in excess of £35,000. According to Murray, he would expect to be able to pay two top-notch players from that pot of cash. It didn't prevent Advocaat from window-shopping in the Italian style capital, though, with striker Filippo Maniero among his other targets at the Rossoneri as he browsed the designer end of the football market.

Within a matter of weeks, Advocaat had broken the club transfer record he himself had created when he'd signed Arthur Numan. The man who took on the dubious honour of becoming the club's most expensive recruit was Fiorentina winger Andrei Kanchelskis, who returned to Britain, having previously done stints with Manchester United and Everton. He cost £5.5 million on the day that French goalkeeper Lionel Charbonnier moved to Govan from Auxerre for £1.2 million – with the two deals taking the summer spending past the £20-million mark.

Murray said:

> Rangers have to operate at the top end of football, to compete and play at the highest level. This is a sign that we can compete. I've noticed many comments in the press recently about players maybe not wanting to come to Scotland, but I know for a fact that

Newcastle and Middlesbrough were interested in Andrei – so once again the club jet has come in useful.

There's a massive rebuilding process to be done at Rangers and we're not finished yet. We didn't win the championship last year, so initially we want to become No.1 in Scotland again and I'm trying my hardest with the board to put the best team on the park. These are exciting times with Dick coming here and we are trying to make as many resources available to him as possible.

Leeds United live wire Rod Wallace, a rare free transfer, was next to hang his hat on the Ibrox coatrack and was followed through the door by Romanian defender Daniel Prodan, a £2-million buy from Atletico Madrid. The move proved ill-fated. Prodan had an injury nightmare, failing to kick a ball in Scotland after his big-money move and serving as a demonstration of the fact that huge sums of money were being parted with in such a way that it appeared as if value for money was well down the list of priorities.

Mind you, once bitten, twice shy. Some of Advocaat's targets were not landed due to Murray's new-found caution. The attempt to recruit John Hartson from Wimbledon in the summer of 2000 was a case in point as, stung by the Prodan saga, a rigorous new medical deemed the Welshman not fit to sign. He did, of course, prove the experts wrong by bagging goal after goal for Celtic, but the incident at least proved that the lessons of the past had been learned when it came to due diligence over prospective new faces.

There was also a new air of patience pervading, with Murray stressing that his decision to bankroll the major rebuilding exercise was not designed to guarantee instant success. Indeed, he went so far as to plead for calm before Advocaat's team had even kicked a ball in anger. Speaking on the eve of the 1998–99 season, he said: 'Dick doesn't have a magic wand. He's putting the building blocks in place that we hope will bring us success, but he needs time.'

It was not an era of blind spending, with Murray playing hardball in a number of negotiations. The protracted bid to lure Colin Hendry north was a case in point, with the Ibrox owner going head to head with Blackburn Rovers counterpart Jack Walker as they haggled over the asking price. Rovers wanted more than £5 million; Rangers were prepared to pay just half of that.

Typically, Rangers had been cute about the process. Hendry knew a four-year deal was on the table for him in Glasgow, with the carrot of the captaincy apparently also waved under his nose. It was that which led him to put pressure on Blackburn to grant him his 'dream move'.

Murray vowed to 'take a long play' and gently reminded the English side that he was used to getting his own way, adding, 'We are very keen to sign Colin and he is keen to come here as well.'

What he hadn't bargained on was fellow steel magnate Walker and his team's stubborn resistance, and eventually it cost close to £4 million to land the Scotland captain.

There were suggestions that the very public courtship of another club's star man could lead to trouble for Murray, who stood accused of 'tapping up' Hendry. Walker dispelled that notion, admitting: 'We've been friends for 30 years in the steel business, so we're not about to end that over this.'

Murray's forceful approach to the pursuit of signing targets often raised eyebrows and ire among the football fraternity. There were murmurs of illicit approaches to Aberdeen's Eoin Jess as well as murmurs of discontent from Newcastle United after their bid for AB Copenhagen starlet Peter Løvenkrands was allegedly hijacked by the Gers at the eleventh hour.

The deal to land Hendry was an expensive piece of business when the defender's fast-approaching 33rd birthday was taken into account, and it edged Advocaat's spending close to the £30-million mark in just a few short months.

The proof of the pudding, as always, would be in the eating. Results were encouraging, aside from a minor wobble: a 2–1 defeat against Hearts in the first league game of the new era. Apart from that, Advocaat's team of all stars looked excellent, with impressive defence performances married to liberal scoring at the other end.

The manager had arrived on a two-year contract, and even before his first six months were up, there were efforts to tie him to a longer deal. The Dutchman was non-committal. The chairman, in turn, was unconcerned. Murray remarked:

> I believe that a handshake is sometimes stronger and more binding than any other form of agreement. Dick and I shook hands on the Rangers job a year ago and I've no reason to believe he would want to leave Ibrox.

The work ethic of the new manager was often hailed by his boss, who pointed to late-night calls from the Dutchman as a sign of his unstinting efforts to improve the team he had inherited. It was not uncommon for chairman and manager to be hatching transfer plans while others were settling down to go to sleep.

The reward for his devotion to the cause was instant success. The first trophy of the 1998–99 season was collected when Advocaat steered his side to the League Cup with a 2–1 victory over St Johnstone. Jörg Albertz was on target along with Stéphane Guivarc'h. The Frenchman had lost his aversion to the Scottish game and had finally arrived in Glasgow, via an unhappy stint at Newcastle United, to link up with Advocaat.

It marked the beginning of a memorable run for the Little General. It seemed he could do no wrong in his maiden season. The league title was sewn up and secured in style with a 3–0 win at Parkhead; then, with the only goal of the game, Rod Wallace clinched the treble as Rangers landed the Scottish Cup in an Old Firm final at Hampden.

In Advocaat's second season, the 1999–2000 campaign, he bolstered the squad with the exciting signing of £4-million man Michael Mols from Utrecht, with the striker looking surefooted and accomplished from the outset.

The league was won again – this time with a 21-point lead over closest challengers Celtic. The silverware continued to stack up when the Scottish Cup was claimed with a 4–0 victory in the final against Aberdeen.

It was not enough. European success was what the manager and chairman both craved, and it would take further investment to achieve that goal. Or so the theory went. The investment followed, but the European trophy did not.

Towards the end of the 1999–2000 season the club made a record-breaking bid of £12 million for Dynamo Kiev attacker Serhiy Rebrov, although the cash carrot was not enough to lure the in-demand man to Scotland.

There was greater success just a few months into 2000–01 when the Scottish transfer record tumbled yet again. Tore André Flo arrived after a £12-million fee was sanctioned by the Ibrox board. It was brave and it was bold – but ultimately the gamble failed to pay off. Flo was steady but unspectacular and he would not help his new side to a single trophy.

Flo's arrival in the closing weeks of 2000 for the astronomical fee was a headline-grabber. Flo himself pocketed in the region of £1.2 million of that sum, with Chelsea and Rangers haggling over who would pay the Norwegian his slice of the cake before agreement was reached. Rangers were 15 points adrift of Celtic at that stage and the deal for the Stamford Bridge striker smacked of desperation. Murray said:

> There is a maximum for everything at this club and we would not
> put the club at risk. However, the supporters can rest assured that

> Dick Advocaat and myself are doing our utmost on and off the park
> to get things right and bring the club out of the difficult situation
> we have been experiencing recently.

As PR stunts go, it was a costly one in the long run. The transfer dwarfed the Scottish record held by Celtic after their capture of Chris Sutton that summer and is unlikely to be broken any time soon.

The Scandinavian had never set foot on Scottish soil before being given the red-carpet treatment by Rangers, flown north on Murray's private jet to conclude negotiations. He had been Chelsea's leading scorer the previous term, with 19 goals for the Blues, but had been languishing on the bench when Advocaat made his move.

Flo has often been remembered as an Ibrox flop, although it was perhaps his hefty price tag rather than his performances on the park that was largely responsible for that feeling. In truth, he was somewhere between a flop and a £12-million player. He could not do enough to improve the side's ailing fortunes.

As the 2001–02 season loomed, the pressure was on Advocaat's shoulders for the first time and he could do nothing to shift it, with signs of strain beginning to show.

During the Dutchman's stay on Clydeside, there were whispers that the chairman was taking a greater interest in team affairs than at any point previously. For example, it was suggested that Murray had been the key protagonist in the move for Scotland skipper Colin Hendry.

In later years, the player himself strenuously denied that Murray had gone behind the manager's back to broker the deal – even though he admitted his face-to-face dealings had been solely with the chairman. He claimed it was 'a myth' that Advocaat had not been central to the transfer. However, as Hendry stated, even if it had been the case that Murray had instigated the move, surely it would be the owner's prerogative to have a major influence on the recruitment policy.

There were also ructions when Gordon Strachan, then in charge at Coventry, claimed that Murray had sanctioned a deal to sell fans' favourite Jörg Albertz before reneging when it became clear that the German was still part of his manager's plans.

A similar claim surfaced during Alex McLeish's tenure, when Brazilian midfielder Emerson insisted it was Murray and not McLeish who had taken him to Glasgow. He made the allegations after being binned from the team and they were firmly refuted by McLeish.

Regardless of player recruitment policy, there was still plenty of scope for Advocaat to make his own mark. In 2001, the Dutch contingent grew when Jan Wouters, the former Ajax coach, joined Advocaat's staff. It was on the back of what the chairman admitted had been a 'disastrous' season and represented another vote of confidence for the embattled manager.

That summer's spending spree continued with the arrival of Claudio Caniggia from Dundee, a signing Murray claimed was 'only the beginning'.

Christian Nerlinger checked in from Borussia Dortmund, a snip at £3 million, or so they thought, and Russell Latapy, from the bargain shelf in comparison, joined the list of new faces. At one stage, Real Madrid's Samuel Eto'o was quoted as a potential target, although that was one that Murray was quick to dismiss as a bridge too far. The procurement of England international Michael Ball for £6.5 million from Everton was not, however, and the defender duly signed on the dotted line.

By the start of December 2001, the tide was beginning to turn. Murray had always claimed he would listen to supporters ahead of opinion from other quarters, and when the fans began to turn on Advocaat as a result of another Old Firm defeat and a ten-point deficit in the title race, the manager's future began to be the subject of serious discussion at board level.

Those talks led to a quick announcement on the strategy for the road ahead – with Advocaat offered a supervisory role as new boss Alex McLeish was installed and promised funds to rebuild the team. Murray quipped: 'Everybody writes our death wish [sic] – but people tend to forget that I'm not short of a bob or two.'

It was a dream move for McLeish, who appeared comfortable with the prospect of working under his predecessor. For the up-and-coming Scot, having the wily Continental coach on hand was viewed as a boon rather than a burden. He had already had a close encounter with Advocaat when, as a rookie taking his first tentative steps on the managerial road with Motherwell, he'd travelled to PSV Eindhoven to observe Advocaat and his staff in action. He did, however, point out he was working 'with' rather than 'for' the Dutchman at Ibrox.

Advocaat agreed to a two-year stint as director of football, although, given that he expressed doubts about his suitability for the back-seat role, there was always the chance it would be a more of a short-term appointment.

Within months, Advocaat had been tempted back onto the training field when the Dutch FA installed him as coach of the national team for a second stint at international level, combining that job initially with his Rangers commitments and revelling in the opportunity to get back to basics and enjoy regular contact with players on the training ground and in the dressing-room.

By September 2002, the connection had been severed, with Advocaat leaving Ibrox to concentrate fully on his job with his home country. Murray paid a glowing tribute, remarking:

> Dick Advocaat's achievements with Rangers should not be underestimated in any way. There is no doubt that he will be remembered as an Ibrox great. Twice voted manager of the year, he won a double and a treble with the first team. His determination in creating training and youth-development facilities benefiting our club has created a solid foundation for the future.

It had been a flamboyant, exciting and invigorating experiment at the start. At times, it became a frustrating and infuriating journey, as the man from the land of the Oranje proved not to have the golden touch that his first two seasons had suggested.

Scottish football had welcomed his legion of foreign stars with open arms, treated to a wave of top-quality internationals who, in the main, embraced the culture of their adopted country and the traditions of the club they served.

But it had also been a costly exercise. The departure of Advocaat and the arrival of McLeish heralded a large dose of realism. The carefree early days of the Dutchman's tenure were a fading memory, and a new, more frugal era was about to kick in.

CHAPTER 17

'This is my fourth manager at Rangers and I still get
a buzz at the start of every new era.'

David Murray, 2006

AFTER THE EXTRAVAGANCE came thrift; after the idealism came
pragmatism. After Dick Advocaat came Alex McLeish, to restore some
good old-fashioned Scottish values to Ibrox and bring an end to the
experiment with foreign management at one of the country's proud old
institutions once and for all. Or so we thought.

Between 2001 and 2006, there was the calm of McLeish. Then came
the storm of Paul Le Guen as David Murray returned to scratch the
itch of foreign coaching for a second and final time. He experienced
the best of times, with the Champions League run under his fiery Scot,
and the worst of times, as the quirky Frenchman's tenure stuttered to
an ignominious end.

The McLeish and Le Guen years will go down as among the most
turbulent in a chairmanship that otherwise benefited from a relatively
smooth passage, oiled by the success savoured under Graeme Souness,
Walter Smith and Dick Advocaat.

Since leaving Ibrox, McLeish has gone on to great things. He has
managed his country, scripted the fairy tale of Birmingham's Carling
Cup final victory against the might of Arsenal and established himself
as a Premier League manager with Aston Villa. But if life after Rangers
has been eventful, those years have been nothing in comparison with
the whirlwind he found himself at the centre of during his stay in the
Gers manager's office.

After walking through the door in 2001 and hanging his jacket on the
peg once used by luminaries such as Bill Struth and Willie Waddell,
McLeish led his side to the league title twice, the Scottish Cup two times
and the League Cup three times in his action-packed stint in charge.

During that period, he also made swingeing cuts to the wage bill as the megabucks signings of the Advocaat era slowly ebbed away to be replaced with more cost-effective solutions. The Dutchman had spent big on Arthur Numan, Ronald de Boer and Giovanni van Bronckhorst. McLeish was down in the bargain bucket as the likes of Marvin Andrews, Gavin Rae and Steven Thompson were brought in during a book-balancing exercise.

Initially, results were encouraging, but ultimately the credit-crunch menu was not fulfilling enough for a success-hungry chairman, and Le Guen was sent for to breathe new life into the club.

The solid start enjoyed by McLeish ensured loyalty from his owner but could not preserve his future when the going got too tough. He found his early success had won him Murray's backing during turbulent periods. Still, he also found that the chairman did not mince his words. Late in 2005, Murray, while giving McLeish qualified support to overcome a difficult period of results, admitted that he already had a plan in place to replace his manager if fortunes did not improve. While Murray stressed it would be disrespectful to name names while McLeish was still fighting for his future, he did admit:

> At all times you are looking at alternatives. I wouldn't be doing my job if I didn't know what route I was going to go down. We know what we would do, but I hope we don't have to do it . . . We must see a marked improvement. If not, we have to look at his forward relationship with the club. If it doesn't work out, Alex would have to go.

It was the vote of confidence, Murray style.

Rumours of negotiations behind the scenes with French coach Le Guen soon began to circulate, with the Continental manager doing little to quash the claims. Bizarrely, Murray took the opportunity of the escalating newspaper talk to inform McLeish of his recruitment drive. He said:

> Alex knows who the next manager of Rangers will be if he has to go. Alex has had a run of bad luck and I told him I'd have to put a backstop on it. But I am very loyal to people. My word is my bond and one thing I can't recover if I break it is my reputation.

McLeish and Murray held talks in November 2005, which gave the manager a stay of execution, but dialogue between the two men became far more frequent as the situation became critical. Day in and day out,

Murray and McLeish would talk over the plans for progress.

Guiding the club into the last 16 of the Champions League provided McLeish with the ticket to see through the campaign. The £5-million windfall that the safe passage through to that stage guaranteed was unashamedly one of the factors that decided Murray about his manager's future.

Funds were swiftly reinvested, with Kris Boyd recruited for £450,000 in a shrewd piece of business, but the raft of new faces promised by Murray failed to materialise. By that stage, Rangers' clout in the transfer market had diminished substantially from the heady days of Dick Advocaat's honeymoon period at Ibrox. When McLeish bid £450,000 for Derek Riordan of Hibs, the Easter Road club dismissed the bid out of hand – claiming it would have taken three years for Rangers to complete the instalment programme they had offered.

The lack of fresh blood led to the first sign of demonstrations against Murray, with the tables turning as the manager was forced to leap to the defence of his chairman. McLeish said:

> David made those statements [promising new signings] thinking there would be quite a bit of investment coming in. That hasn't happened yet. Also, we had about ten players down at the time. If that was still the case, and the injury crisis had persisted, we would have been forced into going into the market and maybe spending over budget.

Days after that staunch defence, McLeish was sacked. It was announced in February 2006 that he would step down at the end of the season and confirmed that his successor was already in place, although the name would not be released until the following month. Murray said: 'The decision had to be made. It's a premature announcement, but it takes away the grey area. We want to get down to winning some football matches.'

He added:

> Alex McLeish has enjoyed a highly successful period, winning seven trophies over four and a half years, and during this time there have been significant financial constraints throughout the football environment.
>
> When he took over at Rangers, it was a very difficult period. The club was in the red, so he was having to deal with getting free-transfer players, players on loan, and that's not Rangers Football Club. He never moaned about it. He got on with it and he's kept his

dignity fantastically well. He's always been really strong that way, Alex. It's never been a problem for him.

The front-runners to replace the manager included Le Guen, Souness, Ottmar Hitzfeld, Alan Curbishley and former Light Blues skipper Terry Butcher, then at Motherwell. Soon, it became clear that Le Guen was in fact the only runner in a one-horse race.

In March, the announcement was made: the Frenchman was on his way. Murray greeted the confirmation with the proclamation that Le Guen represented a 'big capture' and claimed the appointment would give Scotland as a nation a stronger identity in the world game. Murray insisted his new manager could have had his pick of the major European clubs and commented: 'This is my fourth manager at Rangers and I still get a buzz at the start of every new era. If I didn't, I wouldn't be doing this any more.'

His new man's credentials were impressive, to say the least. Between 2002 and 2005, he guided Olympique Lyonnais to three French championships, three domestic cup triumphs and – crucially, when Murray's ambitions were taken into account – to the quarter-finals of the UEFA Cup twice in as many years.

Intriguingly, given the precarious finances at Rangers, he had done all of that with a relatively small group of players. In his homeland, he had unearthed rough diamonds like Shabani Nonda and El Hadji Diouf. Unlike Advocaat, he did not fit the identikit of a cheque-book manager.

When asked the secret of his success with Lyon by FIFA.com, Le Guen said:

> We had wonderful players, of course, and an excellent team spirit. The players were always exceptional on the pitch, and despite the fact that the squad was never more than 17 or 18 strong, they were a tight-knit group. Not only were the players technically impressive they were mentally strong as well. It was a fantastic time for me.

The task was to try to repeat his consistent success in Scotland. It was the same game but a different country and a different set of people from those he had left behind in France. Everything had changed and he would have to learn on the job.

In came a clutch of players, most unheard of previously in Scotland and none carrying the type of price tag entertained by Dick Advocaat just a few years earlier.

Jérémy Clément, a £1.1-million recruit from Lyon, was to be the new midfield linchpin. There was strike sensation Filip Sebo from Austria Vienna, Swedish stopper Karl Svensson and veteran French forward Jean-Claude Darcheville.

Sasa Papac, another of the less-than-glamorous recruits, turned out to be the one unlikely diamond in the rough. He was the Le Guen signing who stood the test of time at Ibrox – unlike Czech winger Libor Sionko, who came, saw and went away again. Remember young French winger William Stanger? No, and nor would you be expected to – he was another of the new-regime recruits who failed to set the heather alight.

The chairman and directors backed their new boss, even if there was an element of unease about his signing policy. Results, they figured, would be the telling factor.

But by November 2006, the wagons were circling around Le Guen, after a miserable start to his time in charge, with hundreds of supporters protesting. Murray kept a dignified, or calculated, silence before coming out all guns blazing. It was the players, not the manager, who should carry the can, according to the chairman.

Murray, who held a summit with his players, said: 'These players have to realise the responsibility of pulling on the blue jersey. They have to learn and they have to learn quick. I hope we get a response in the positive manner.'

As if to prove his loyalty to the Frenchman, Murray backed his manager in his decision to strip Barry Ferguson of the captaincy. At least Le Guen claimed that was the case. The Ferguson affair proved to be the beginning of the end for the manager, who walked away in February 2007.

Le Guen stated:

> I am disappointed to leave the club, but I think it is the best solution for all concerned. I would like to thank all the people who helped me and my team during my spell in Scotland. In particular, I would like to thank the directors, who at all times gave me their total support.

But did he walk? While it was portrayed that way in the media, the strong suspicion was that *le manager* had been given some encouragement to return to the Continent and leave Rangers to get on with the business of rebuilding a team that had descended into chaos. The suggestion that he had quit the post protected his reputation and also painted the club in a more favourable light than might have been the case if he had been binned so early in his tenure. After all, he was a coach held in high regard throughout Europe and his failure to succeed in Scotland could have been viewed as as much of an indictment of the state of the SPL as it was an indication of Le Guen's abilities on the training field.

Murray, speaking as he conducted interviews to mark his 20th anniversary in the owner's seat in 2008, shed some light on the departure and painted a picture that reflected the mood at the time. He said:

> It was his call. He made it easier by falling on his sword. I don't know if he had been tapped for the Paris Saint-Germain job. He said he hadn't. What made me think he had was when he didn't take any money for going. He sent me a text three weeks before he decided to go saying, 'Thanks for your support.' I thought, 'That's fine, he's OK,' then him and Barry Ferguson had words, blah, blah, blah. I was in Paris, in a brasserie having a glass of wine, when I got a call saying he had dropped Ferguson, so I flew back immediately. I met him in the Norton House Hotel, asked how he saw it, and he said he would like to go. I said, 'Just sign this bit of paper then,' because he had two years on a contract to go. I took the view that if he wanted to walk out on us and we were prepared to let him go, we shouldn't be financially paying out.

It might not have cost a large sum in compensation, but the departure of the Frenchman was not entirely without pain. He had been well rewarded during his time in Glasgow and had also spent money on players who ultimately failed to provide value for money. There were costs other than financial ones; the time spent on the underwhelming experiment was impossible to recover and many more months would need to be invested to repair the damage and build again for the future.

What on paper had looked to be a textbook appointment proved to be an unmitigated disaster, save for the advantage of proving that a lack of understanding of the Scottish game is not something an Old Firm manager can afford. It appeared from start to finish that Le Guen had underestimated the enormity of the challenge at Rangers and the peculiar demands placed on the Ibrox boss. He quickly discovered, to his cost, that the SPL would be no walk in the park. Take an average player from the Continent and place him in Scotland and he remains an average player – something Le Guen appeared not to have factored into his calculations when he crossed the Channel with blueprint in hand.

All in all, it had not been Murray's finest hour; his judgement had wavered. Had he trusted his instinct and backed away at the very beginning, the whole situation could have been averted.

Murray admitted that first impressions had not been good but said he had been swayed by his target's impressive credentials and had gone through with the appointment regardless of the omens.

In a 2008 interview with *The Times*, the chairman reflected:

> I have tried to change the menu with players and managers. I brought Dick Advocaat in and it was a success until, amazingly, he ran out of steam. Alex McLeish was able to take on his players and win a treble. Paul Le Guen is a real disappointment because there is no doubt he was the most chased manager of the time.
>
> I went to Dinard in December 2005 to meet him. Martin Bain and I flew to Dinard, we were on a private plane and the weather was atrocious. We were the only plane to land that day and there was nobody to take us from the airport. I had to climb on a Land Rover trailer that belonged to the fire brigade. I said to Martin, 'I hope this bastard is good!' It wasn't a very good meeting – he was quite cold – but then we brought him and his whole team to my house in Perth to discuss things.

That meeting went better and the deal was sealed to take Le Guen and his staff to Scotland. In the weeks leading up to his arrival, there was incredible anticipation. He was new, interesting and carried an element of intrigue. What followed was a surprise to everyone, media included. He should have breezed into Glasgow with Gallic flair and fresh ideas, taking the dear old SPL in his stride. But he didn't; he was knocked sideways by the pace and intensity of it all and left looking like a lost soul devoid of inspiration and struggling to get his ideas across to a group of players who, by and large, failed to embrace the French revolution. Even those imported by Le Guen could not lift the mood with their performances for the embattled coach.

It took just a matter of months for a fear of failure to creep in at Ibrox, as Murray and his directors began to grasp the very real prospect of having to take swift and decisive action over the future of a man who had been expected to be a long-term solution to the search for a settled managerial set-up. It had dawned on the chairman that the theory of the appointment was very different from the practice and that expectations were far and away above what was being delivered at ground level by the manager and his charges.

Murray later admitted:

> All the credentials, all the CV was good but, when he came here, I don't think he prepared himself for what he was coming into. I

don't think he understood the game, and the players he bought did not make the grade here. Paul Le Guen was offered money and did not spend it. Any manager can blame the tools but, with the greatest of respect, he did spend a bit of money and the tools weren't the right ones for the job.

It is surely an unusual complaint from any chairman, that his manager is unwilling to splash the cash. It was not that Le Guen did not invest at all; after all, there were plenty of new recruits during his short time in Scotland. The problem was more one of scale: there were no blockbuster signings, no record-breaking arrivals to whet the appetites of chairman and supporters alike. Le Guen appeared determined to live by his own rules and shun the established logic that as Rangers manager he must spend big in order to make his mark on the club.

Mind you, it was not a marquee signing who first set the chairman thinking that he might have made a mistake with Le Guen – rather a tried-and-tested Scottish veteran who had been over the course with Rangers before, albeit during his formative years as a professional player. Murray, when pressed on the moment he realised he had made the wrong appointment, said:

> It's very basic but when Steven Pressley was available, I suggested we sign him to shore up the back. We didn't have that sort of centre-half and I wanted to bring a Scot into the backroom staff. The one thing I never do is override anybody. When you do that you are as well not having them. I offered Le Guen money to sign players and, when he said he didn't want the money around November, December, that's what started the alarm bells in my head.

When Le Guen departed, he had been in charge for fewer than 200 days. His only achievement was an unwanted one: becoming the shortest-serving manager ever to lead Rangers. He left the country and returned to his homeland to think again about his brief sojourn in Scotland.

Not that Le Guen was idle for long. Within ten days, he had been installed at Paris Saint-Germain, proving that his failure with Rangers had done nothing to damage his reputation in French football. He was tasked with steering PSG clear of relegation and did that, going on to slowly rebuild the Parisian outfit and turn them back into championship challengers.

An interested bystander was former Ibrox striker Stéphane Guivarc'h, who, in his role as a television pundit with Canal+, was able to analyse the impact Le Guen had on PSG. Guivarc'h, speaking in an interview with the *Sunday Mail* in 2009, said:

> There is one big difference between Le Guen at Rangers and Paris Saint-Germain: time. In Scotland, for some reason, they took one look at him and decided they didn't like him. After seven months, he was gone with only a simple '*au revoir*' as a way of thank you. No one can say that is enough time to make your mark on a club.
>
> He arrived from another country, a foreign culture, and spoke a different language. His ideas were always going to take time to implement, but the pressure is so intense in Glasgow he wasn't given that luxury. Paul is not a quick-fix manager. He takes time to get into the heads of his players and make the fans understand his philosophies. He should have been treated better than only being given seven months then getting the sack before anyone knew what he could do as a coach.

Le Guen endured turbulent times early in his PSG reign, escaping by the skin of his teeth with his job intact. Guivarc'h added:

> PSG could easily have done what Rangers did and got rid of him in their first season. He had a difficult year and results weren't much better than they were before his arrival. Because PSG have a history of sacking coaches, the writing seemed on the wall. There is a long way to go, but the future looks bright for the club now again, and it could have been the same at Rangers if he was still there. In football, there are no guarantees. Maybe they would have continued to suffer if Paul stayed, but perhaps Rangers would have won the league.
>
> If fans had bought in to his ideas, Rangers could be the big force in Scotland. People say the pressure is huge in Glasgow, but it's the same in Paris. They are the capital's side, a team that has traditionally spent a lot of money, and their fans have high expectations.

After the burden of trying to live up to the demands at Rangers, Le Guen must have been ready to face anything football could throw at him. He never criticised his Scottish experience, no doubt classing it as character building.

What he and his predecessor McLeish had in common was decorum when dealing with their unexpected exits. Neither had a bad word to say about David Murray; both felt they had been treated fairly.

When criticism of Murray was at its strongest, it was McLeish who was among the first to leap to his defence. The former Aberdeen star could have been forgiven for being less than complimentary to the man who had sacked him from his dream job with Rangers, but he was the opposite, full of praise for Murray's achievements. Speaking in 2009, he said:

> I don't think the criticism is fair at all, given what David's done for the club over 20 years. That man has done everything he possibly can to make Rangers successful. He's ambitious, a winner.
>
> Long term, I've absolutely no doubts that David Murray's heart is in Rangers. In everything that he's done and everything he's still trying to do, he's trying to get Rangers back to the top again. I just cannot see David Murray not wanting to do the very best for Rangers.
>
> Rangers are a massive club and you definitely believe that they can compete with the very best, but it's unrealistic in this day and age, finances wise.

McLeish had seen life from the other side of the fence by then, operating in the promised land of the English Premier League. Even perennial strugglers like Birmingham could outgun the Old Firm in the wages stakes and in terms of transfer fees, putting the struggles of the Glasgow pair in stark relief for the former Ibrox gaffer. This perspective must have served to intensify his appreciation of Murray's efforts in keeping Rangers competitive for as long as he did, and with a certain degree of panache and style.

Speaking in September 2011, after his former chairman had departed the club, McLeish claimed:

> I think he has worked wonders for Rangers. He tried to inject his personal money into having a go at the Champions League. For a Scottish team to do that is almost impossible because they don't have the backing of the top English and Spanish teams financially. It would need the personal wealth of an owner like David Murray. He tried really hard for Rangers to achieve that dream.

CHAPTER 18

'I've said before I'd rather see success in Europe
than nine in a row and I stand by that now.'
David Murray, 1996

WHEN THE DUST eventually settles and there is time to reflect on the Murray years at Rangers, the big questions will almost certainly revolve around the ignominious manner in which the era drew to a close. With debts piling up, banks closing in and indifference from the supporters, it was not the way the influential owner would have wanted to depart.

He would far rather have left having held aloft a European trophy on the front doorstep of Ibrox to an adoring crowd. That was the dream; that was the masterplan. That was what kept him coming back for more, year after year and million after million. Unfortunately, it was that aim that ultimately can be traced to the root of the problems that caused the chairman the most angst.

For one thing, European glory proved to be an ever-elusive holy grail. It was there in the distance, within touching distance at times, but cruelly snatched away on more than one occasion to leave all associated wondering what might have been. So near, so far, so terribly painful.

Secondly, tens of millions of pounds had been staked on one day, just maybe one day, hitting the jackpot in Europe. It was the prize that the owner wanted more than any other in football and he took huge risks to try to make the dream happen. Those risks, stacked up season after season, were the biggest financial drain on the club.

Ironically, the two nearest misses on the Continental stage came during periods of calm in the sea of spending. Both were at the hand of Walter Smith, more than a decade apart, in 1993 and then 2008, and both relied on the traditional Rangers qualities of organisation, a team ethic and flourishes of individual flair.

Sandwiched between was the Dick Advocaat era, a period of huge investment under an experienced European coach. Stacked high with promises, what was delivered, in Europe at least, paled in comparison. What the experience taught the owner was that money can't buy you happiness.

The thrill of the UEFA Cup chase in 2008, even in the face of the crushing disappointment that night in Manchester, brought far greater enrichment, on a relative shoestring, than any of the Advocaat-led campaigns. Murray fell back in love with football.

As the club prepared for the showdown with Zenit St Petersburg in 2008, the owner admitted as much when he said:

> Recently, I have really enjoyed being involved with Rangers. Since Walter Smith came back I have shown renewed enthusiasm. Reaching the UEFA Cup final in Manchester is a wonderful achievement by the management and players. I have been involved with the club for 20 years and can't remember anything better. I don't think we will realise what a remarkable time it was until we look back on it.

The incredible adventure, Murray's most successful run in a tenure at the helm spanning almost quarter of a century, might have ended in defeat – but in a sense it also provided vindication. The dream that had been chased for many years at great expense was not as implausible as it perhaps had sounded. For a team – even one as big as Rangers – from a league the size of the SPL, with all of the limitations that go hand in hand with that, to reach a showpiece European final was indeed a remarkable achievement.

What Walter Smith had proved was that Rangers could do it. Had it been for a touch more guile, a cutting edge and a big slice of luck, the result in the final could have been different and Murray's reign would have had the crowning glory he had always hoped for.

The owner's burning desire to achieve at the very top level put him at odds with his managers at times, although they must surely have appreciated his unstinting determination to live the Euro dream.

In 1996, during the thrill of the chase of a ninth championship, Murray claimed, 'I've said before I'd rather see success in Europe than nine in a row and I stand by that now.'

The arrival of Advocaat and the flood of high-profile players that accompanied the Dutchman's appointment brought renewed hope for Murray. At the start of the 1999–2000 season, he insisted, 'I believe Europe is more important to us than the championship this season.

We've won the league so many times – but we've not achieved success in the Champions League.'

In one sentence, he laid bare his desire, almost desperation, to explore new territories and to conquer them. The assertion of the shift in priorities drew an acerbic response from his team boss, who appeared less optimistic about Rangers' chances of emerging victorious from European competition. Advocaat said, 'I have to disagree with the chairman. How else are we going to qualify for the Champions League if we are not the champions?'

He had a point, after all. Domestic success, as sweet as it tasted each season, would always open the door to the promised land governed by UEFA – even if that door had a nasty habit of slamming shut again.

The first demonstration of that came before Murray even had his car in the chairman's parking space. As Murray engaged in negotiations with Lawrence Marlborough over the purchase of the club in the winter of 1988, Graeme Souness and his team were trying to negotiate their way through the UEFA Cup.

Success against Polish side GKS Katowice in the first round paved the way for a second-round contest against FC Köln. With the new owner waiting in the wings and hoping for a money-spinning extended run in the competition, disaster struck.

A 2–0 defeat in the first leg in Germany was compounded by a red card for Ally McCoist and his subsequent suspension. An injury to Ray Wilkins in the build-up made matters worse and, despite a Kevin Drinkell goal in the return match, an equaliser from the visitors made it 3–1 on aggregate.

Souness said:

> Circumstances combined to knock us out this time. But we know that given a reasonable share of the breaks, and given the chance to play our best side, then we will get that long run in Europe that the fans want so much. Listen, we want it too.

Neither the manager nor the chairman could have appreciated just how difficult it would prove to push their domestically dominant team forward on foreign shores. Their first season as a partnership, in 1989–90, brought first-round defeat in the European Cup against Bayern Munich. The following term it was Red Star Belgrade, in the second round, who bumped Rangers out of the tournament, and in 1991–92 it was Sparta Prague, in the first round, who did the damage.

Bayern aside, it was not a stellar cast of big-earning megastars who were the cause of the problems. Rather it was the methodical and efficient men from the Eastern bloc who dashed the hopes of the expensively assembled outfit of the Souness revolution.

Things had to change and, with Walter Smith taking control, there was an immediate upturn in fortunes. When Rangers welcomed the Danes of Lyngby BK to Ibrox on 16 September 1992, it marked the first instalment in what would be the most memorable of stories. It was the first-ever season of the Champions League, as the European Cup had been rebranded, and it would soon see the name of Rangers Football Club up in lights. A neat and tidy 2–0 win against the Scandinavians in the first leg of the qualifying tie was the small acorn from which the oak of that giant season would grow.

Remember Leeds United, the Battle of Britain? Who could forget? McCoist and Hateley were too hot to handle for the Elland Road side and it was game, set and match to the tartan crusaders who had ventured south to teach the Auld Enemy a thing or two about good football, good attitude and good tactics.

Then onwards to the group stages as the European football public waited with bated breath for the business end of the Continent's newest and most prestigious competition.

Rangers were drawn in Group A, and when they opened with a 2–2 draw at home to Marseille, it set a marker for what was to follow in a tense and closely contested pool. Victory on neutral territory in Germany against CSKA Moscow and a draw in Belgium against Club Brugge were only offset by a frustrating defeat against the Belgians at Ibrox.

A rousing 1–1 draw against the highly fancied, and highly paid, Marseille in a feverish South of France atmosphere was not enough to secure passage to the final, with a 0–0 draw at home to the Muscovites in the final match bringing the curtain down on an impressive Champions League debut.

Marseille were the team to progress from the group, and it was they who went on to win the trophy, although their victory was later tainted somewhat by allegations of match-fixing in French league matches during the 1992–93 season.

The final at the Olympic Stadium in Munich could, and arguably should, have featured Rangers against the might of AC Milan. It didn't, though, and there were only thoughts of what could have been to carry the club through the summer months.

Speaking in the aftermath, Murray said:

> What Rangers have achieved in Europe this season is against all the odds. The current domestic set-up is not conducive to any Scottish

club doing well in Europe. Remember, our players have been brought up in the hurly-burly of the Premier League. In addition, your typical Marseille player has taken part in perhaps only 36 games this season. David Robertson, for example, has played in 54.

Despite all that our current squad have shown they are good enough to play at the highest level in Europe. It has been a classic case of boys becoming men. Rangers, and our supporters, have made the Champions League a huge success this season. Our run in Europe has been crucial because it has reduced borrowings, increased gate money and boosted profit.

And there was the crux of the matter. European success could provide kudos and incredible Old Firm bragging rights – but it also brought financial benefits capable of dwarfing anything available in Scotland. There were plentiful reasons for hoping for more great European nights akin to those sampled during the heady 1992–93 Champions League run.

What followed was a horrible lull. First-round exits at the hands of Levski Sofia and then AEK Athens ensured Ibrox was bereft of the seductive glamour of the Champions League group stages. Then, in 1995–96, the Light Blues returned to the big stage. Results were not encouraging, with the Group C campaign ending without a win from six matches against Steaua Bucharest, Borussia Dortmund and Juventus. The following term was little better, with a group featuring Ajax and Auxerre as well as dark horses Grasshopper bringing the meagre return of just a single victory against the Swiss men.

Smith, after his initial success, had failed to deliver, and it was time to move aside and let Dick Advocaat put his experience to good use. Or at least that was the idea, with tens of millions of pounds lavished on the squad to give the Dutchman more than a fighting chance.

There were highlights along the way – the stirring UEFA Cup win at Bayer Leverkusen in 1998–99, the 2–0 win at home to Parma and the 4–1 thumping of PSV Eindhoven at Ibrox the following term – but the tangible results were limited as Advocaat's side failed to hit top gear when it mattered most.

There was the brief hope of salvation when talk of the Atlantic League began to resurface. When Celtic initially attended discussions regarding a proposal from Ajax to form an Atlantic League as the new millennium loomed, Rangers declined their invitation. The Champions League, Murray declared, was the future for his club, rather than any poor imitation of the Continent's elite competition that could be contrived.

By the start of the 2000–01 campaign, that attitude had certainly softened, and Rangers agreed in principle to proposals for a European league involving leading lights from the Netherlands, Belgium, Portugal and the Scandinavian associations. Murray remarked:

> I'm changing my opinion. We are now hindering Scottish football. Perhaps it will be better for other clubs not to financially strain themselves trying to keep up with Rangers and Celtic. There is merit in the idea of Rangers and Celtic joining the new league if it can be worked out with UEFA.

The pipe dream turned out to be exactly that, with UEFA nipping the breakaway notion in the bud. Eventually, the Europa League would come to pass, under the strict auspices of UEFA itself, but in the meantime it was a case of making do within the existing structure.

The quest for glory on the Continent was a mission not without dilemmas, none more so than in the 2001–02 season. There was no doubting how much the owner craved European success; he had admitted it himself. But not at any price, surely? The answer came in that campaign as Murray went to war with UEFA, threatening to do the unthinkable and withdraw his team from European competition.

The saga began when Rangers were drawn against Anzhi Makhachkala in the UEFA Cup early that term. The opposition were based in the war-torn Russian region of Dagestan, and Murray made a firm and determined early stance that he would not risk the lives of his players, officials or staff by making them travel to the troubled area. He lodged a formal request for the away tie to be relocated to a safe neutral venue, but the proposal was instantly rejected by UEFA, who were adamant that the show must go on.

The decision came just days after a car bomb had exploded in the area surrounding the stadium; it was the second device to be detonated in the run-up to the tie. The Foreign Office and the SFA had both expressed grave reservations about the Rangers party travelling; at the time, Dagestan and neighbouring Chechnya were no-go areas for all Westerners due to kidnapping fears.

It left the Ibrox chairman facing what he described as the 'hardest decision I have ever had to make', and he threatened to pull the club out of the competition. He justified his stance by pointing out that 'this is not about football and money now – this is about safety', and added, 'We are dealing with human beings and their safety is far more important than playing a football match.'

Pulling out of the UEFA Cup would have brought severe sanctions, with a two-year European ban and a heavy financial penalty in prospect. Rangers lodged an appeal to the Court of Arbitration for Sport as they frantically explored every avenue available to them in the days leading up to the proposed trip.

In the midst of the controversy, the world was rocked by the 9/11 atrocities in the US. It was the starkest illustration of the grip that terror had on the world during that period, yet UEFA refused to bend. The situation had escalated into deadlock.

As the Court of Arbitration met, the clock was ticking. On the day the panel gathered in Switzerland, Rangers had until 4 p.m. to arrive in Russia to comply with UEFA rules. The decision came late in the day and fell in favour of the governing body, with Rangers ordered to make the trip. The only concession was a rescheduled date, the result of a decision to postpone ties in light of the 9/11 attack.

The Scottish government waded into the dispute, vowing to do all it could to support the club and gaining cross-party support for its stance. Govan MSP Gordon Jackson described it as 'beyond belief' that Rangers were expected to make the treacherous journey.

The British Government was even called upon by UEFA to become involved and meet with Russian counterparts to assess security provision for the tie as the issue was referred to the highest levels across Europe in a bid to reach a satisfactory outcome.

Captain Barry Ferguson entered the debate when he insisted he would not travel under any circumstances. Ferguson said, 'It is as simple as that – you can't go to Dagestan. I want to see my boys grow up.'

When the club's insurers withdrew cover for the squad to make the trip, UEFA finally reversed their hard-line stance and ordered a one-off tie to be played in the more agreeable surroundings of Warsaw. In a statement, UEFA said it had a 'duty to ensure that participants can play safely and securely'. David Murray 1, UEFA 0.

The result was welcomed by SFA chief executive David Taylor, who said:

> Rangers took a brave stance, knowing that they could have faced serious consequences for failing to fulfil a UEFA Cup tie and I am delighted that the concerted campaign by the club, the SFA, the media and the Government has finally been successful.

David Murray was magnanimous in victory, praising the game's rulers for being 'even-handed' in their final decision and adding, 'We cannot emphasise how happy we are that this decision has been made.' That was the public approach; you have to imagine that, in private, there was at least a raised glass in celebration.

Murray had been involved in heated discussions with UEFA chief executive Gerhard Aigner for days when the decision was finally overturned, emphasising during his final arguments that there had been fighting in the region surrounding the stadium in the days leading up to the scheduled fixture.

The Russian club accused Rangers and UEFA of being involved in what they described as 'backstage intrigues'; they reacted furiously to the move to Poland, claiming it represented discrimination against the club, Dagestan and Russia.

The switch to a single tie on neutral territory cost Rangers hundreds of thousands of pounds in lost gate receipts from the forfeited Ibrox home leg – but more important was the victory for common sense.

As an aside, that was a European campaign that took the Light Blues past Dynamo Moscow and Paris Saint-Germain before they fell to Feyenoord in the fourth round as Advocaat made way for Alex McLeish.

McLeish, of far more humble coaching origins than Advocaat, more Motherwell than Maastricht, would provide one of the great contradictions of Rangers in recent times. Whereas his lauded Dutch predecessor had the benefit of Murray's mint to lavish on his squad, Big Eck found his wings clipped in the transfer market. Yet it was McLeish who delivered a place in the last 16 of the Champions League with that plucky run in 2005–06 that proved he had the mettle to succeed at the very highest level.

While, on a football level, there were plaudits for the resilience required by the team to reach that stage, Murray's own thoughts understandably turned to the knock-on benefits the extended run brought. Speaking during what was otherwise a disappointing season, the chairman said:

> Alex has managed to a higher level of success in Europe than ever before in a period of less resources. Rangers were mocked before about European success but we're in there now and this season we're going to make as much as in the last three years of European football.

That was just a warm-up, though; the best was yet to follow. The second coming of Walter Smith brought the championship-winning smile back to the collective Ibrox face, but it also heralded a new high in the club's modern European history.

What Smith achieved in taking his (in relative terms) inexpensively assembled team through to the final of the UEFA Cup was nothing short of a minor football miracle. Panathinaikos fell, Werder Bremen were toppled and Sporting Lisbon were brushed aside. When Fiorentina were taken care of in the semi-final penalty shoot-out, on the back of two ties without a goal, the path was clear to the showpiece final in Manchester.

The build-up to the match-up with Dick Advocaat and his Zenit St Petersburg side naturally drew comparisons with the previous European final.

Barcelona, 1972, Dynamo Moscow, Willie Johnston, Colin Stein, sun, sangria and celebrations. It had taken 36 years to match the achievements of Willie Waddell's team in reaching a final, and the class of '72 found themselves thrust back into the spotlight, facing a barrage of media requests.

What Murray made of that blast from the past is anyone's guess. For years, there had been a sense among some of the Barça Bears that their achievement was a weight around the neck of the big-spending chairman as he tried to recreate the glories of yesteryear.

Willie Mathieson, a hero of the team that stormed to victory in the European Cup-Winners' Cup, was one of those who questioned the recognition, or lack of it, afforded to his peers. He has said:

> I don't think the 1972 team has ever got the credit it deserves. It's almost as though we're an embarrassment because the club hasn't been able to repeat it. If you contrast that with Celtic, you can't get past the front door at Parkhead without seeing a picture of the Lisbon Lions team of 1967 or a replica of the European Cup. While the Celtic team are included in everything, we seem to be kept out of sight. That saddens me. We all share a love of Rangers and it's a team and an achievement that deserves to be remembered.

The creation of Bar 72 at Ibrox in 2006 did help to put Mathieson and his team back on the agenda, although, unlike their Celtic and Aberdeen counterparts, they have never been given an official testimonial to mark the achievements of the '70s.

But perhaps Murray simply did not like to live in the past. In any case, he certainly revelled in the present when it was his turn to fulfil the role of chairman for a European final experience. As he discovered, it was a whole new level, above anything experienced before.

Murray said in the build-up to the Zenit tie:

> I have been inundated with requests for tickets. The guy who did

209

my gates five years ago sent me a card. I even heard from a friend in New Zealand who I hadn't spoken to in 17 years. By rights, we should not be there. The team which beat Fiorentina in the semi-final cost £9 million. A club like Derby County has a bigger wage bill.

As we now know, reaching the final was, in a way, the easy part. Winning it would be an altogether different proposition – a task not helped by ructions back in Scotland.

A huge row arose between Murray and the SPL when the league refused to postpone the fixture scheduled for the weekend prior to the Manchester occasion, not to mention scheduling seven games in eighteen days. The conflict was an unwanted distraction from the job in hand. Murray said:

> Throughout the world people will laugh at this decision in disbelief, and none more so than in Russia, as their own association have done everything they can to assist. We were not asking that all games be called off, simply one match prior to such a prestigious European final.

Talks between Murray, club chief executive Martin Bain and SPL leader Lex Gold were scheduled. Gold had claimed that there was no way of altering the fixture list compiled by the league. Pleas for the season to be extended to aid Rangers were rejected out of hand.

Gold had said:

> It is a matter of public record that we were unable to agree a request from Rangers FC to extend the season still further. This decision was made on the basis that there had been no material change in circumstances since we published the revised fixture list.
>
> The SFA indicated late yesterday that they wished to discuss whether there was any help they could provide. The meeting took place in a constructive atmosphere. But no viable alternatives to the fixture list emerged that did not place the integrity of the SPL competition at risk.
>
> Given the stage we have now reached in our competition, both in terms of the title chase and in relation to the European places, it's not possible to modify the closing date of the season without placing at serious risk the fairness to all of our competition.

Murray said he was angered but not surprised by the SPL's decision. He claimed, 'What has happened here is footballing authorities not being proactive in their assistance but only at this late stage by being reactive through embarrassment.'

There was even the oddity of tiny Queen of the South, surprise opponents for the Gers in the Scottish Cup final, being canvassed on their opinion as to whether their big day should be changed to ease the burden on Walter Smith's team. The answer? No, of course. Gordon Smith, then chief executive of the SFA, agreed.

Whether fixture congestion had any bearing on the final result is anybody's guess. Would a bit more gas in the tank have been of benefit against the well-drilled and energetic Zenit? Most probably, yes. But even that might not have been enough. In the end, the most enjoyable of journeys ended in defeat. Rangers were beaten but far from disgraced.

The arrests on the day of the final and the troubles on the streets of Manchester did much more to leave a sour taste in the mouths of all decent Rangers people, from the very top at boardroom level to the humble supporter. The fallout from those events would be long-lasting, with the hangover from the football-related issues not so protracted.

A clear-the-air meeting between the SPL and Rangers chiefs took place before the 2008–09 campaign kicked off. The drama, tension and excitement of the previous season was a fading memory. It was time to start again in the quest to recapture the spirit of '72.

CHAPTER 19

'They are like two old girls on Sauchiehall Street
lifting their skirts at every league that walks by.'
                                        Keith Wyness, 2001

THE OLD FIRM. You can't live with them, you can't live without them. The relationship between Rangers, Celtic and the rest of Scottish football has been a dysfunctional one to say the least. The schism that has existed for generations shows no sign of closing and events of recent times have done little to help bridge the gap.

As the administrators settled into the Ibrox offices, new questions began to arise. Would administration lead to relegation? If liquidation were to happen, would a reformed Rangers be allowed a back-door return straight into the SPL or would the other top-flight sides vote to kick them out and force them to start from scratch in the lower reaches of the league? Many questions, few immediate answers.

While there was clear dissent from within the SPL about the possibility of Rangers escaping scot-free, common sense suggested that the league could not survive without them. Sponsorship, television revenue and gate receipts would all take a hammering without the men in light blue.

The issue of where Rangers, post-administration or liquidation, would play their football brought bitter divides back to the surface. The root of the problem lay not in Scotland, but over Hadrian's Wall in the green and promised land of England.

What at times appeared to be an obsession with seeking fresh pastures had sent the rest of the SPL onto the back foot and into full defensive mode in recent years. And the best form of defence was attack for clubs who feared being left behind in a vacuum devoid of the interest, and money, generated by the big two.

Aberdeen chief executive Keith Wyness famously led the way as he and his fellow power brokers came out fighting. The Dons supremo, while discussing the Old Firm and their attempts to court their English Premier League rivals, memorably commented:

> They are like two old girls on Sauchiehall Street lifting their skirts at every league that walks by. They have just had 20 punters go by who have said, 'No.' What is it going to take for them to realise that they should be putting their energies back into Scottish football?

The colourful characterisation came on the back of an eventful period in the history of the leagues on both sides of the border, late in 2001. The issue of Old Firm participation in the English Premier League was put to a vote by the 20 elite clubs south of the border. The result was an emphatic 20–0 drubbing for the Glasgow pair.

It should, you would have thought, have put the issue to bed once and for all. But it didn't. Rangers and Celtic had enviously eyed the pot of gold at the end of the rainbow stretching from Scotland into neighbouring territory for years up to that point, and they have continued to sit uneasily at the SPL's top table in subsequent seasons, unsettled by the knowledge that there was a far more glamorous party next door, where all of the beautiful people were hanging out. For now, at least, there is no invitation in the post.

Money has been the root cause of the fractious relationship between Rangers and the Scottish game. As television revenues have dried up, gates have stagnated and sponsorship opportunities have contracted, there has been a natural feeling that a club with an average attendance of 50,000 has perhaps outgrown its home surroundings.

Commercial possibilities in England dwarf those in Scotland and the all-important bottom line is that both Rangers and Celtic would be far better off in a league in which they would be big fish in a big pond, rather than in the goldfish bowl of their own division.

It has, however, not always been like that. Once upon a time there was parity between the Scottish and English games. It was a time when Rangers could attract the England captain Terry Butcher, the England goalkeeper Chris Woods and fellow England stars Gary Stevens, Trevor Steven, Ray Wilkins . . . the list goes on.

Freddie Fletcher is a man with a unique perspective on the debate about the Old Firm and the English game. Greenock born and bred, Fletcher has held high office with both Rangers and Newcastle United.

He was appointed commercial director at Ibrox in the mid-1980s, having already been a trusted lieutenant of new owner Lawrence Marlborough in his other business ventures, and went on to play a key role in the early days of the Graeme Souness revolution.

Fletcher told me: 'When we went to Rangers, when the Lawrence Group bought the club, we were in a position to sign top English internationals. During my time at the club, our vision was to go out and bring those quality players to Scotland – and we were able to do that.

'When we arrived there was very little debt and the stadium had been rebuilt already, so it was a football and management job rather than a complete rebuilding process. The challenge in my era was boosting a very low average attendance that was being attracted to a beautiful stadium at Ibrox and putting a winning team on the park.

'I was fortunate to benefit from the genius and vision of two men – Willie Waddell and Hugh Adam – who through the creation of the Rangers Pools had rebuilt the stadium to create a ground that was ahead of its time. It was their response to the Ibrox disaster. Our mission was to get the place rocking and rolling again and we achieved that.

'When we went in, Rangers hadn't won the Premier Division championship for nine years. Attendances were averaging 17,000. What we did was go out and appoint Graeme Souness as player-manager, bring in Walter Smith from Dundee United, sign England's goalkeeper in Chris Woods and their captain in Terry Butcher. It was an indication of our ambitions for the club.

'English football was on a par with our own game, financially speaking. It meant we were able to make those types of signings. So the thought of Rangers playing in the English game was not something that was ever discussed.

'Now everything has changed. You can see the logic in the Old Firm clubs looking towards England, because the earning potential is far greater, primarily because of the television revenue. It stands to reason that a country of five million people, like Scotland, has less bargaining power than a nation of England's size. There is not only a bigger population to draw upon but a deeper pool of clubs to make the league more attractive.

'The club that got relegated from the English Premier League last season got a £35-million television payment. Rangers, as champions of Scotland, got just £3 million. That is the problem laid bare.'

Fletcher departed Ibrox when David Murray took control. He returned to his role with the Lawrence Group's remaining enterprises, but it was not long until he was tempted back into football south of the border.

He said: 'Personally, if you asked me if Rangers and Celtic would enhance the English Premier League, my answer would be yes. There are some clubs at the top level in England, and fair play to them, who don't have the history or the supporter base of the Old Firm. If you had 20 clubs with the same tradition and support, then I think the league down here would be far more competitive.

'From a business perspective, it would benefit Rangers and Celtic – and I also don't think it would harm Scottish football. The remaining clubs would be on a level playing field and that would be certain to stimulate interest in the SPL. Yes, the wages would be lower for players left in the Scottish league – but players would still be earning more than a bricklayer or average working man.

'The perception of the Old Firm in England is good. People see Rangers and Celtic as big clubs and enjoy watching the Old Firm games. But what people aren't interested in is watching the likes of St Mirren versus Dunfermline – that is where the chances of attracting a decent broadcast deal for the SPL falls down.'

The lure of the megabucks television deals on offer to English clubs is what has driven Rangers to continually push for a way into that market, but Fletcher insists the fascination is not a two-way affair.

He added: 'The prospect of Rangers and Celtic joining the Premier League has never been a serious discussion in England. These things tend to happen when there are people who want them to happen, and there just isn't that appetite. You can never say never, but it is not something even on the agenda for the English clubs.

'The English Premier League is changing. What we see now is effectively four leagues in one – the big four who are virtually guaranteed the Champions League places, another group of clubs just below challenging to get into those spots each year, a group in the middle who are safe and the fourth group scrapping away against relegation at the bottom.

'Rather than worrying about the Old Firm wanting to get in, the league in England is more concerned with finding a way to make their own competition more competitive as it stands at the moment. Unless a double-double billionaire buys them, there is little chance of any of the mid-table clubs competing with Manchester United, Chelsea or Manchester City.'

Fletcher is convinced the Glasgow giants have huge advantages over many of the current English top-flight teams, but knows prudent stewardship is the key to unlocking their potential.

He said: 'Three things make a successful football club. The first is a history and tradition of football. The second is a good population catchment. The third is good management, on and off the field. The first two you've either got or not got. The third is something that can be brought to any club if the right people are in charge.

216

'Some clubs flip over the first two and get by with simply being well run – but I would argue it cannot be sustained unless you have that tradition and fan base to draw upon.

'When we went to Rangers, we clearly had the first two, even if crowds were down at that stage. I would also class my time at Rangers as a success. We won the league for the first time in nine years and really got things moving again.

'Newcastle was a bigger challenge in a bigger pond, but they were similar in many ways. After leaving Rangers when the new owner came in, I remained a director of John Lawrence Group. Scottish and Newcastle Breweries, whom I had brought into Rangers as sponsors through McEwan's Lager, also sponsored Newcastle United through the Blue Star brand, and the managing director got in touch to discuss the situation at Newcastle.

'They had received a call to say Barclays Bank was thinking of liquidating the club, which was in the Second Division at that stage and favourite for relegation. Obviously, that was a major concern for everyone in the North-east and John Hall, who had just built the Metro Centre, was worried for the future of the club. John wanted to help but was also worried about football as a business and wanted to talk to me about it. We met a few times and eventually John decided he would buy Newcastle if I would come and run it for him.

'The club was bankrupt and looked certain to be relegated – but I had confidence in my ability and thought with John's backing it could be turned around. We avoided relegation, won the Championship the following year and then qualified for Europe every year after that. We didn't quite make it to where we wanted to be, in that we finished second in the Premiership rather than winning it, but we did reach two FA Cup finals and had a successful time. I spent ten years with the club and thrived on the challenge.'

Fletcher remains active in business as a director of the Esh Group, a major construction company, and through an involvement with his son's legal company, Square One Law. He is also the part-owner of security company the Protector Group with Lord Stevens, the former Metropolitan Police commissioner, and runs the Mercer Street marketing consultancy. Taking it easy is not on Fletcher's agenda, even though it is almost half a century since he first began to make waves with his career moves.

He said: 'In 1966, I was a Liberal councillor when we became the first Liberal-controlled council in Britain, which was as much a privilege and an honour as it was to serve as a director with three wonderful football clubs.

'I served my football apprenticeship as a director of Morton for seven years, where my mentors were Hal Stewart and Hugh Curry, a director of Scott Lithgow, the shipbuilding company that owned the club.

'I had always been a Morton supporter – my mum had bought me my first season ticket when I was a five-year-old – and it was when I became a councillor and then provost of Inverclyde in the 1970s that I was invited to join the board at Cappielow.

'I was provost of Inverclyde between 1977 and 1980, and it was during that period that I first met Lawrence Marlborough. He invited me to join the board of the Lawrence Group and it built from there, with Lawrence inviting me to become a director at Rangers when he gained control of the club.'

Fletcher, still a regular at Newcastle United home games and an occasional guest at Ibrox, has seen football change beyond all recognition during his lifetime. He would never have envisaged the prospect of Rangers deserting the Scottish game when he first took office at the club.

That was an attitude shared by David Murray when he first arrived on the scene, to begin with at least. Murray was a chairman quite content with his team's role as the dominant force in the Scottish Premier Division.

When interviewed by the *Press and Journal* in 1989, just months into his tenure, Murray was unequivocal about his desire to keep Rangers embedded in Scottish football. He said:

> We would not break away from Scottish football. That's not in our remit at all. I think the clubs will do it collectively if there is a European league. It is all hypothetical at the moment in the sense that, as we have the money and the wherewithal to do it, we'll be ready for it. If a European league came, and we're talking about massive crowds from the likes of Barcelona, my job is to make Ibrox ready for the fans. I can't let such a change happen and then prepare things, which is why things are going ahead just now. In business and football we'll always be like the club motto states – ready.

That European set-up did come to fruition in the shape of the Champions League and Europa League, but, in time, it became clear that the riches from those UEFA-run competitions were neither guaranteed nor sufficient to keep Rangers in the manner the fans had become accustomed to during the glorious years in which world-class stars graced the Ibrox turf.

In European circles, the gap between rich and poor was widening with every season and it was domestic budgets that held the key. Clubs from England and Spain were riding high on the wave created by the hype surrounding the Premier League and La Liga, with broadcast companies and commercial partners lining up to shower money on teams in those divisions. Meanwhile, back in Scotland, Rangers and Celtic attempted to keep pace while feeding from the crumbs of the Premier Division table. Something had to change, and in 1997 it did.

It was at that time that Murray was accused of holding a 'gun to the head' of Scotland's small clubs by Livingston chairman Bill Hunter. The fierce criticism came as plans for a breakaway league gathered pace, with the Rangers chairman leaping to the support of Hibs chief Lex Gold after the Easter Road man had driven forward the idea of forming an elite division.

With lower league sides understandably reluctant to wave farewell to their money-spinning stablemates, the heavyweights began to get restless at the lack of progress.

Murray said at the time:

> I will confirm again that the new league will happen. If this has to be achieved without the agreement of the smaller clubs then so be it. Such a situation, however, must threaten the proposed support package. If for any reason the support package is not available to the smaller clubs, how will they fare then? Could they continue to operate? How would they generate additional revenue? This opportunity must be taken or a massive backward step will materialise.

On the table was the formation of a ten-team Premier League, what would become the SPL when it was eventually pushed through. Murray and his fellow top-flight chairmen envisaged moving to a 12-team structure within a matter of years, with scope for Scottish Football League teams to win promotion if they could meet strict new criteria regarding facilities.

It was clear that the big teams were offering the SFL a stark ultimatum: agree and be cut adrift with financial support, or oppose the change and be cut adrift without any funding being drip-fed down to the First Division and beyond.

Murray admitted:

> I can understand that when these proposals were first presented there may have been some concerns among the smaller clubs that

they would be adversely affected by the changes. That is why we have guaranteed that no club will be any worse off as a result of the initiative. Indeed, we have proposed that we would work with the Scottish League to maximise additional revenue to them. We are under no obligation to provide the support package, but we are committed to the game as a whole in Scotland.

Although the Old Firm were at the forefront of the scheme, Murray was quick to spread responsibility for the divisive plans. He said: 'There has been a view expressed that the current initiative has been masterminded by David Murray and Fergus McCann. This is simply not the case.'

The 30 clubs set to be sliced free from the top sides were presented with a legal document outlining the proposed breakaway early in December 1997, prompting a flurry of board meetings and votes. Lex Gold, the man appointed as the figurehead for the SPL formation, made it clear that it was a non-negotiable offer. The deal was £1.7 million per year for a minimum of four years.

The outcasts were given seven days to decide whether to accept the olive branch of a financial support package, having frustrated the revenue-generating breakaway clubs with their stubborn refusal to embrace change. Murray's intervention was the equivalent of wheeling out the big gun for a final blast at a group who had established themselves as the enemy.

For the clubs being left behind in the SFL, the plans for the elite league were viewed as selfish. For those being carried along with the Old Firm, it represented a new and intriguing time, with doors opening that previously had been bolted shut. For a period, it looked like the promised land had been discovered on their own doorstep.

Roger Mitchell was appointed chief executive of the new SPL, a young and driven individual who had won the seal of approval from the game's power brokers. It was a reciprocal relationship, with Mitchell, who came from a background in the music industry, not slow to sing the praises of the game's boardroom giants. Speaking following his appointment, Mitchell said:

Guys like Stewart Milne, Geoff Brown, David Murray, Fergus McCann and Chris Robinson have a lot in common. They are winners in life, successful businessmen who don't like losing any fight. They haven't got where they are by making wrong decisions or by being quitters. They are men who won't rest until this league is back at the top.

The SPL strategy was rewarded in staggering fashion in the summer of 1998 when Sky announced they had completed a £45-million deal to secure the rights to screen SPL football. It was a windfall that Scottish clubs could previously only have dreamt of landing and it led to a wave of optimism washing through the game. The contract represented a four-year agreement to cover thirty live matches per season.

Despite the massive financial benefit, there were dissenting voices from supporters sceptical about the prospect of clubs dancing to the tune of a television company, which planned to screen matches at five past six on a Sunday evening, as well as complaints about the lack of terrestrial coverage.

Murray said at the time:

> We have worked hard to balance the best interests of the regular paying supporter and the armchair fan, while at the same time maximising the revenue coming into the game.
>
> In recent years, we've all seen the improvements to the English Premiership, which is due in no small part to the additional revenue and strong marketing which Sky has helped bring to the game. We're extremely confident this deal will similarly help improve the quality and raise the profile of Scottish football.

All in all, with additional television rights deals, a bounty of £60 million was raked in to get the new-look top flight off on a solid footing. With ambitious plans for pay-per-view packages, the future looked bright.

With the benefit of glorious hindsight, where every Scottish club went wrong was in believing the hype. They were too quick to accept that the new format would instantly create a league that would become measurably more appealing to outside organisations and that the long-term future was secure. Money came in, money flowed back out again as clubs spent the proceeds of the brave new era almost as quickly as they received them.

In defence of the chairmen who sanctioned the expenditure on transfer fees and player wages, it was difficult to envisage the way in which Scottish football finances would shift in a relatively short period of time. In those early days, in the glow of the SPL honeymoon, there was a belief that there was a sustainable business model.

The response from the commercial sector certainly strengthened that belief, with several huge deals conducted throughout the country during that period. The Old Firm, understandably, were at the forefront of the drive to exploit the early interest in the newly formed SPL, and concluded some ambitious pieces of business to underline the potential that existed for the two biggest clubs during the boom years of the league.

Rangers and Celtic joined forces in 1999 to secure a joint sponsorship deal, with American cable operator NTL rumoured to have paid in the region of £12 million to have its name plastered on both Glasgow kits. Murray had taken a leading role in the discussions in what was a groundbreaking deal to ensure maximum exposure for the new partner. It was a unique agreement, since the C.R. Smith backing of both clubs in the early 1980s had come as the result of individual negotiations rather than the dual approach adopted in the 1990s. In some areas at least, there was a new-found unity between the two clubs, particularly where there was a profit to be made.

The problem was that profit was not enough. Competing in Europe had always been at the top of the agenda, and it quickly became clear that whatever the SPL could do, the English Premier League could do bigger and better. As a result, the Manchester Uniteds, Chelseas and Arsenals of the world were getting richer and their squads getting stronger.

Against a gloomy financial backdrop, both at Rangers and in the wider football community, suggestions that a leap into the English top flight would be preferable began to grow louder – with Murray himself admitting that he believed it might be better for clubs on both sides of the border if the Old Firm made the move.

He floated the possibility of retaining a Scottish league interest with an Under-21 or B team filling the void, following the Spanish model. It was a debate that rumbled on throughout the remainder of the owner's tenure, with both Celtic and Rangers making plays for a place at the table for the feast of television and sponsorship revenue being served up in England. Each push was met with stern resistance from the Premiership. The idea was branded 'illogical' by Southampton's Rupert Lowe as he sought to protect his team's place in the promised land, and many others echoed those sentiments.

Indeed, SNP MSP Adam Ingram branded the two Glasgow sides 'a parcel of rogues' for their expression of interest in jumping the fence to greener pastures. Alex Salmond climbed on the same bandwagon, criticising the clubs for seeking a place in the English game, but that would not be enough to put them off the idea.

Both Rangers and Celtic wanted a piece of the action, and by 2001 the pipe dream looked to be morphing into the realms of reality as changes in the structure in England were mooted. First Division clubs, with big hitters Wolves and Manchester City among them, were eager to create a second tier to the Premier League. That, in theory, could have thrown open a door to the Scottish prospective members.

What they could not have bargained for was the fierce resistance from the existing 20 clubs in the English top flight. First they voted 19–1 against the concept of a second tier. Then all 20 of them roundly rejected the notion of inviting the outsiders in. Richard Scudamore, then chief executive of the English Premier League, said after the meeting:

> There has been an overwhelming dismissal of the notion of a Premier League Two. And the Premier League can see absolutely no practical way nor any proof of sound commercial reasons why Celtic and Rangers should enter the English system – and certainly not that they should be parachuted straight into the Premiership. I have never known the clubs to be so firmly against an idea.

The big clubs weren't interested in seeing their share of the loot split further than it already was while the smaller outfits, battling against relegation, would never accept a plan that would create greater competition on the field and leave them more likely to be relegated. It was the old 'turkeys voting for Christmas' question. Scudamore added:

> The Premiership is a huge success story so of course people want to be involved. But there is no value in changing it or diluting it. There is no evidence that cherry-picking other big clubs will add anything to its value.

Publicly, Rangers were calm about the rejection, with manager Dick Advocaat fielding questions on the matter and doing his level best to appear indifferent. Celtic took a different approach, claiming they knew nothing of any meeting and insisting they would pursue options to broaden their horizons.

Meanwhile, the rest of the SPL was growing restless with the constant speculation about the future of the league's two biggest commercial assets. Over to Keith Wyness, emerging as the most potent mouthpiece for the majority. The Pittodrie chief executive said:

> There is no doubt Aberdeen as a club want an Old Firm committed to the SPL. However, the key word there is committed. We do not appreciate the way they are sitting on the fence just now.
>
> I really believe that if the Old Firm work with us in the SPL then we can repackage its look and feel into a more trendy and fashionable product, internationally as well as domestically. We can go a long

way to helping them meet their financial concerns and needs.

I have been asking for a coalition of the Scottish film industry, music industry and fashion industry to get together to try and rework the SPL package. The Premier League has done a great job of it in England and I think we can do it in a smaller, different way.

The vision of one big happy Scottish football family was laudable, but it was also laughable. With clubs desperate to protect and preserve their own positions, reaching a consensus among the top clubs proved to be an impossibility.

In 2002, the non-Old Firm clubs grew tired of the hankerings from Rangers and Celtic for a passage to England. They attempted to call their bluff, announcing plans for a breakaway league of ten teams that would exclude the Glasgow giants. It came on the back of haggling over television deals, with the Old Firm blocking the launch of SPL TV because they were adamant more lucrative offers could be attracted from established broadcasters.

Murray pointed out that the Old Firm represented 80 per cent of the media value of the SPL and revealed fears that the proposed SPL television channel could prove to be a liability rather than a revenue generator. The SPL TV concept had been the brainchild of the league's chief executive, Roger Mitchell, as he attempted to negotiate a path through tangled woods in a landscape that saw appetite for Scottish football among broadcasters suppressed and a general malaise beginning to creep in across professional sport. It was an innovative solution, but one that carried no promise of a decent return for the partners.

Rod Petrie, of Hibs, hit back by claiming: 'None of us are frightened of Scottish football without Rangers or Celtic. If they are not committed to Scottish football – if they have some other agenda or some other plan – it's about time they removed the uncertainty.'

A £16-million offer from the BBC, favoured by the gang of ten, did nothing to tempt Rangers and Celtic to add their support and the row rumbled on. It was a fraction of what had been stumped up by Sky at the outset of the SPL and a bitter pill to swallow for the Old Firm as they sought to protect the revenue that helped cover the substantial overheads being generated at Ibrox and Parkhead.

All the time, the issue of a switch to England was bubbling away on the back burner and ready to boil over at any point. In the summer of 2002, the Old Firm anticipated an invitation from the Nationwide League to join them in England's second tier. It drew a furious response from their rival teams in Scotland, with Keith Wyness once again leading the charge and accusing Rangers and Celtic of greed as well as launching into a tirade against the English chiefs who were attempting to 'steal' Scottish football's prized assets.

With the league south of the border reeling from the collapse of ITV Digital, the Scottish teams were considered a viable shot in the arm. In the end, the plans were abandoned by the Nationwide League power brokers, perhaps stung by the fierce criticism that the idea had generated on both sides of the border.

Back in the north, there was a breakthrough in the summer of 2002 in the stalemate that had brought the national sport to its knees. A change in the voting structure signalled a path forward. Previously 11–1 was the required ratio for decisions in the SPL – it altered to 8–4 in 2002. Rangers and Celtic also dropped their right to 40 per cent each of the television revenue, settling for one third instead. Both were key developments and designed to end the deadlock that was strangling the game, with a BBC broadcast deal agreed after great delay.

It was an uneasy compromise, although just two years later there was greater cheer when it was announced that the SPL had come through lean years to clinch a broadcast deal with Setanta worth £35 million.

In 2006, that agreement was renegotiated, with the revenues pushed up to £54.5 million over a four-year period. It was the biggest such deal in the history of the Scottish game. Everything was rosy; life was good.

In 2008, the association with Setanta was extended again, although both sides of the Old Firm and Aberdeen argued against the deal. They wanted to take a smaller package offered by Sky, arguing it was a more stable firm to be working with.

And they were right. In the summer of 2009, the collapse of the satellite station left the SPL staring into a broadcast black hole. Clubs big and small were damaged by the failure of the Irish television firm, although a replacement deal was struck with ESPN.

If only they had listened to David Murray in the first place. As far back as 2004, the Rangers owner had been voicing concern about the longevity of Setanta as a company and its ability to keep up with the payments scheduled in its contract with the SPL. At the time, in an interview with the *Sunday Herald*, he said:

> I'd have done the BBC deal without a shadow of a doubt. It's safe, it's secure, it's not as many games being shown live. I would rather have certainty. There must be uncertainty at the moment because we're doing due diligence on Setanta. What the SPL have done is like buying a house without doing a survey first. I don't think it's in the best interests of Scottish football.

It was not like the flamboyant Murray to urge caution, but the instinct that carried him through his business life had proved correct once again. He had told the *Sunday Herald*:

> I think there is no doubt that football's at the bottom now in terms of its media value and it will improve, definitely. I think Setanta has done a great job for itself – it has picked us off when we've been most vulnerable. It's timing's been brilliant and that's why it has gone on for four years. I hope it works, because it has to. If it doesn't work, that's Scottish football in a right mess. I hope I'm wrong, but I have serious reservations about the way it's been negotiated and the final outcome.

The final outcome was the disappearance of Setanta and a late scurry around to find a broadcaster willing to take a gamble on the Scottish game. It was a period of huge uncertainty at a time when Rangers could ill afford a dent on the balance-sheet, and nor could any of their SPL rivals. One of the few occasions when David Murray had been overruled had ended in financial disaster for his club and every other top-flight side in the land.

It only intensified the desire to jump ship and find new avenues in England to explore, all without success. With Craig Whyte and his board expressing a similar desire just months after taking over at Rangers, the debate showed no signs of abating.

CHAPTER 20

'Business is about averages. I have no God-given
right to get everything I do correct.'

David Murray, 1991

FOR YEARS, IT has been claimed that Rangers have been given an easy
ride by Scotland's media. There has been, we are told, a campaign
among members of the Fourth Estate to protect the club and send out
a positive message surrounding all things Ibrox-related. In essence, it
has been a conspiracy. A conspiracy, according to the keyboard warriors
laying down battle lines in the online forums, designed to benefit
Rangers and besmirch Celtic.

That is the theory, at least. What about the practice, though? The
rather less exciting truth of the matter is that there are no conspiracies,
no press packs gathered in darkened rooms talking in hushed tones
about the next move in the propaganda campaign.

There may have been, admittedly, issues that were not scrutinised or
covered exhaustively. The financial problems, for example, and the
threat posed by the huge tax bill that lingered over the club for years.
The thorny issue of sectarianism is another in the same category.

The explanations are many and varied but none are quite as dramatic
as a pro-Rangers conspiracy. Rightly or wrongly, the prime reason is
the age-old assumption throughout the media that sports fans want to
read about sport in their sports pages. Not entirely radical as a concept.
Business analysis and social commentary have never been staples of the
football writer's work diet and never will be.

There have been exceptions to that rule, but generally there is no
appetite to stray from the tried-and-tested menu of transfer stories,
match reports and player and manager interviews. It is recipe that has
worked. Deviate from it, and the risk is alienating readers – or worse,
boring them, something no newspaper can risk in the current climate.

There is also a certain safety to be had in refraining from digging too deeply into matters that by their very nature are complex legally and technically. Misplaced or misguided exposés relating to an issue that could have an impact on a company's trading future could be catastrophic and have huge implications for any publication or journalist responsible for bringing them to print. That does not apply only to football clubs but to all companies.

An erroneous report on a Monday morning suggesting Joe Bloggs' Bakery is on a shaky financial footing could see suppliers jumping ship by the Tuesday, all credit facilities removed. By the Wednesday, there'd be no flour in the cupboard, by Thursday no bread on the shelves and by Friday a closed sign on the door. That is the chain of events that any newspaper report can cause by speculating on the financial health of a business, which is why, in general, you will not see those articles either in the sports pages or anywhere else in a newspaper. An angry Joe Bloggs could, after all, be beating a path to his lawyer to hold the newspaper, its editor and the journalist to account for their irresponsible actions.

Of course, annual accounts, issued through Companies House, have always been fair game. So too have the financial debates at annual general meetings. But the level of detail given will, ordinarily, be relatively minimal and entirely safe, with reporters tending to stick to the headline figures.

Attempting to unravel the finer points would take time, resources and a level of commitment to the story that simply would not compute with the level of anticipated interest from readers. Far better to concentrate on the signing scoop that would stand a better chance of drawing in readers; for every one interested in the accounting minutiae, there would be another ten desperate to find out who the new £5-million striker is.

Setting aside the issue of the detail of the coverage of the economic ins and outs at Rangers, there is also the assertion that the media were somehow enamoured of Sir David Murray and Walter Smith in a way that they simply never were with their Celtic equivalents at various stages.

The theorists cry 'conspiracy!' But could it simply be that Murray and Smith were more sophisticated in their handling of the media? The latter is most certainly the case. While international man of mystery Dermott Desmond remained frustratingly elusive for the Scottish media, his Ibrox adversary Sir David was happy to pick up the phone and take calls from trusted members of the press corps. Relationships were cultivated over time, contacts built up, and there was a mutual understanding that the press needed Rangers as much as Rangers needed the press. Better to work together than go head to head with the type of siege mentality that has all too often emanated from other clubs. Sir Alex Ferguson is the past master in the 'them versus us' approach and as a result has won few friends in either press or broadcast circles. Only his staggering success has won a begrudging acceptance.

Walter Smith, too, has been a friend to the media. While Martin O'Neill and Gordon Strachan were firing acerbic asides in the direction of the press gallery, picking what at times appeared to be petty fights, the veteran Rangers coach was living in harmony with the self-same journalists. That is not to say he was a soft touch; every reporter was aware that crossing Smith was not a sensible course of action. But, again, there was a two-way spirit of cooperation.

Murray was prepared to show his teeth when he deemed it necessary. He believed he had the measure of the press gang. As results foundered in the midst of the 2000–01 season, Murray hit out at the country's media corps, claiming:

> The press are attacking Dick Advocaat and his players – yet can't get on the plane quick enough for a European trip. Our task is to support him 100 per cent and give him all the encouragement we can. I find these articles to be unacceptable and out of all proportion.

When the dust settled, all was forgiven and it was back to the mutually supportive relationship that had been a hallmark of the Murray chairmanship. So, no conspiracy – just good old-fashioned courtesy and a dose of common-sense media savvy. It is what you would expect from a club owner who never viewed the media as the enemy.

He was happy in the limelight, never one to shy away from publicity or hide his light under a bushel. He also appreciated that the media was a business like any other and that everyone had a role to play, whether sportswriter or editor, and that getting it right was not always easy. Murray's own bitter experiences of the newspaper game had taught him that much.

His willingness to embrace the media stretched as far as a decision to found his own newspaper. It was the early 1990s and a time long before the Internet threatened the very fabric of the industry.

Having already dabbled with the world of public relations and made modest returns, Murray aimed high with the launch of the *Sunday Scot*. It was a venture that, if successful, would provide power, status and riches.

Months of planning and recruitment led up to the first edition on 10 March 1991. Then, on 11 July that year, the *Sunday Scot* closed its doors. Owner David Murray addressed staff at the St Vincent Street base in Glasgow, informing them that the dream was over. After four months, the nation's youngest paper disappeared from news-stands once and for all.

Failure was not something Murray had been accustomed to in his business career to that point. Indeed, he was referred to as Scotland's 'golden boy' in reports charting the demise of his ailing media enterprise.

At the time, Murray told *The Herald*:

> We had a poor launch. The product was poor in the early stages and then we were always fighting against it. I still believe there is a place in the market for a paper like ours but 300,000 people read the paper when it was poor at the start and we never recovered. But 70,000 people are still buying it and that's more than *Scotland on Sunday* and the *Sunday Times*.

A circulation of 70,000 in the modern media marketplace would be reason for cheer. The *Sunday Herald* would salivate at those figures; so too would *Scotland on Sunday* in the 2012 landscape. For the staff at the *Sunday Scot*, the problem was that in the 1990s that was simply not a readership capable of sustaining the costs associated with producing a national title.

Murray Media, the parent company behind the *Sunday Scot*, had employed big hitters to try to get the launch right. Jack Irvine, one-time editor of the *Scottish Sun*, was at the helm as managing director, while Steve Sampson, formerly of the parish of the *Daily Record*, was in charge as editor. The pair had a formidable reputation in the industry and were characters not to be messed with – likened, albeit tongue in cheek, to the sector's equivalent of the Kray twins. Their brief was simple as they sought to nudge the competition out of the way and corner the Sunday market.

It was Irvine, with his *Sun* editor's hat on, who had broken the story of Mo Johnston's decision to join Rangers. He still cites that exclusive as the proudest moment in a long and distinguished media career and the one that turned the tide for *The Sun* in its battle against the *Record*.

When it first appeared in the spring of 1991, the *Sunday Scot* was pitched as a natural alternative to the likes of the *Sunday Post* and *Sunday Mail*, with the more upmarket *Mail on Sunday* also in its sights.

The first edition led with a front-page story about security at Scotland's nuclear military bases and unveiled Kenny Dalglish as a star columnist. The main promotion was a competition offering £100,000 worth of cars as prizes.

The verdict at the time was very much 'worthy but dull'. The first edition sold 300,000 copies, no doubt boosted by the intrigue about Murray's latest pet project, but in a matter of weeks the circulation slumped below six figures and the writing was on the wall. The briefest of flirtations with life as a newspaper proprietor had cost the Murray organisation £3 million, according to his own estimate.

Murray, in an interview carried in *The Herald* in 1991, explained:

> It was a very difficult decision. There are some good people in that paper and I felt sorry for them. Two or three weeks ago we were contemplating a relaunch or a daily to run in tandem with the Sunday. The problem was we had seven days' overheads and only one day's income. We had to stop the wound bleeding.

Murray was defiant about the potentially embarrassing decision to cut his losses. He added:

> I haven't lost yet, have I? Business is about averages. I have no God-given right to get everything I do correct. The Murray International Group is in what I consider to be 44 positions. We've got Rangers and we've got this and we've got that. OK, so we got one wrong. We have no right to get it right every time. The product was wrong at the start and we have to own up to that. We got it wrong.

When asked if he could afford to take the £3-million hit, he replied:

> Of course I can. One shouldn't be smug and say 'of course I can' just like that because, in truth, one can't afford to lose a pound, but our steel and property business has never been better. We are doing admirably well under the market conditions. Murray International is doing very, very well.

Referring back to the doomed *Sunday Scot*, he said: 'We are taking a step back so that we can review the situation. This closure doesn't mean that we won't have another go in another guise. OK, I'm down, but don't count me out yet.'

Another tilt at the newspaper trade never did materialise, leaving Murray to ponder in private why his first attempt had gone awry. Jack Irvine, his MD at the time, is in no doubt. While the Mo Johnston story was his proudest moment, when asked recently by the website allmediascotland.com what his most embarrassing episode in the media had been he stated: 'Closure of the *Sunday Scot*. Lesson learned was – don't join a business that is underfunded.'

Murray could never stand accused of being thrifty in relation to his other high-profile business, Rangers FC, but it appears he had his business head on when it came to the *Sunday Scot*. It was no ego trip. If it didn't turn a profit, the plug had to be pulled. The disappointing launch issue was a major stumbling block, but others have been cited. Among them are the problems experienced with new and untested editorial systems, and poor preparation has also been mentioned in discussions about the *Scot*'s closure.

Murray had obviously been confident that the *Sunday Scot* could hold its own in a notoriously fierce sector, dominated by established brands with loyal readerships. New launches tended not to set the heather alight, as the rise and fall of the *Sunday Standard* in the 1980s proved. Founded by *Herald* owner George Outram, the *Standard* soon disappeared from the scene after advertising revenues proved to be disappointing. It was George Outram and Co. who were eventually contracted to print the *Sunday Scot* by Murray's new media company, offering them a guaranteed weekly return for services rendered with no outlay.

Just as the decision to buy Rangers can be laid at the door of Graeme Souness, in a roundabout way, the move to establish the *Sunday Scot* was also instigated by the Ibrox manager.

It was Souness who had introduced Irvine to Murray, and their conversations turned to the notion of founding a Sunday newspaper. Irvine and Murray took the idea and ran with it, formulating an ambitious business plan based on shifting 250,000 copies each weekend. At the time of closure, the circulation figure sat nearer 70,000.

Opting for a standalone Sunday title, rather than adding a daily stablemate, was an error in judgement according to the owner, and one that proved terminal to the future of his fledgling media company. Murray insisted at the time: 'It was a difficult decision and one takes no pleasure from it, but you have to stand up and move on. It was important that I protected our group's resources.'

Observers, looking at the tabloid roots of both the managing director Irvine and editor Sampson, had expected a *News of the World*-style offering, packed with gritty and sensational material. In the end, the proprietor was keen to set the bar slightly higher. Murray said: 'That was said in the beginning because of Jack's background on *The Sun*. I wouldn't allow the standard to drop down to that level, but I didn't have to tell him that. He didn't need to be told.'

That was the script, but according to those on the shop floor, the quality the paper was aiming for never materialised and what remained was a disappointing compromise that stood no chance of attracting or retaining the type of readership required to satisfy the advertisers who would bankroll the project.

The established Scottish tabloids were plundered for staff, with big-name journalistic transfers akin to those Murray was more used to masterminding in football with Rangers.

If *The Sun* and *Daily Record* were the red-top equivalent of the Old Firm, the *Sunday Scot* was a Gretna – and the new kid on the block went out and snatched the most established, and most expensive, talent from the big guns.

Sport was naturally a key component of the new paper and the renowned Ken Gallacher, a hugely respected figure in the industry who rose to become a senior figure with both the *Daily Record* and *The Sun*, was among those lured to the promised land of the *Sunday Scot*.

Ian Broadley, another experienced newspaperman recruited during that exhilarating pre-launch period, remembers the time well. Broadley, now a freelance writer working for the *Daily Record* amongst other titles, told me: 'It was Ken Gallacher who asked me if I fancied moving to the *Sunday Scot*. Obviously, one of the questions I asked was "What's the deal?" – and it was terrific. The money was fantastic, I got a nice new Volkswagen car, company phone and a weekly expense allowance running into hundreds of pounds.

'Initially, I was offered a three-month contract but I said no to that – I'd been 25 years with the *Record* at that point. They came back and agreed to six months, which wasn't ideal, but it was better at least, and the fact it was on good money made it worth taking a chance on. My role was to cover the east-coast football beat, everything from the Highlands through to Aberdeen and Dundee, as well as doing a golf column.

'The paper was sold to us as being a mix between the *Mail on Sunday* and the *Sunday Mail*. We were told the paper would be given two and a half years to establish itself in the marketplace.

'The *Mail on Sunday* was very anglicised and very Tory, while there was the impression that people were growing tired of the *Sunday Mail*. It felt as though there was a real chance of taking advantage – but it didn't work out that way.'

The build-up to the launch day was a whirl of activity, with an experienced editorial team recruited and the look and tone of the paper plotted by the management team. When the big day arrived, there was a sense of relief and celebration in the air as the presses started rolling. Broadley recalls: 'We were all summoned to St Vincent Street on the night the first edition was put to bed and I can remember the champagne flowing and the cheers going up.

'While some were cheering, I looked at the first edition and thought, "We're finished." It was abysmal, full of stock features from the Press Association and lots of grey and boring pages. What had been built up to be a quality tabloid product looked downmarket and no better than the *Sunday Sport*. In fact, the *Sunday Sport* was better presented.

'If it had been taken back to the start and designed as a proper alternative to the *Mail on Sunday* and the *Sunday Mail*, then it might have had a chance. It had been rushed onto the streets, for what reason I've no idea. The paper looked like a dog's breakfast and from that day on it was doomed to failure. There was no way back from that first edition. I knew that night that it was all over.

'I wouldn't blame the rank-and-file staff. I think it was more a case of the wrong people in charge. When you heard cheering after this absurd paper had come off the presses, you knew all was not well. We were told two and a half years was the minimum lifespan – but in the end it got something like seventeen weeks. In truth, even if it had been given ten years I don't think it would have recovered from that first issue.'

While there was joy in the offices on launch night, the atmosphere soon turned to despair as staff realised the brave new dawn was a false one. The sun was setting on the *Sunday Scot* once and for all.

Broadley said: 'I was at Gleneagles covering golf when I was called back to Glasgow. It was a Thursday, day one of the tournament, and mid-morning when we were told the news. There had been a lot of interest in the paper's launch and there was just as much interest in its demise, with camera crews and reporters waiting outside after the announcement to get reaction. It wasn't a complete surprise. In the weeks before that, all the talk had been that advertising had fallen through the floor and sales of the paper were dreadful.

'I'm not an excitable type of person, but I was when it came to the *Sunday Scot* at the beginning. The concept was clear – we were going to be a high-end tabloid newspaper. If that had been followed through, there was every chance the paper would have hit the mark – there was a real feeling that Scotland was ready for a new national newspaper. There was even talk of going daily if the Sunday was a success. Instead, it was taken downmarket and that very first edition put paid to any hopes of making it last.

'The plug had been pulled far earlier than we had been promised at the outset. In the end, it was all about money and the investment wasn't going to be there in the long term when it became obvious there wasn't a profit in the paper. Jim MacDonald was the main man with Murray

International Holdings and I think Jim had always advised against the project. I doubt he would have been too open to keeping it going for long if it was running at a loss. When it came to the end, I had to haggle to get a proper severance package. The money that had been washing around at the start wasn't there at the end.'

Just as quickly as the project had taken shape, the lights went out at St Vincent Street. The staff scattered to the four corners of the Scottish media industry and were left to reflect on the motivation behind the decision to launch in the first place.

Broadley added: 'I've worked for him, but I've never spoken to David Murray in my life. I was recruited by Jack Irvine via Ken Gallacher. I never saw him in the office, although I was working out on the road most of the time and didn't spend too much time at my desk.

'To me, it looked as though David Murray needed the oxygen of publicity and thought he could get his message across in his own paper. With your own newspaper you are in a position to try and dictate what people think about certain issues – it is a unique position.

'He was still early in his days as Rangers owner, but there is no mistaking the fact he was already a very powerful man in Scotland. He would have been even more powerful if the paper had become established in the way we all hoped it would.

'The press barons, led by Rupert Murdoch, were hugely important figures in the 1990s and Murray wanted to be part of that. Unfortunately, the product and the plan were flawed, The *Sunday Scot* never stood a chance. If we had taken our time and got the product right, it could have been different.

'Looking at Rangers, there have been similarities with some of the flaws. Too much time has been spent trying to upstage Celtic instead of keeping the house in order at Ibrox. Trying to spend fivers when Celtic were spending pennies is what got Rangers into trouble. As a club, Rangers had a tradition of going about their business efficiently but quietly – that all changed in the Murray years.'

While Broadley has remained entrenched in the newspaper industry, others turned their back on print to venture into different areas on the back of the *Sunday Scot*'s demise. Initially, Murray had vowed to retain the services of Irvine and Sampson to spearhead another, unspecified media venture. The paper's owner had said: 'I'm not going to say too much about what they will be doing, but everybody who knows me will realise that I'm not going to take this lying down.'

When Irvine did resurface, it was to stand on his own two feet, forming communications and PR company Media House International after the ill-fated *Sunday Scot* adventure. He had spent more than two decades with the *Daily Record*, *The Herald* and *The Sun* but branched out to turn from poacher to gamekeeper as part of the public-relations set. Crisis management became one of Media House's key strengths, and a long list of blue-chip clients has been added to its credits. Rangers Football Club also sat on that list of clients during the Murray years – no hard feelings, it would appear.

When Craig Whyte took over the mantle of Rangers chief, the question was whether he too would be able to cultivate the type of relationship Murray had enjoyed with the media.

Like his predecessor, Whyte had media minders to fall back on. His chosen partners were Hay McKerron Associates, based in Glasgow and led by experienced journalists Ian McKerron and Gordon Hay. He also leant on Jack Irvine at Media House for support.

For him, unlike for his predecessor, there was no honeymoon period. High-profile media organisations scented blood very early in Whyte's chairmanship – none more than the BBC, which lit the blue touchpaper (no pun intended) with its television exposé entitled *Rangers: The Inside Story* in October 2011.

The programme delved into the club owner's past business dealings and highlighted a string of associates who did not fit the image of those you might expect to have influence with those walking the corridors of power at Ibrox. It also brought to light the fact that Whyte had been disqualified as a company director in 2000 for a seven-year spell.

There was no attempt at a charm offensive to smooth the rubble dislodged by the high-profile BBC1 news special. Instead, Whyte threatened legal action, banned the BBC from talking to any Rangers staff and made his own accusations of bias by the corporation against the club.

The BBC strenuously denied those claims and also had its allegations about Whyte's record as a company director vindicated when it was confirmed in 2012 that the chairman had indeed failed to disclose his previous disqualification – leading to a £50,000 fine by PLUS Stock Exchange, on which the club's shares were listed.

His quickness to threaten court proceedings demonstrated Whyte's unwillingness to play the media game, to take what was thrown in his direction. He would pick and choose his interview opportunities, talking when he had a message to send out but not indiscriminately.

Ultimately as the financial trapdoor began to open up, the choice was taken out of his hands. The headline writers were sharpening their pencils and the previously unknown figure was set to take centre stage once more – only this time he was not in control; the administrators were.

CHAPTER 21

'Cricket grounds and muddy rugby pitches are not the places to put £50- or £60-million worth of players.'

David Murray, 2001

THE ONSET OF the administration process in 2012 brought much talk about the value of Rangers: the worth of the famous name and of the tradition and the support the club enjoys, the potential transfer fees a fire sale of the Ibrox squad might bring in. Ultimately, though, it became clear that the biggest assets did not wear football boots or have the glitter of silverware. No, the biggest assets were bricks and mortar.

Who would own the property when the process was complete, and whether Craig Whyte would profit, was the subject of much debate. What was clear, however, was that those assets, developed over time, gave at least a glimmer of hope.

It was David Murray who had played a key role in building the property portfolio. The training ground bearing his name is the most obvious contribution to Rangers infrastructure over the past quarter of a century, but the very fabric of Ibrox has also changed almost beyond recognition in that time. The proud façade of the Main Stand remains the traditional public face of the club; the marble staircase provides that most grand of entrances, and features such as the Blue Room and the Trophy Room have been virtually untouched. But otherwise the ground has been consistently and comprehensively reworked and remodelled to keep pace with the modern game.

Much is made of the investment made in the playing staff since the beginning of the Graeme Souness revolution. Tens of millions were pumped into the squad, but massive sums were also ploughed into facilities in the same period. That expenditure was not sexy or glamorous and would never attract the interest from supporters or the media that a Brian Laudrup or Paul Gascoigne type signing would, but arguably it was the spending that in the long term provided best value.

From his first day in the seat of power, Murray recognised the need to look after the family home. It was not only a symbolic gesture, a desire to give players and fans alike a stadium they could be proud of, but also a passion born of sound economic principles. By expanding and improving, Rangers could accommodate more people and offer more hospitality provision to gain more vital revenue.

Murray had inherited a modern ground that was already well developed, in no small part thanks to the vision and drive of Willie Waddell in the aftermath of the Ibrox disaster. The completion of the Govan Stand in 1981 marked the end of a flurry of construction activity that had begun in the late 1970s as the Copland Road and Broomloan stands quickly took shape. All in all, a figure topping £10 million is estimated to have been spent on the complete reshaping of the ground in the aftermath of the Ibrox disaster.

The new owner set about evolving Ibrox to form the stadium as we know it now. When Murray took control, the ground comprised four separate stands, with a capacity of 44,000. It meant that, on the back of the early success inspired by Graeme Souness, a 'closed gate' policy was in operation for many games and fans were being locked out.

The majority was seated, save for the remaining terraced enclosure tucked at the base of the Main Stand – the last bastion of the bygone era. My first experience of an Old Firm game came in the swaying mass of bodies on that terrace while still a young schoolboy in the late 1980s. It was exhilarating, intimidating and a football education at a time when the writing was on the wall for standing areas.

Murray's hand was forced in removing the terracing – the Taylor Report saw to that – but the other major changes to the fabric of the club were his own creation, with a helping hand from Edinburgh-based Gareth Hutchison Architects, the firm enlisted to put a sympathetic slant on the modernisation of the design classic that is the Main Stand as well as to create executive boxes in the Govan Stand.

The blueprint for the Main Stand, when it was delivered, was spectacular. Hutchison's solution was ambitious yet seamlessly blended new with old. A third tier was to be added on top of the building, leaving the façade untouched. A huge girder spanning the length of the stand, all 141 metres, was hoisted into position to support a new level holding close to 7,000 seats as well as the all-important revenue-generating collection of more than 20 executive boxes. The two glass stairwells, now part and parcel of Ibrox, were the most visible aspect from street level and complemented the original Archibald Leitch design perfectly.

It was the culmination of a planning exercise that began almost as soon as the ink had dried on the documents transferring ownership to Murray. Outlining his plans for Rangers in an interview with the *Press and Journal* shortly after taking control in 1988, Murray said:

> Everything has been written about accommodating wealthy supporters, but nothing about the ordinary supporter. What must be remembered is that, whatever we are doing to the ground, nothing is being taken away. We are only adding to our facilities.
>
> We believe the optimum support for Rangers on a regular basis is 52,000. The Govan Stand works begin in four weeks and will be ready by December, providing thirty-eight boxes, which will give us an additional revenue of £900,000 a year. It should be remembered it's not just gate money that is going to pay for this.
>
> Over and above that, a year from now work will begin on the new upper deck on the Main Stand and will be done in the two summer 'weather windows' – erection work will be done in the summer months – and we hope to be open two years from now with a capacity of 52,000, of which only 9,000 will be standing.
>
> In the light of recent events in football, the continuation of standing came about by the demand of our own fans. Letters from them indicated that nine to one preferred to stand. We'll always consider safety first of all, but also what the fans want.
>
> Rangers are moving to another level again. We initially had the Lawrence Group taking the club to a certain size and – I'm not being egotistical about this – I think it was important for someone, like myself, to come in and take it to another level.

The only thing that did not materialise from those early promises was the retention of a standing section, for reasons outwith the club's control.

At around the same time as the stadium was undergoing its mini-rebuild, the future of the Albion training ground across the road was also up for debate. The old base had been part and parcel of life for generations of players from the 1960s onwards. But, landlocked in urban Govan, it was deemed not fit for purpose and plans were hatched to expand the Albion, the site of a dog-racing track before being adopted by Rangers. However, the scheme was eventually rejected by Glasgow City Council.

That left the club looking for alternative training facilities, dotting from place to place throughout the 1990s in a daily routine hardly befitting a club among the biggest in the world.

While the training conundrum occupied the thoughts of the management team, there was the issue of what to do with the by then empty land at the Albion for directors to consider. Murray International Holdings wanted to pay £2 million for the land, which had permission to be turned into a retail site, with a view to creating an industrial and office development. However, eventually, the old training ground had to be transformed into car parking to meet conditions of the planning permission required for the stadium expansion.

It took 18 months to complete work on the new Club Deck, which was said to have cost £20 million to construct. With the enclosure at the foot of the Main Stand transformed into a seated area and the new section atop, the already impressive grandstand took on new and magnificent proportions.

Further developments saw, in 1996, the corners between the Govan Stand and the two end stands filled to add further seating and the jumbotron screens. In 2006, additional Govan Stand seating, boosting capacity by 1,000, was installed to tie in with the creation of the Bar 72 area, a nod to the past with a big emphasis on future profits from the bar and hospitality facilities.

In 2001, plans for a family section were announced. It was to be located in the Broomloan Stand, and there were promises that any form of unacceptable behaviour in the new pocket would not be tolerated. Murray said: 'Rangers recognises the importance of our young supporters as fans of the future and our market research has proved there is a huge demand for a family area in the stadium.'

Ibrox, as it had always been, remained the largest tangible asset for the club. When debts spiralled in 2004, rumours circulated that the ground could be sold to one of David Murray's companies to ease the financial problems at the club. Chairman John McClelland moved swiftly to allay those separation fears, insisting Ibrox would remain 'safely' in Rangers' ownership. The ground and surrounding land were valued at anywhere up to £100 million at that point – and they were about to get even more valuable.

In September 2005, the club was granted planning permission for a £120-million casino development, incorporating hotel accommodation and other leisure and community facilities, as Rangers attempted to utilise the land for the club's benefit. Murray said he was cautious but confident about the prospects of seeing the plans turn to reality.

Nothing was guaranteed, however, as the board entered into a lottery of their own. The Westminster government had announced plans to allow one 'super-casino' in Britain, with a licence to install Las Vegas-style machines with the potential for unlimited prizes. It would make the winning bidder a mecca for gamblers from across the country, and the attraction was obvious for Rangers, who estimated that the facility would create 2,000 jobs if it came to fruition. With Glasgow City Council desperate to attract the super-casino to their patch, there was added weight to the Ibrox bid.

A further advantage was the involvement of the Las Vegas Sands corporation, which was ready to go into partnership with the football club to create the complex. More familiar with Sinatra and the Rat Pack, the Sands directors were eager to bring a touch of Nevada glitz to Govan, and together with Rangers they were said to have ploughed £1.5 million into the project simply to take it to the planning stages. Las Vegas Sands had entered into a similar agreement with Sheffield United as they set their sights on the lucrative British gaming market.

Grand artists' impressions for the Glasgow site, depicting the casino complete with 140-bed hotel, conference centre, Rangers club shop, entertainment complex and a community centre with a floodlit rooftop pitch, were unveiled as the ambitious venture gathered pace. The plan was for the club to lease the site to the American developers, initially for a 25-year period, with options for that agreement to be extended.

David Jolliffe, Rangers' finance director at the time, said:

> We are the first in the UK with planning permission from a council that wants a casino. It's a powerful combination. We're investing £200 million, creating 2,000 jobs, at least half of which will be recruited locally. Our plan is perfect for the wider Govan area.

The runners and riders in the competition to land the country's sole super-casino licence were Glasgow, Manchester, Blackpool, Greenwich, Cardiff, Newcastle and Sheffield. The Ibrox scheme was not the only proposal in Glasgow, with alternative schemes proposed on the riverside as well as at the SECC and in the city centre at St Enoch Square. However, with planning permission in the bag, it appeared Rangers were at the head of the queue.

Local rivalry became inconsequential on 30 January 2007, when the announcement was made: Glasgow had lost out. Instead, it was the East End of Manchester that was picked for the regeneration scheme, and Rangers in an instant had dreams of money-spinning redevelopment of the Ibrox site blown out of the water.

The directors went away and regrouped, tackling the issue head-on at the annual meeting in the summer of 2007. At that point, chief executive Martin Bain made it clear that redevelopment of the under-utilised land was still on the agenda and that he and his board were looking to draft a new masterplan, which would include commercial activity to benefit club coffers.

Murray, pointing towards burgeoning demand for family-section places, had already intimated his desire to increase capacity at the ground to 54,000, and at that point it was revealed that several possibilities were being considered with that in mind. The simplest idea was to remove the big screens in the corners of the ground and replace them with additional seats, while a more labour-intensive proposal was to lower the pitch and add extra rows of seats around the perimeter of the park.

By the time Murray made his exit, the capacity for fans in hospitality areas, including executive boxes, was 1,200, with just over 51,000 seats within the stands. Both of the potential expansion schemes would have required investment, and in difficult financial climes neither was deemed a necessity.

While the money-spinning casino never did get off the ground, in 2008 permission was granted for a revised scheme, again proposing a project running to hundreds of millions of pounds, featuring retail and hotel accommodation. Such was the scale of it that Murray hoped to attract partners to share the cost of the development. The club hailed the decision to grant planning permission as 'a significant step in an exciting project' and remarked on the hopes for regenerating Govan as part of the wider revamp for the city that the council was intent on pushing forward.

The £350-million scheme would see flats in the Hinshelwood area transformed into a hotel and retail outlets, with Murray stressing: 'We have a masterplan which will hopefully be of financial benefit to Rangers. The funds will go to the club, nobody else.'

A spokesman for Glasgow City Council added:

> The Ibrox redevelopment proposals are part of the overall regeneration plan for the Govan area. At times when markets are experiencing difficulties, the council needs to be more adventurous about how it uses its own land to encourage economic development and generate investment.

What had quietly slipped from the various ideas under consideration was the substantial redevelopment of the stadium itself that had been mooted by the club. Murray and Bain had looked at French side Lyon's plans for a new ground and liked what they saw, with visions of an all-singing, all-dancing 70,000-seat ground with only the Main Stand façade retained. The sums did not add up, though, and it was put on the back burner.

The same can be said for the regeneration of the surrounding land. As Rangers – and, more importantly, the banks – battened down the hatches, the project remained firmly on the drawing board.

All of the grand visions and ambitious proposals appeared to be disintegrating around the club for a plethora of reasons, most of which were influenced by outside organisations and decisions.

Had it not been for the Government's choice of Manchester for the super-casino, the years following that decision could have been very different for Rangers and its directors. The cash injection from the Las Vegas Sands corporation would have been hugely beneficial, and the spin-offs from the regeneration of the Ibrox area would undoubtedly have been positive. It was not to be.

Similarly, had finance been forthcoming for the redevelopment plans approved in 2008, the area would look very different today. So too would the club's bank balance, as the plan was to plough millions of pounds of profit back into Rangers. Right idea, wrong time, as the property markets stagnated and potential commercial partners ran for cover. Instead, the land lies vacant and ripe for redevelopment.

Of course, not all of the plans fell by the wayside. Perhaps the most significant bricks-and-mortar legacy left by David Murray is the one bearing his name: Murray Park. While the creation of the Club Deck and the modernisation of Ibrox to its current guise were important in infrastructure terms, the creation of the country's first, and arguably finest, purpose-built modern football training complex should have a greater impact on performances on the pitch and the future health of the club's youth-development department.

Murray Park opened for business on 4 July 2001, named in honour of the club's chairman by the board and supporters' groups. It was viewed as a fitting tribute to his contribution in more than a decade at the helm.

Equally appropriately, the complex had been created in a fashion that the owner of the club could be proud of. No corners cut, no scrimping or saving. It was a beautifully appointed facility completed with a level of attention to detail that Bill Struth, the visionary former manager who had created unprecedented indoor training facilities buried deep in the bowels of Ibrox decades earlier, would have approved of. While some have argued that Struth's name would have been a better fit on the gates of the training complex, it should be remembered that it was Murray who sanctioned the renaming of the Bill Struth

Main Stand in tribute to the club legend in 2005.

The 38-acre Murray Park site in Auchenhowie included six full-size pitches as well as two half-size parks, an indoor pitch and a training centre. The facilities were split into two halves, so that first-team and youth players were able to work side by side and benefit from shared medical and gym facilities as well as the hydrotherapy pool on site. Annual running costs were estimated at £1.25 million when it opened its doors.

The £14-million investment represented a massive leap forward from the days of training in local parks and begging and borrowing facilities from cricket clubs, amongst others.

It prompted Advocaat to take a swipe at his predecessors, who he claimed were only interested in spending the club's cash on players rather than on infrastructure – a rich claim when you consider the amounts the Dutchman spent on his squad.

Murray himself admitted at the time of the opening:

> Cricket grounds and muddy rugby pitches are not the places to put £50- or £60-million worth of players. It is something every Rangers supporter can be very proud of. We do follow a lot of other countries but this is a very positive step.

The creation of the SPL in 1998 brought a wish list for the future of the Scottish game. Indoor facilities and purpose-built training centres were at the heart of that blueprint – and it was Rangers who led the way.

While the likes of Hearts, Hibs and Celtic have followed suit in recent years, there was a frustrating lack of progress during the early years. Only at Ibrox was there a commitment to investing in modern facilities, and from that shoot of an idea grew the leafy complex that was christened Murray Park.

The plans had been on the drawing board for a number of years but moved forward apace following Advocaat's arrival with his entourage, who had been tasked with getting to grips with the thorny issue of promotion from within the club's youth ranks.

Murray, speaking in 2001, acknowledged the role played by Advocaat in the creation of the new centre – which had been a prerequisite of the Dutchman's agreement to pledge his future to the club. The chairman said: 'He gave it added impetus. If the club has a future, we must train our own players – it is something we have not done enough of recently and hopefully that will happen more now.'

Ironically, the greatest return from the Murray Park investment is likely to present itself to the new owners. The emergence of Jamie Ness, the now departed Gregg Wylde and Ross Perry, to name but three, under Ally McCoist suggests that the conveyor belt put in place a decade ago is beginning to bring finished products to the first-team dressing-room.

For those who have benefited from working in the refined environs of Murray Park, there is no doubt that the facility will play a key role in the long-term health of the club. George Adams was one of those men. The renowned talent-spotter, who learned his trade under Alex Ferguson at Aberdeen before Celtic and Motherwell tapped into his expertise to unearth a batch of potential young stars, was recruited by Rangers in 2003 to completely overhaul the youth set-up. His mission was to make sure the raw ingredients were available and the systems were in place to ensure the shiny new training complex was not wasted.

The results are tangible. Adams told me: 'The home-grown players who you see in the Rangers team now were all recruited while I was at the club. That was almost ten years ago in some cases, but now the benefits can be seen and that shows how long the process can be. Youth is a long-term commitment.

'A steady stream of the boys who joined during that period have been fed into the Rangers team and that type of pool of talent will have saved the club millions in transfer fees. That has to be the way forward, not just for Rangers but for every club at every level.'

Adams, now director of football at Ross County, is proud of the work he did in two and a half years at Murray Park, only leaving in 2005 when he and chief executive Martin Bain's working relationship broke down. He said: 'I loved working there and knew Rangers would reap the benefits, as they are now.'

When the gates to Murray Park opened, there was still a lot of legwork to be done. The Rangers community programme was completely revamped, new policies were put in place and the coaching staff overhauled. Scouting, a particular area of expertise for Adams, was stepped up and the network of coaching centres was expanded to take in outlying areas, including his old stamping-ground in Aberdeen.

Adams stressed: 'Murray Park was under-used, so we had to make sure we were using it to its full capability. I think that was important. We had the best facility and had to use that to the full to push the players through the system.

'Murray Park is among the best of its kind and the facilities are important – but only as long as the vision is there in the first place at a club. The manager has to be youth-orientated and that was something I had in my time at Rangers with Alex McLeish. Alex was brought up by Fergie, a manager who was never frightened to give kids a chance.

'There have to be pathways and possibilities of playing in the first team for young players, although it is not all about facilities and structures. The most important thing in football is player recruitment. It's also about good coaching and there is plenty of that available at Murray Park. There are good people at Rangers developing the raw material and allowing Ally McCoist and Kenny McDowall to take it to the highest level.'

Adams stressed that all of that means nothing without a quality that money simply cannot buy: good old-fashioned heart. He said: 'There's nothing to beat the allegiance you get from boys who support the clubs they play for – whether it's Rangers, Celtic, Hearts or Aberdeen. They want to play for their clubs, but it's difficult at the Old Firm because the pressure is always on to deliver league and cup success.

'However, Rangers have found a formula to help the kids develop. Walter Smith had the confidence to pitch in lads such as Darren Cole and Kyle Hutton at Champions League level. He also had enough faith in Jamie Ness to hand him a start against Celtic. I am sure that will continue under Ally McCoist.'

While the benefits for McCoist are obvious, from a business perspective it stands to reason that if even one of the current crop moves on for a similar fee to the £9 million Alan Hutton commanded when he transferred to Tottenham in 2008, the initial outlay on the training ground facilities will have been recouped.

The one quirk to that model emerged in 2004, when the club created a new company, Rangers Youth Development Limited, in an administrative move that appeared, from the outside, to be designed to safeguard the assets within the youth structure.

Martin Bain explained the system when he said: 'With transfers, Rangers will negotiate with Rangers Youth Development Limited and hopefully we'll come to an agreement. But if we can't we'll use the FIFA transfer model to agree a fee.'

The company was designed to be self-funding and the club was at pains to stress it was wholly owned by Rangers, despite using outside investment when it was established. The new firm would own the youngsters coming through the ranks and would receive a fee from the club when they stepped up to the first team.

Bain added:

I can see how it sounds strange but, if you take the running costs of Murray Park, Rangers are actually committing £2 million every year to this company. If Allan Hutton is sold, for example, to

Liverpool at the moment, the money goes to Rangers Football Club. But if Bajram Fetai, who is owned by the new company, is sold to Liverpool, then the money goes to the development company. And that money is used to further fund more players.

If I'm very honest, the focus was on the first team for most of the nine years that I've been here. But we created this Murray Park facility and you have to offset some of the running costs – and you have to protect the youth side.

Alan Hutton did indeed find a new home and the revenue was a welcome shot in the arm. Hutton's peer Charlie Adam has also found a place in England's elite, along with fellow Ibrox apprentice Danny Wilson, at Liverpool, while Alan McGregor has emerged as a saleable asset too.

Detractors have criticised Murray Park for a lack of end product, but it was always intended as a long-term project. Now, more than a decade since it opened its gates for the first time, it is a facility that will be relied on more and more as every club looks towards home-reared players.

The investment in the buildings and grounds has not been in isolation, with an emphasis also placed on appointing quality personnel. Jimmy Sinclair was lured from his position as the SFA's head of youth development in 2006 to lead the Murray Park revolution, following on from the initial incumbent Tommy McLean and then George Adams, who had established a reputation as one of the country's best-qualified star-finders.

There was a recognition within the club that the youth-development strategy had to be ripped up and started from scratch, with a new focus on spreading the net far and wide to find young talent. That extended abroad, with the likes of Hamed Namouchi, on a wage representing a fraction of those earned by established first-team players, brought in to add depth to the playing resources.

Mitchell has had an extended run at the head of the youth-development department and has brought stability behind the scenes. Circumstances in many ways have made his job easier, with a lack of transfer funds leading Walter Smith and then McCoist to delve into the youth resources for solutions to gaps in their squads.

A clear pathway from the youth ranks to the first team has been established, and obstacles that once stood in the way have been removed. Murray's millions and the superstar players brought to the club through the nine-in-a-row years created those barriers, but his commitment to Murray Park in the second half of his reign has given the club the tools to at least become partly self-sufficient in what promise to be testing years ahead. Football's own version of the good life may hold the key to the rebuilding of a proud football club, from the grass roots up.

CHAPTER 22

'I have returned to the role of chairman with
renewed enthusiasm and vigour for the challenges
ahead – together we will bring the good times
back to Ibrox.'

David Murray, 2004

WHEN THE FRONT door of Ibrox was locked on 30 June 2004, it was
very much an ordinary evening. What nobody on the outside could
quite appreciate was that behind the sturdy façade of red brick and
mortar a financial house of cards was stacking up to a perilous height.

It was the financial year up to that date that saw Rangers' debts hit
the record-breaking total of £73.9 million. It was a black day for the
club as the scale of the fiscal plight began to reach a level that set alarm
bells ringing among the rank-and-file supporters.

The mounting debt was, of course, just one of the figures that
brought concern. The interest payments were, as a result of the huge
deficit, topping £4 million annually or £80,000 per week at that stage.
The near £74-million debt had accumulated after another year of loss-
making at Ibrox, with a £5.9-million deficit in the year up to 30 June
2004 recorded.

It was at that stage that Murray was planning his share issue, a last
throw of the dice designed to wipe £50 million from the debt. He
maintained typical bravado and, when announcing the record debt
levels, insisted:

Despite what the critics may say, our club retains great strength.

I do, however, recognise that our greatest asset is the backing
of our loyal fans and shareholders and I would like to thank you
all for your continued support. I have returned to the role of
chairman with renewed enthusiasm and vigour for the challenges

ahead – together we will bring the good times back to Ibrox.

John McClelland and the executive team have performed well in executing our business plan. It was, however, apparent that a solution would eventually be required to resolve the club's historic debt position and the board had been considering options for restructuring finances for some time.

At the same time, I have consistently confirmed my willingness to play a leading part in whatever type of long-term financial solution was deemed to be appropriate. While trading performance has improved significantly in recent years, the reduction of the historic debt eliminates negative media attention, removes the significant interest burden and enhances the club's net asset position.

For a man confirming his firm's near £6-million loss for the financial year and debts a whisker away from £74 million, it was a remarkably bullish stance, but entirely credible. It had long been argued that the level of debt was only an issue when it could not be serviced, and the nation as a whole was riding high on a wave of readily available credit in the first half of the decade.

Rangers appeared guilty of little more than the corporate equivalent of flashing the plastic a few too many times; there was still time to bring down the balance. The trading loss for the year up to July 2002 had been a whopping £31.9 million, so there was reason to be optimistic, just not wildly so.

The £74-million figure was the spur to bring the house in order, and the huge share issue was the vehicle for doing that. Still, Murray remained adamant that quality on the park would remain central to the business model. He said:

> Although the fund-raising will not alter our basic business strategy, which is to maintain a balanced approach to on and off-field activity, it will enable us to reinvest operational cash flow which would otherwise have gone to service the debt. Our past ambition was financed by large capital investment and the promise of media revenues that did not materialise. We must now operate within our budgetary constraints. We will, however, always endeavour to field the best possible team operating within our available financial resources.

Rewind back to the Advocaat era, the time in which the near £32-million loss of the 2001–02 campaign was racked up. At the time, the chairman and owner was convinced the splurge was worthwhile.

The bulk of the debt burden could be traced back to the excesses of that period. Speaking in November 2001, Murray said: 'This year has seen our highest spend – taking into consideration player acquisition, contract extensions and the new training ground. Including recent player movements, our total investment exceeds £40 million.'

By the following year, there was no sign of the international shopping spree abating. Murray said in the autumn of 2002:

> Last year, like previous years, saw a combination of investment both for current and long-term success. Expenditure of £55 million over the last three years on the current playing squad has created a team of European quality. At the same time our investment of £15 million in the Murray Park training facility is to ensure we can maintain this standard in the future without incurring the scale of expenditure previously seen on transfers in.

There was a multitude of reasons why the board was comfortable with the levels of expenditure – and the levels of debt that went hand in hand with the loose purse strings. One was that the club's owner had always made it clear that he and his parent company would be on hand to shore things up if the road got particularly rocky. Another was the manner in which the debts were structured. By 2002, they had crept over the £50-million mark, but chairman John McClelland was at pains to stress to shareholders at the annual meeting that year that only £6 million of that figure was what he classed as 'short-term' debt, in other words loans that could be called in at any point.

The rest was tied up in long-term arrangements, the equivalent of 15- or 25-year mortgages secured against the club's assets. As long as repayments were being met, those were not deemed to be a major cause for fear or alarm. It was, as McClelland put it, all 'under control'.

The chairman had been left to explain the situation to shareholders during that 2002 AGM, with David Murray taking the unusual decision to bypass the meeting and make a video presentation instead. McClelland dismissed any notion that Murray's absence was significant, saying:

> David has asked me to take over the chairman's role and that meant he was taking a step back from some of the day-to-day activities of the club – including the AGM. David was anxious, as was I, that Alex McLeish and I move forward as a team. David is on holiday right now and he deserves it. I don't think the general body of the

meeting feel that, in any way, David's 14 years have been anything other than outstanding.

However, there were admissions at around that time that losses of the level of the one reported in 2002 could not be sustained, and efforts were made to cut back on the extravagances of the past.

Speaking on Radio Clyde in January 2004, Murray said: 'We have been guilty of being overambitious and I don't remember too many voices of discontent at the time. But I am here to make it clear that I am prepared to accept my share of responsibility.'

He claimed the debt would be capped at £65 million unless the Murray Group made further funds available to the club, insisting he was relaxed about the situation.

He added:

> We have got one of the best training facilities in Europe, we spent a lot of money on the retail side of the business, refurbished the ground and we have bought some football players. It is all very well having £65 million of debt as long as your assets are worth more than that. We have a stadium which is worth anything between £50 million and £100 million, a training ground worth whatever valuation.

Just months earlier, chairman John McClelland had leapt to the club owner's defence at the annual meeting in 2003. McClelland claimed criticism of Murray's management of the finances was not valid, saying:

> There was a very ambitious investment programme in the squad and the infrastructure, but £15 million of the £68-million debt was spent on Murray Park and I think we are seeing the benefits of it. Undoubtedly, towards the end of our investment programme we lost our way a little bit in the Champions League, which would have been a great source of income. Last season we had nearly no European income when the previous year we had £5 million.

McClelland, who the previous year at the annual meeting had told supporters to think of the multimillion-pound annual interest charges being paid by the club as the equivalent of the single wage of a top-class player, was understandably supportive of Murray and the rest of the board. They had all been in it together, confident that the heavy borrowing could be sustained – and it could have been, had it not been for the small matter of the financial collapse that threatened to bring the world to its knees.

The root of the problem lies in the global banking crisis and the meltdown that ensued. Collapses, mergers, streamlining – the banking sector went through it all and swept its corporate clients along with it.

David Murray and his empire had a long and established relationship with the Bank of Scotland. Edinburgh-based, they were the perfect financial partner to understand the complex and varying needs of the group.

Murray was one of a string of bright young things backed by the bank's own rising star, Gavin Masterton. It was Masterton, a Fifer by birth who worked his way up through the ranks to eventually become managing director, to whom BoS turned when they decided to dip a toe into the world of management buyouts and substantial corporate lending as the 1980s dawned. He was on his way to becoming the most powerful banker in Scotland. Indeed, you can still see Masterston's signature on banknotes today.

Masterton threw his weight behind the ambitious plans of Murray, Tom Hunter, Tom Farmer and mobile-phone entrepreneur Richard Emmanuel. He was given licence to fund those business brains in their formative years and put his intuition, not to mention the skills developed during his studies at Harvard, to good use. Speaking in a *Sunday Herald* interview about the type of individuals he staked his organisation's money on, Masterton said: 'They either have the spark in their eyes or they don't.' He added:

> I think the style of the individuals we backed fitted in with Bank of Scotland's entrepreneurial style. Such people are difficult to describe. For a start, it's difficult to stop them talking. They have a high level of energy, they work their pants off and they have a very strong sense of conviction. They bring a good knowledge of their market and huge belief in what they are doing, and you end up wanting to be part of it. They have passion and you can't help but buy into that.

Masterton retired from the BoS in 2001, before the wheels came off the industry. At the time, his bank were in the process of a merger with Halifax to become HBoS. Then, seven years later, as the blocks the British banks were built upon crumbled, the organisation was taken over by Lloyds TSB in a £12-billion deal that had been pushed for by a government terrified about the future of HBoS.

Lloyds TSB was considered a strong and well-capitalised bank, well placed to steady the rocking HBoS ship, but they were not immune to the issues that led to the bail-outs. Public money was pumped in, ensuring the urgency surrounding the new super-group stepped up a level.

Senior managers began examining the inherited client list, poring over accounts and shoring up any that threatened greater problems than they already faced. Rangers would not be the worst offenders, given the high ratio of turnover to debt, not to mention tangible assets in the land owned by the club, but the club still came under close scrutiny as Lloyds sought to claw back money from borrowers.

Their pursuit of Rangers was different; it had to be subtle to try to allay the obvious fears of a public backlash. A bank spokesman admitted: 'We understand that the football club is an intrinsic part of Scottish life. We are working with Rangers to look at a long-term sustainable solution to the issue of its debt.'

There were echoes of a velvet glove encasing an iron fist as it soon became clear that the liberal borrowing enjoyed during the peak years of the Murray-BoS relationship was very much consigned to the history books. Existing banking covenants were ripped up; new rules were in play, and they were far tougher than ever before as the world woke up to the debt mountain that had been built up over time. Putting pressure on a business to toe the line would be unpopular in any sector, but in football it was a knife-edge situation. The whispers that Rangers could have been pushed into administration struck fear into the heart of every Ibrox supporter. It was a necessary evil as the bank battled to restore some sort of order to its book of big business loans.

In saying that, even after the banks began to get tough there was still leeway for bad habits to resurface. At the annual meeting in the summer of 2007, Murray laid a portion of the responsibility for the continued struggles to balance the books at the door of manager Walter Smith, claiming they had spent almost £3 million over the agreed transfer budget of £7 million. Those figures were small change compared with the money changing hands in the heady days when spending £3 million wouldn't have mustered as much as a frown in the Ibrox boardroom.

The banks had been swept along on a romantic notion that the game could pay its way. Even Masterton, a dyed-in-the-wool banker who should have had prudence as his middle name, was bitten by the football bug himself, joining the board of his home-town club, Dunfermline Athletic, in 1990 and going on to become the major shareholder in the Pars when he shelled out £825,000 to take control of the East End Park side in 2006 as the club struggled at the wrong end of the SPL table and also attempted to tackle rising debts, which would eventually force wage cuts. Masterton knew that the beautiful game hid some ugly finances, with his own group of companies, Stadia, established to invest in the Scottish game but hitting rocky times from 2004 and eventually closing.

It should not be forgotten that Rangers were far from alone in over-indulging during the boom years. Given the earning potential through season-ticket sales and massive gates, Murray and his board were positively reserved when you begin to examine some of the other financial horror stories that the Scottish game has been party to in the not-too-distant past.

Exhibit A: Dundee Football Club. Oddly, nobody raised an eyebrow when Dundee, supported by average attendances in the four-figure bracket, brought World Cup superstar Claudio Cannigia, Italian international Fabrizio Ravanelli and Scotland mainstay Craig Burley to Dens Park. Rather than delving too deeply into the detail, most were content to revel in the moment and put the absurdity of the situation firmly to one side – so far to the side that it dropped off the agenda completely. For a few glorious months, Dundee fans and the rest of Scottish football got up caught in the moment.

Then, in November 2003, reality began to bite. Faced with debts reported to be in the region of £20 million, the club's owners, brothers Jimmy and Peter Marr, had no option but to call in the administrators. At that stage, the weekly losses were said to be in the region of £100,000 – and that for a club with gates a fraction of the size attracted by Rangers.

Ravanelli and Burley were among the casualties as 25 members of staff were culled in the first instance, with manager Jim Duffy tasked with delivering the body blow to his shell-shocked players. Duffy said at the time:

> I'd like to send a message to all football clubs to have a look at their finances and if they are contemplating going into administration to clear some of their debts. They should realise how much of a devastating blow it is to people's lives.

For every Ravanelli and Burley, stars who had already grown rich on the back of the game, there was a Gavin Beith, Tom Cowan or Barry Forbes. Players, either journeymen or youngsters, who relied on their pay cheque to keep a roof over their head and food on their family's table. In an instant, they lost their bread and butter because of the recklessness of others.

The 25-person reduction from the staff included 15 players. With one stroke, the administrator had shaved 45 per cent from a weekly wage bill that was crippling the once-proud club.

The Marr brothers had been chasing an impossible dream, throwing money at the squad in an attempt to compete with the big-hitting Old Firm. They did not act alone, with the banks and organisations that extended the hand with credit facilities arguably just as culpable for the fiscal mess that enveloped Dens Park in the winter of 2003.

After the pain of administration, Dundee did live to fight another day. Not that the lessons of the past counted for much, with the club's slide into administration in 2010 proving that once bitten does not necessarily mean twice shy in the weird and wonderful world of football.

The modern-day precedent had been set by Motherwell, with the Fir Park side entering administration in 2002 after fighting a losing battle against debts in the region of £8 million. Charismatic chairman John Boyle was said to have ploughed £10 million of his own money into the Steelmen on top of that figure as he too attempted to use cash to help a provincial side punch above its weight.

On that occasion, nineteen players were binned, with ten sacked and nine released from their contracts as administrators got to grips with a business sector like no other. It took until 2003 for the books to be set straight and creditors dealt with, leaving manager Terry Butcher to galvanise what was left of his squad and build on a crop of young, and inexpensive, players. In essence, Motherwell came out of the process leaner and stronger in every department, proving that a club's fortunes can be turned around with strong and purposeful management on and off the park.

Livingston proved to be the other side of the coin. Placed in administration early in 2004, with debts reported to be in the region of £3.5 million, the Lions went on to lurch from one crisis to another.

Scottish players' union chief Tony Higgins warned at the time: 'Clubs have taken a big gamble in the past and the ones who suffer are the players. We've been predicting these kinds of problems for two or three years.'

Livi, Motherwell and Dundee all went into administration before the SPL had taken the decision to implement a ten-point penalty for clubs finding themselves in that situation. The playing penalty was seen as a deterrent strong enough to persuade clubs to put their financial houses in order – but not all toed the line.

In March 2008, Gretna's fairy-tale rise to the elite of the Scottish game turned into a nightmare when benefactor Brooks Mileson's financial backing disappeared, with the enigmatic owner in ill health and disappearing from the football scene he had featured so prominently in during the years in which the minnows were in the ascendant.

There were redundancies for 22 players and a clutch of other staff as the battle to save the club began – but it was all in vain. By June that year, the club, docked ten points and then relegated as results failed to pick up, was out of business, brought to its knees by debts of £4 million, and league status was relinquished. It was a dramatic bust after the boom years.

Gordon Smith, then chief executive of the SFA, said:

> The SFA, the SFL, the SPL will need to look very closely at these aspects of how the game is structured and financed.
>
> It's very sad. Unfortunately, the problem with Gretna was their success was down to the money of one person and there was no stability behind it because of that. That's something that maybe lessons have to be learned about, the stability in the game.
>
> If someone is putting a lot of money into a team and it's getting a bit of success for a while, is there any future for that team if that one person pulls out? I think all of us in Scottish football need to look at that, all the bodies, everybody involved in the game.

The trail of creditors stung by Gretna's demise ran to 139 individuals, organisations and companies. On that long list were the former players and staff as well as HM Revenue and Customs and a string of suppliers.

The club had managed to rack up debts of £3.7 million despite holding assets, primarily the stadium and surrounding ground, valued at just over £800,000. The debt figure included £1.7 million that was said to be due to Brooks Mileson, in the form of a loan to the club, while the taxman had an unpaid bill of £500,000 on the Raydale Park doormat.

It was a sorry mess, but a perfect example of the perils facing any club if the man who has propped up the business gives up his involvement and takes his cheque book with him.

Could the same thing ever happen to a big club, a club the size of Rangers? The assets are far more valuable and income is huge in comparison with a club like Gretna with relative handfuls of supporters. The same thing shouldn't happen to a big club, but it was not impossible by any means.

Motherwell proved that administration does not have to be the end of the road for a football club, but it is far from an easy option. The pain felt by players, staff and supporters of the Scottish clubs who had fallen into the trap previously was palpable and the stigma takes a long, long time to wear away.

Almost every club in the SPL, and even down into the SFL, has been guilty of carrying too much debt at one stage or another. Some have tackled the issue head-on and successfully managed to get their figures in order; others have been stuck in limbo as they face up to a future with reduced borrowing possibilities and diminishing revenue-generating opportunities as broadcast cash dries up and fans tighten their belts.

David Glen, of the accountancy firm PricewaterhouseCoopers, has become established as the leading authority on Scottish football's finances. He has taken responsibility for compiling the firm's highly respected annual report on the state of the national game's affairs. The annual study was first published at the end of the 1988–89 season, coincidentally David Murray's first full term with Rangers, when Glen's predecessor Ian Dewar launched the research.

The experts have watched with interest as the business of the sport has changed almost beyond recognition. Glen, who conducted a special review to mark 21 years of the company's analysis, said:

> Undoubtedly the clubs have been through something of a financial roller-coaster during that period, with income soaring from £24 million to £197 million – but this was matched by debts spiralling out of control from £9 million to peak at £186 million, wages, rising from £10 million to £110 million, being the principal culprit.
>
> Our reports have covered administrations and liquidations – including a near miss by Celtic for what now seems like a paltry figure of debt, for the club, of around £6 million – while on the park we had nine in a row and not one but two UEFA Cup finals.

According to Glen, a number of issues have been 'clarified' by events since 1989. He explained:

> The SPL does not generate a sufficient audience to attract the major media contracts that are to be had in a number of the other European leagues, particularly those secured by our neighbours in England, and access to the riches of the Champions League is increasingly becoming a lottery as Scotland's ranking continues to slip amongst the European nations.
>
> This lack of, and uncertainty over, levels of income does not create a sound platform for investors who seek solid cash flows to fund their investment. There are too many examples of those who have found this out to their cost and therefore the prospect of further investment in the SPL in the short- to medium-term does not look good, whether this be the banks providing loans and overdrafts, or an investing entrepreneur.

In many ways the SPL has suffered from the rampant financial success elsewhere, particularly in England. Simply, the SPL cannot compete financially – it can no longer match the transfer fees or the wages demands of the top talent to be competitive on the global stage and the worrying part of this is that it can be an increasingly downward spiral.

To counter this there will have to be a period of consolidation. The clubs will survive by nurturing their own talent but ultimately with a view to selling that talent on to the richer leagues. The fees generated from these transfers out will dictate the level of transfers in, with a balance being earmarked to keep debt levels in check.

This will perhaps be more apparent with the Old Firm – the smaller clubs have been working with this model already and I would cite Hibernian as a club who have been successfully operating in such a fashion for a number of years now, though not always to the delight of the Hibs fans.

Glen appreciates that it will take far more than some prudent bookkeeping to take Scottish clubs back to the days when they did not have to live in fear of their English counterparts appearing with cheque book in hand, when Rangers could attract the very best of talent from south of the border. Those days may never return, but he does believe the existing gulf may at least narrow.

Glen added:

In the medium term, if things are to get back onto an even keel there will need to be some sort of 'levelling' event. For example, whilst the English Premier League attracts enormous income, the clubs are equally adept at spending it and more, resulting in a substantial debt mountain. There are already signs that some clubs are struggling to service this debt.

When combined with the fact that BSkyB is coming under pressure from the regulator over the wholesale price of its sports channel, the renewal of the EPL television contract in 2013 may prove to be a significant event if the terms of renewal prove not to be what the EPL clubs hope for. A reduction in their budgets would bring the financial playing field closer to the SPL's level.

Failing this, and assuming it is still the ambition of principally the Old Firm to compete and be competitive on the highest European stage, then I believe the clubs will have to seek additional revenues from outside Scotland.

A move to the English leagues has been talked about on and off for many years and remains a possibility but, in my view, if it is to happen at all it will be driven not by the English clubs but by television and a desire by the broadcaster to see things 'spiced up'. If this remains an outside bet, then maybe it is time to resurrect the idea of an Atlantic League in conjunction with the Scandinavian and Benelux countries? This week's fixtures: Rangers v. Ajax, Anderlecht v. Celtic, Hibernian v. Rosenberg, Gothenburg v. Hearts . . .

Until a radical vision such as that becomes reality, the SPL will have to concentrate on getting its own house in order to safeguard the future of its current clubs. There have been warnings down through the years, in fact as far back as Third Lanark's unfortunate demise, about the dangers of not being able to match income to expenditure. Events at Motherwell, Livingston and Gretna have rammed home the message in more recent times and the Rangers saga screamed out that all was not well in the garden of the Scottish game.

Now it is up to the rest of the SPL to sit up, take notice and make positive strides towards addressing the problems by grabbing the bull by the horns and ensuring Rangers are the last club to face the ignominy of administration and the pain and suffering that brings.

CHAPTER 23

'If you were to do a financial analysis on Scottish football as a business, it is basically bankrupt – that is the fact of the matter.'

David Murray, 2001

SIMPLICITY HAS NOT been a feature of the finances of Rangers Football Club over the course of the past quarter of a century. From share issues to cash injections and right back to the very beginning with the debenture scheme at the start of the 1990s, the methods for raising funds have been many and varied. Some have been successful, others less so. Ultimately, time, and the balance-sheet, conspired to show that the constant efforts to keep the overdraft at bay were stemming the tide rather than turning it from the Ibrox door.

When David Murray collected the keys to the front door, he inherited a team, a stadium, a proud tradition and a £7-million overdraft. He also had tucked under his arm a blueprint for the future, a masterplan for success on and off the field of play.

Key to his business plan was finding room for more spectators and the revenue they would bring. The only hitch was finding the £12.5 million required to create the new and improved vision for Ibrox at the heart of that plan. There was no blank cheque and, on this occasion at least, no application to the bank. The supporters proved to be the first port of call.

It was in 1990, in the infancy of Murray's time as owner, that the club launched the Main Stand debenture scheme. The target was to sell more than 6,800 bonds at up to £1,650 each to pull in around £8.5 million towards the cost of expanding the ground with an extra tier on the Main Stand, as well as the switch to an all-seated layout. The remaining £4 million was to be paid by the club and through grants available for stadium development as the rush to comply with the Taylor Report criteria gathered pace.

While individual supporters were eligible for the bonds on offer under the scheme, the corporate market was very much a target. Murray, such a keen rugby follower, had taken his lead from the SRU and Murrayfield when he'd formulated the fund-raising initiative with the help of financial advisors.

In return for their four-figure outlay, bond holders would be entitled to purchase the season ticket for 'their' seat for life. They would also get first call on tickets for big European nights and they would get their name engraved on that seat. Within a week, Gers from across the world had pledged £2 million of the total and the money continued to roll in as more than 6,000 of the seats were snapped up.

The owner led the sales pitch, telling fans:

> It has always been our intention to provide our supporters with the finest stadium possible. The Rangers bond gives us the mechanism to make that dream a reality. This method of financing the reconstruction of the stand will ensure that Rangers can continue to make money available to Graeme to invest in the best available players and keep the club at the forefront.

A £300,000 advertising campaign was plotted to educate supporters on the ins and outs of the debenture model, which would allow the bonds to be passed down through generations or be sold in a secondary market. Think time share, but in a football stadium. And without the sun.

Just a few short months into the Murray era, it was clear that Rangers would be prepared to push the boundaries and try new ways of raising finance. It went way beyond the traditional and accepted methods, which up to that point had extended, for most Scottish clubs, as far as shirt sponsorship and advertising hoardings.

The income from sponsorship had already been ramped up during the early days of the Murray regime, with a £5-million deal struck with Scottish Brewers to keep the McEwan's logo on the front of the shirt. Part of the deal brokered with the company had also given them an option to purchase a 10 per cent stake of the club. The option was never exercised by the drinks firm.

As the club galloped through nine in a row, there was concerted yet controlled investment in the squad, first under Souness and then during Walter Smith's tenure. Rangers hogged the football headlines, with the financial aspects of Ibrox life deep in the distance.

It was in the late 1990s that the accounts began to take dramatic and unexpected twists, starting in January 1997 with the massive investment from the mysterious figure of Joe Lewis.

Lewis's was not a name most Rangers supporters were familiar with, but that was about to change. Shortly after the bells had chimed to bring in the New Year, it was announced that the Londoner had purchased a share of the club from David Murray in exchange for a £40-million windfall. It took Murray's stake down to 61 per cent, but that was a small price to pay for the introduction of welcome funds at a time when the transfer market was adjusting to the Bosman ruling and clubs found a vital revenue stream cut off at source.

Lewis, a billionaire and one of Britain's richest men, spent most of his time at his Caribbean mansion in the Bahamas. He also had bases in London, Florida and Argentina. He had no football or sporting background, aside from a reputation for enjoying the American football betting markets. His highest-profile extravagance was art, with a collection of Impressionist and modernist pieces worth as much as his share in Rangers had cost him.

Through his holding company the English National Investment Company (ENIC), Lewis also began to collect football teams as he played his part in the muddied waters across the board in European football – with various organisations taking stakes in clubs in an array of leagues across the Continent.

At one stage in the late 1990s, ENIC, in addition to a 20 per cent share in Rangers, owned AEK Athens and also had slices of Vicenza in Italy as well as Czech outfit Slavia Prague.

The blurred ownership lines in the game in general prompted UEFA to introduce stricter controls and regulations, limiting clubs with shared ownership from entering the same European competition. The get-out clause was that the conditions only applied to majority shareholders, not those, such as ENIC, who held minority stakes.

What the involvement of Lewis did do was raise the question of wider interest in Rangers Football Club as a business. Was it time to realise its full potential and float on the stock market? Murray remained unconvinced. Speaking at the time of the Lewis investment, the chairman said:

> I have consistently stated that I do not believe it is appropriate to float Rangers until the uncertainties arising from Bosman, pay-per-view television and the expansion of European club competitions are resolved.
>
> I am delighted to have raised £40 million of new capital from a single investor at this time, providing us with the financial strength

to develop the club further while these changes take effect. I believe that Rangers is now in a much stronger position to realise our ambitions for footballing and commercial success.

Part of the masterplan included the introduction in 1998 of fresh ideas at the top, with the arrival of a chief executive for the first time since Alan Montgomery had held the post in the late 1980s.

The appointment was an indication that the scale of the business had extended far beyond the traditional reach of a part-time board of directors juggling football commitments with their day-to-day commercial interests.

The man selected by Murray to carry through his plans was Bob Brannan, a former management consultant who had spent four years as managing director of William Grant & Sons Distillers before being headhunted by the Rangers supremo.

The Dundonian was a young man, just into his 40s, but arrived with glowing praise from his new employer. His mission was to expand commercial opportunities and offer a new and more rigid management structure, fit for the rapidly approaching twenty-first century.

Brannan lasted all of ten months, resigning after deciding that football was not his career of choice. It had not been a roaring success, with no sign of the major sponsorship it had been hoped the addition of a permanent commercial figurehead would attract. He later reappeared in a similar capacity at Dundee, although that was not a lasting relationship.

Murray decided he would resume day-to-day control of club affairs, although he would later return to a structure incorporating a chief executive, mirroring developments throughout Scottish football.

The arrival of Fergus McCann in the green half of Glasgow brought Rangers' great rivals kicking and screaming into the modern era in the mid-1990s and forced Murray to keep his eye on the ball commercially. It intensified the competition on the pitch, but at board level there was a new spirit of unity developing as the two clubs embraced their global appeal.

In 1999, a £13-million sponsorship deal was announced, giving US-based cable television firm NTL shirt sponsorship rights for both Celtic and Rangers for a four-year period. NTL's managing director, Frank Cullen, hit the business nail on the head when he remarked: 'We are delighted to be associated with both clubs, two of Europe's biggest and most famous clubs. We believe this is a case of the Old Firm teaming up with a new firm.'

In time, the sponsorship mushroomed to include a media partnership running to tens of millions of pounds as Rangers and NTL worked in tandem to develop television and Internet opportunities, taking advantage of the firm's expertise as plans for Rangers TV were formulated. NTL's snaring of Glasgow's giants was no new tactic. C.R. Smith had got in at the beginning with an Old Firm double in the 1980s, and others followed, including Carling and Tennent's in more recent times.

The boom in sponsorship was hugely important for Rangers during the 1990s, with cash flowing out of the Ibrox account as quickly as it was accumulated.

Supporters often found themselves carrying the can for the financial handcuffs that Scottish football imposed on the club. With television revenues not coming close to competing with those afforded to comparable English clubs, season-ticket prices during the Dick Advocaat era were cranked up and the increase justified by Murray.

As the sales push for the 1999–2000 season began in earnest, the Ibrox chairman defended a 15 per cent hike by claiming:

> We want to compete at the highest level but we are not competing on a level playing field in terms of transfer fees and wages. Many of the clubs we are competing with are playing in a league where the revenue they get from TV money and other income is far greater. These are the facts of life and we have to compensate for that in as many ways as we can.

In fairness, the following term saw prices come down again.

Still, behind the scenes there were rumbles of discontent about the levels to which Advocaat had been allowed to spend. In the summer of 1999, Howard Stanton quit as a director after a short period on the board. The ENIC chairman cited personal commitments as the reason for his departure, but it was suggested that he and Murray were at loggerheads over spending plans that appeared, from the outside at least, to be unsustainable.

As the millennium celebrations loomed, Rangers announced plans for a major share issue. The blueprint was designed to raise in the region of £40 million and it was hoped the opportunity would entice big hitters from home and abroad.

Tom Hunter, cash rich following the sale of his Sports Division chain for £250 million, was among the figures quoted as taking an interest in purchasing a chunk of the club, although his investment did not materialise.

The timing of the share issue coincided with soaring debts, which had peaked at around £20 million at that stage, a figure that the club had admitted was a concern.

Qualification for the Champions League group stages, with an unexpected victory against Palma during qualification, had eased the pressure. Indeed, Murray conceded at that stage that reaching the lucrative group phase was a necessity rather than a bonus after the excesses of the early months of Advocaat's tenure. It appeared that the rising debt and difficulties in eating away at the deficit had served as a wake-up call for the board of directors and their figurehead.

There were admissions that the 'high-risk' strategy of running with substantial debt had been an error in judgement and promises that there would be no repeat in the future.

The short-term remedy came in the spring of 2000 when it was confirmed that South Africa-based supporter Dave King was to pump £20 million of capital into the Ibrox accounts. King, who had made his fortune in the financial services industry, claimed the money would take the club to a 'new level'.

It formed part of a revised share issue that would see Murray make an investment of £32.3 million in new shares through Murray Sports and its wholly owned subsidiary RFC Investment Holdings. Shades of financial smoke and mirrors perhaps, but the headline-grabbing figure was a combined shot in the arm in the region of £53 million.

There were grand plans for that pot of gold. Investing in new players, paying down some of the debt, building a new training ground . . . not to mention keeping more than £10 million aside in the bank.

It transpired that even £50 million was not enough to keep the club ahead of the game, however, and a worrying pattern began to emerge as the problem of matching income to soaring outgoings began to raise its head more and more frequently.

Belt-tightening, for the first time, was on the agenda, and priorities were scrutinised. The club got tough, with Murray never shirking the opportunity to play hardball. Early in 2000, they went as far as arresting Airdrie's share of gate receipts from a Scottish Cup tie after the Diamonds had stalled on paying a £30,000 debt to one of Murray's many firms. The Lanarkshire side was stumbling towards extinction at that stage, with spiralling money troubles, but there was no mercy despite the relatively minor bill due to Murray – who accused them of playing on Rangers' 'good nature'. It proved to be one of the straws that broke the camel's back, with Airdrie going into liquidation a day after the move to claw back the outstanding money.

Across the board, there was a new, more prudent approach and it extended to the playing staff. While lavish salaries were showered on the Ibrox superstars, it was not a bottomless pit of generosity. When John Brown was awarded a lucrative testimonial match in 2001, Murray made it clear he expected the stalwart's benefit game to be the last hosted by the club. He claimed that the player power of the post-Bosman era meant that the revenue-generating spin-offs were a thing of the past.

This coincided with a stark overview of the national sport, with Murray claiming: 'If you were to do a financial analysis on Scottish football as a business, it is basically bankrupt – that is the fact of the matter.'

While he countered that dire assessment by pointing out the commercial potential of his own club and rivals Celtic, he warned that as many as ten clubs could fold within five years. His predictions proved wide of the mark, but the boom and bust of Gretna proved his fears about the difficulties facing smaller sides were far from unfounded. He insisted wage bills would remain stagnant but rightly guessed that squads would reduce in size across the board as clubs attempted to get more bang for their buck.

Clubs would have to get smarter, more efficient. With that in mind, in November 2001 there was a key appointment when director John McClelland stepped up to become vice chairman. McClelland was tasked with overseeing business activities in tandem with a four-man executive board. The restructuring was carried out to allow Murray to concentrate on the football side of the organisation. McClelland had an impressive CV, with IBM and Philips among his former employers.

Speaking in the winter of 2001, Murray admitted:

> As chairman of this club I have run a high-risk strategy which has worked for us in the past. We are sitting here today with a good playing squad, an excellent stadium – which we own – and a fabulous training ground. However, if we were to continue with the same strategy then there is no doubt we would face serious financial problems in the long term. It is clear that some clubs are continuing with a high-risk strategy. What I would say to our supporters and shareholders is that we will have to run a tighter ship in future. In the current financial climate we need more prudent management. I genuinely feel a major club could go bust.

He claimed at that stage that debts of £30 million would be manageable and argued that he had invested £25 million himself in the past 13 years – with the promise of more to come if necessary.

In July 2002, Murray stunned the football world when he announced his decision to step down from the post of chairman. McClelland took over in the top job, although his predecessor retained his 66 per cent shareholding. Murray said:

> It has been a great honour to have held the position of chairman for 14 years but I feel a change of management style would be beneficial for the club as the whole industry faces new challenges. A strong team is now in place to assist John in reaching our financial, commercial and football targets, which collectively must be more realistic as recently costs have soared and incomes remained static. These facts are facing all clubs at present. I will still be available for support and advice when required. This move will also allow me personally to focus more time on my role as chairman of Murray International Holdings.

McClelland, who described himself as a 'challenge-oholic', said:

> I believe we can still achieve success but we will have to achieve it in a different way. We will definitely not have as much to spend and need to concentrate more on bringing on home-grown players. It's a challenge but I thrive on this kind of thing. The fact that one of David Murray's numerous bold decisions was to build Murray Park gives us a great chance of doing just that.

In August 2004, Murray, who had been awarded the title of honorary chairman in his absence from the top seat at the boardroom table, returned to the chairmanship. McClelland returned to his previous role as vice chairman

It coincided with Murray's decision to buy out ENIC's 20 per cent stake in the club for close to £9 million. ENIC had been looking for an exit, with chief executive Daniel Levy, a lifelong Tottenham fan, setting his sights on developing Spurs.

It took Murray's share to more than 86 per cent and paved the way for a major share issue designed to pour £57 million into the debt-ridden club. Existing shareholders would be given the opportunity to buy one new share for £1 for every existing share already held, with Murray underwriting the issue to the tune of £50 million to ensure the revenue target was met.

Murray insisted it would not lead to a windfall for manager Alex McLeish. In a show of modesty, he said:

Even if we didn't have debt, we're not generating enough money to
buy players. I'm not an Abramovich. I'm David Murray in Scotland.
I give the club everything I can financially and I've put my money
where my mouth is today.

In the final analysis, the 2004 issue pulled in £51.4 million – although
£50.3 million of that had come from Murray International Holdings
as underwriters of the scheme, taking Murray's stake in Rangers to
91.8 per cent. The remaining £1.1 million came from existing and new
shareholders, with 4,500 investors contributing to the total.

With a new sense of purpose surrounding the commercial operation,
the decision was taken to promote Martin Bain from his position as
director of football business to the role of chief executive.

Bain had been groomed for a key position from his early days at
Ibrox, joining in 1996 and working his way up the ladder. Speaking at
the time of his appointment, Bain said:

The way the club runs at the moment is extremely efficiently.
There is a great team of people here at Rangers, many of whom I
have grown up with over the past few years. At board level, I've
certainly got the support of the directors, hence my appointment
today, and the chairman David Murray, who has been a mentor to
me over a number of years. He has certainly taught me a lot and,
having served my apprenticeship, I can hopefully fulfil my
objectives within the role, for the board, for Rangers and for the
supporters.

In a familiar pattern, cash flowed in and ebbed back out again. There
was a seemingly constant need for new funds, and in February 2006
Murray tantalisingly announced that 'significant amounts of money'
would soon be flowing into Ibrox, admitting that it was obvious that
'real money' had to be invested in the playing staff.

In March that year, a £48-million tie-up with JJB Sports was
announced. The ten-year licence agreement comprised an initial
payment of £18 million and then an annual payment of at least £3
million. In return, JJB were granted exclusive rights to retail all Rangers'
branded kit and merchandise at the chain's 439 UK stores. Meeting
targets for sales would lead to additional bonus payments.

Murray said:

This innovative licence agreement will allow for the reduction of
the club's debt and enable further investment to be made in the

team and the club's facilities going forward. The arrangement capitalises on our strong current retail trading position and will enhance future revenue streams through greater availability and continuity of the quality and range of Rangers products.

Again, it appeared it was a case of plugging gaps rather than putting the club on a long-term sound footing. As the dust settled on the 2005–06 season, Murray revealed he was ready to walk away from Ibrox. He claimed he had received tentative approaches from prospective owners but was adamant he would sell only to an individual or group with the funds to invest heavily in Rangers.

The loose timescale set was three years, with the chairman confident he would be in a position to move on by then. He insisted he was as 'determined' as ever, in the meantime, as well as enthusiastic about the major challenges ahead.

There had already been rumblings about potential benefactors in the preceding years, with Internet entrepreneur Alistair Donald emerging as a potential investor, waving a promise of £10 million in front of the directors on the condition that they tackled the debt problem. The Donald interest never did turn into a hard-and-fast offer, with the lifelong Gers fan last seen in Scottish football during a short stint on the Morton board in 2009.

The reports about Donald, whose Duchray Castle was reported to have been placed on the market by his bank in 2011, were typical of the type of publicity generated by would-be investors over the years.

If Murray had a pound for every vague expression of interest in his club, there would have been no need to sell. Some were more credible than others. Some were more mysterious than others.

In the spring of 2007, Northern Ireland Assembly member David Burnside, the Unionist MP for South Antrim, claimed to be in the early stages of mounting a takeover bid for Rangers. The Ulsterman suggested he had backing from powerful figures in the City of London and was preparing to head a consortium. The move came in the run-up to the Stormont elections, although Burnside, a former public-relations director, denied it was a publicity stunt.

The bid failed to materialise, and by the summer of that year Murray admitted for the first time that he would consider transferring the club to foreign ownership as he sought a solution to his desire to exit the Ibrox stage.

For two decades, he had juggled the finances at Rangers, employed new and innovative tactics as well as working as an international salesman to attract investment from as far afield as the Bahamas and South Africa.

When the time came to step aside, the predicted flood of offers from all corners of the globe failed to materialise, and for a sustained period the club had to stumble on with the support of the bank.

Rangers had tried everything from debentures to share issues and from sponsorship deals to licensing agreements, but, eventually, old-fashioned loans and overdrafts proved to be the lifeline that kept the club functioning while a permanent solution to the ownership conundrum was sought. Just who would step in to fill the void Murray's departure would leave? A new chapter was set to unfold.

CHAPTER 24

'Now the bank have taken over the running of the club, they'll have their own ideas and obviously investment isn't one of them.'

Walter Smith, 2009

IT WAS WALTER Smith, the wise old owl of Ibrox, who made the first move in what would prove to be a drawn-out game of poker. Sat around the metaphorical table were Smith, David Murray, the representatives of Lloyds and a select band of prospective owners.

Nobody wanted to blink first, but Smith sought to take matters out of the hands of the 'outsiders' by laying their hand on the table for all to see – or at least attempting to.

When the manager claimed in the autumn of 2009 that Lloyds were effectively running the football club, it brought a swift and forceful rebuttal from the bankers, who up to that point had been content to remain hidden in the shadows.

Smith, a veteran not just on the training pitch but also in the media room, must have known exactly what he was doing when he made his claims in an interview broadcast to the nation by the BBC.

Addressing the issue of strengthening his stretched squad, having been unable to buy a player for a year and a half up to that point, the Ibrox gaffer said:

Now the bank have taken over the running of the club, they'll have their own ideas and obviously investment isn't one of them. I just think there's a stagnation about our club at the present moment.

Rangers' situation is quite simple and we've been fairly honest about it for about a year now. All the players have been up for transfer. If anybody is telling me that's a motivational factor for any player, then they're living in another world from me. Our boys

273

have handled the situation well and did extremely well last season to win the league and the Scottish Cup.

There are things that are outwith everyone's control. David Murray has been fantastic for Rangers over his 20 years. He's had to step away and now the bank have taken over the running of the club. So, therefore, we sit and wait for an owner. The club's been up for sale for a period of time and I don't think all those things going on have helped.

The allegations levelled at the club's bankers clearly touched a nerve in Edinburgh's financial district. Lloyds quickly leapt to their own defence and rubbished Smith's suggestions that they were responsible for dictating transfer policy at the club. In a statement issued on the back of Smith's interview, bank chiefs said:

Lloyds Banking Group is a bank which provides finance to many companies and households across the country. Our interest is in helping those customers grow and prosper. We do not run or manage the companies that we bank. That is, quite properly, the responsibility of the management.

Given the recent press coverage, we would therefore like to be clear that Rangers FC is neither operated or run by Lloyds Banking Group. We would also like to be clear that Sir David Murray's decision to step down as chairman was a personal decision and not at the behest of Lloyds Banking Group.

The board of Rangers FC is developing and implementing a sustainable business plan and we have agreed to support this plan. The group is aware of the unique position that football occupies across many Scottish communities and has been working with Scottish football clubs, including Rangers, for many years.

Despite the denials from the bankers, the standing of Smith in the Scottish game ensured there was only one side the football fraternity, and Rangers supporters in particular, would take. In one short burst of media attention, the veteran boss had set in motion a turn of events that would bring to a head the internal debate over the direction the club was heading in. In one fell swoop, that debate became public and fans began to get an insight into the ructions behind the scenes, although it had been clear for a number of months that all was not as it should be at Ibrox.

The lack of transfer activity inwards had been a clear indication that belts were being tightened to the point of strangling Smith's team-building plans, but it was movement out of the club that caused as much concern.

In January 2009, Murray confirmed that at least one star player would have to be sold in a bid to balance the books, or tip the scales slightly in the club's favour. In truth, the sale of the entire squad at that stage would have been unlikely to set the finances straight.

Kris Boyd, attracting interest from Birmingham City and saddled with a £4-million price tag despite the English club's offer of £1 million less, appeared to be the most saleable asset, and Rangers were in no mood to lose him on the cheap.

Murray told supporters:

> The absence of European competition, together with the economic downturn, has confirmed that the size of the squad was neither sustainable from a financial nor football management point of view. It is our aim to rationalise the squad to a manageable level and integrate the young talent now emerging from Murray Park.

The announcement that the playing staff would be pruned to provide funds prompted the Rangers Supporters Trust and other fans' groups to launch the We Deserve Better campaign, hoping to pressurise the club into changing direction. Removing Murray from the top job appeared to be a logical part of that aim.

Mark Dingwall, a member of the trust board, told me: 'When Davie [Edgar] came up with the idea, I didn't think it would fly. Intellectually, I was in favour, but politically I didn't think it would get traction. But it did.

'A lot of what followed was David Murray hitting back through his allies in the press. He gave us a bit of a battering, but it brought the campaign into the spotlight all the same.

'The whole thrust of the campaign was that it was David Murray who had spent all of the money over the years, spent it wildly and badly. We thought, "If you're the bright businessman, you should be looking after the supporters and the club." You would expect us, as fans, to make mistakes – but as custodian of Rangers he should have been far more careful.

'A familiar pattern had started to emerge. It would be the same every season. We would go through a summer transfer window being told things weren't going too well, let's just get through to Christmas and see how things are then. Then in the January window there would be the same type of thing, with no new faces and supporters being told that the club had been trying to recruit. He could only play that game for so many seasons before people began to ask questions and see the pattern. People knew it was all waffle.'

Initially, the embattled chairman came out fighting. In *The Scotsman*, Murray said:

I can understand the frustration of the fans but I would ask them to look at the reality of the situation. When I sit down and review the economic situation of my business, the football side of it cannot be treated in isolation.

We have to reduce costs at Rangers and that is why, when we received a good offer for Kris Boyd, we accepted it. The debate goes on as to whether he is a good, bad or indifferent player, or whether he would win the club the title, but the fact is most clubs would accept a reasonable offer for their players at the moment.

That is the reality, whether you like David Murray or not. Whether it is me, Stewart Milne, John Boyle, Tom Farmer or Dermot Desmond, these are the people who are the financial backbone holding clubs together.

There is a hysteria out there, driven by people who spend most of their time on websites or trying to get on radio programmes. They go on about mistakes which have been made, but I'm tired of admitting mistakes. I have been doing this for 20 years now and I think I have a better hand on the tiller than anyone else could at the moment.

To an extent, trust members agreed. The criticism was not of Murray's tenure as chairman as a whole, simply of the way in which the club had been run in the years leading up to the We Deserve Better campaign.

Dingwall added: 'It was the Advocaat years that really hit us. I remember counting that over £120 million more had gone out in transfers than had come in during that period.

'Murray's decisiveness had gone. In the early days, he had not hesitated, whether it was effectively sacking Graeme Souness when it became clear he was interested in joining Liverpool or banning Celtic supporters after they had demolished part of Ibrox. He was always quick to act.

'Eventually, decisions began to be dragged out. When there was doubt over Alex McLeish and his future, myself, Davie Edgar and Malcolm McNiven met with the chairman. We told him that the manager was constantly just one game away from a crisis, having presided over the worst set of results in our history, and that a decision had to be made cleanly. Instead it was announced that McLeish would stand down at the end of the season.

'It had been the same when Dick Advocaat had come to leave, with the whole director-of-football appointment being played out despite the fact it was patent nonsense for him to be in that role long term.'

The frustrations of the We Deserve Better campaign were dismissed by Murray initially, but in August 2009 it was announced that he was once again standing down from the chairman's role and also resigning from the board. He was adamant that no outside pressure had been brought to bear on him, lambasting what he described as 'conspiracy theories' about the motivation for his decision.

Murray went so far as to claim that the club was in a 'good position' and that the balance-sheet was 'OK' as he moved on, adding, 'There are no outside factors.'

Alastair Johnston was the man who succeeded him in the chairman's seat. The 61-year-old had been a director of the club for half a decade when he was chosen for promotion.

Murray's statement to the stock exchange read:

> As things stand, I remain the majority shareholder at the club and will always have the best interests of Rangers at heart, but it is time to pass on the chairman's baton. For me personally, it has been a tremendous honour and privilege to serve as chairman of Rangers. There have been so many great moments to savour and it is particularly gratifying to step down when the club are reigning SPL champions, Scottish Cup holders and about to embark on another exciting journey in the Champions League.
>
> The club has the governance and management in place, both in footballing and business terms, to deliver further success in the future and Rangers can go forward with confidence. I would also like to salute the countless Rangers fans around the world who have shown unwavering support for the club, week in, week out. They are the lifeblood of Rangers and many clubs would dearly like to have such a great support.
>
> I am delighted that Alastair Johnston has accepted the chairmanship. He is an internationally renowned and respected businessman and will be an excellent servant to the club.

For the fans' groups, it marked a changing of the guard. Murray was gone but not forgotten. Mark Dingwall told me: 'I think he enjoyed dealing with the supporters' groups, in a roundabout way. He enjoyed the verbal punch-ups. What I always found with David Murray was that he was quick to latch onto an idea if he liked it, to claim it as his own.

'At the same time, he had a complete antipathy towards Colin Glass and David Edgar. He liked to have a bogeyman to single out. But he knew our motives were good – rather than having some slimy salesman in his office trying to sell him thousands of tonnes of steel, he had a group of supporters who weren't after his money. The motivation was always about doing the best thing for the club. I think he appreciated that.

'Personally, I'm still fascinated by David Murray. I still think his legacy will be determined by the outcome of the tax case, but I can't help but wonder what kind of chairman he might have been if he hadn't lost his way a bit. But sport can do that to you. Had he lived 100 years ago, he would have owned racehorses or backed prizefighters. He has that competitive streak. Instead, he found his outlet in football and got caught up in it all.

'The big question surrounds the decision to sell the club to Craig Whyte – was he really "duped", as he claims to have been? As a former Rangers player told members of the trust recently, you'd have to get up pretty early in the morning to dupe David Murray.

'With Craig Whyte, the trust was sceptical from the start. Our own investigations into his background showed no obvious means of supporting the club. Most of his companies had been small, or had not filed accounts in ages. Was it possible he could have done so many deals during his seven years in Monaco that he had hundreds of millions of pounds? I suppose it was possible, but we may never know.

'Unfortunately our fears were confirmed, not just about Craig Whyte but about the way the club had been run in the years before he took ownership. Nobody likes to be right when the outcome is as bad as it was for the club, but it turned out we were entitled to be worried.'

When Murray did hand over the chairmanship, it was to another businessman who had become cloaked in all things Rangers. Johnston, a Glaswegian, graduated from the University of Strathclyde before rising to lead the renowned international sports-management firm IMG. With clients including Tiger Woods and Michael Schumacher, there was no doubting Johnston's ability to operate in the most exclusive sporting circles, and he appeared ideally suited to the role of head of the Rangers family. His credentials as a Bluenose were not in doubt, either. A lifetime's devotion to the club stood him in good stead. Even his cars, tucked away in his garage at the family home in America, bear the registration plates RFC1 and 1BROX. He was brought up on a diet of Baxter, Henderson and Greig – a man who knew the glory days and was determined to keep the trophies coming.

Johnston had first appeared on the board at Rangers in 2004, invited by his close friend Murray to lend his vast experience and base of contacts to the club's executive team. He was, after all, the man who brought a certain Arnold Palmer to the list of Rangers shareholders when he bought the golf legend a token stake in the club as a birthday gift.

Johnston split his time between the States and Scotland during his chairmanship and soon discovered the demands placed on the man occupying one of the toughest roles in football. If he hadn't been aware of the pressure, he could just have asked his predecessor.

Murray claimed to have spent £100 million on his Rangers obsession and intimated a desire to put football to one side and instead take care of demands in other areas of his life. Murray was in reflective mood as he spoke to Jim Traynor of the *Daily Record* in an interview coinciding with his departure. Traynor had a long working relationship with the Rangers owner, having first interviewed him prior to his involvement at Ibrox, when Murray was attempting to purchase Ayr United. Murray said:

> I have neglected too many other important things in my life, so my emotions are mixed. I want to have some time now for family and other commitments, like my business interests. Rangers has taken up a totally inappropriate amount of my time. Normal people finish at 6 p.m. and have a life after that. But if you are Stewart Milne at Aberdeen, John Boyle at Motherwell or David Murray, or anyone else, then it never stops. Football has taken up so much time and, I'm afraid, people simply have no idea how much it takes to run a club. It is seven days a week and the phones just never stop.

Murray pointed to his phone records as a demonstration of his efforts. Of 200 calls, he said, 170 were on Rangers business. He claimed to have decided to stand down in September 2008 and thanked his fellow directors for keeping the plan quiet – and for persuading him to remain long enough to unfurl the championship flag at the start of the 2009–10 season.

He handed over while the club was at a crossroads, in every sense. One of Johnston's first acts was to open talks with Walter Smith over a contract extension. Smith and Ally McCoist would be free to walk away in January 2010 if they chose, and it was an area of great concern after their early success.

Johnston made frequent trips to Glasgow to try to get a grip of the tiller at the club he was attempting to steer through the choppiest of waters. He and Smith had several meetings as they attempted to reach common ground, not necessarily on the terms of the contract but more specifically on the way forward for the team and the business that had to sit side by side under the Rangers Football Club umbrella.

When Johnston was introduced to the country's media in September 2009, he insisted he would not have accepted the chairman's job if he had not been satisfied that he – and not the bank – would have control of the running of the club. Johnston said:

> We have a credit arrangement with the bank with various predetermined covenants. We have to follow those criteria unless there are exceptions we can justify. The bank has been very cooperative. If they were running the club per se, they would be here and I wouldn't.

Within weeks, Johnston's claims were being called into question by Walter Smith – with the manager voicing his concerns that spending was being controlled by the Lloyds Banking Group in Murray's absence.

Soon after Smith had gone public in autumn 2009, a statement was issued insisting no players would have to be sold during the rapidly approaching January transfer window. At the same time, the hierarchy confirmed that 'tentative' enquiries had been made about the possibility of buying Murray's stake, although no firm offers had been tabled.

The issue reached fever pitch late in October 2009 when it was reported that Lloyds had threatened Rangers with administration. That prompted the then Scottish Secretary Jim Murphy to intervene – not least because the banking group was 43 per cent owned by the taxpayer at that stage. According to the Scottish Office, Murphy reminded the bank of the importance of its continued support for one of the country's great sporting institutions.

That forced Lloyds to break its silence and issue its statement denying the claims, although that did nothing to silence the talk of a mass boycott of Lloyds Banking Group by Rangers supporters.

Donald Muir's appointment to the Ibrox board, giving Lloyds their own man among the directors, had set the cat among the pigeons and did nothing to dampen the fears over who was calling the shots.

The Rangers Supporters Assembly, Rangers Worldwide Alliance, Rangers Supporters Trust and Rangers Supporters Association joined forces to release a statement that put pressure on the bank and also urged Murray to sell his stake in the club. The statement said:

Rangers fans have endured unnecessary and damaging uncertainty over the future of the club and it is now time for this to be resolved. We welcome recent statements from Lloyds that they are not running the club. However, the only meaningful way they can do what is in the best interests of Rangers and their fans is to help a takeover be completed quickly.

Many fans are personal and business customers of the Lloyds Banking Group. Lloyds must understand that Rangers fans will quickly withdraw business if there is any risk whatsoever of the club's current situation being worsened by their actions. The situation cannot continue. It is imperative that a change in ownership is completed.

The bad feeling ran throughout the 2009–10 season, with supporters staging a protest at Ibrox in February of that campaign, with banners waved and leaflets distributed. Slogans describing Muir as 'the enemy within' and reiterating the desire for a Lloyds boycott were dotted around the stands.

At the time of his appointment in October 2009, Muir had been described as a 'lifelong fan of the club'. He was hailed as a man with more than 25 years' experience of 'strategy implementation and business transformation activity' in a wealth of industries and companies – including others within the Murray group. He would, according to the spin, help the club meet its 'strategic business objectives'. Supporters, it appeared, remained unconvinced.

Muir's appointment to the board coincided with the arrival of fellow new director Mike McGill, who was finance director at Murray International Holdings and another Rangers supporter since boyhood.

Making way for the new faces was Donald Wilson, chief executive of MIH. He had been a valued director at Ibrox, overseeing the Murray Park development in particular, but was edged out as the structure changed.

Inside Ibrox, there were big changes being implemented. Outside, supporters were beginning to consider their own role in the saga and questioning whether they could solve the growing problems the club faced.

In November 2009, moves to explore a mass-ownership scheme gathered pace. The same four supporters' groups stated:

The organisations are considering the options open to fans to invest in the club on a massive scale and on an accountable basis. We are considering various options for this – whether on our own or in partnership with others. We intend that the future of the club will never again be reliant on the goodwill of a bank or any individual.

One option we are currently discussing with advisors is the changes necessary to turn the trust's Gersave scheme into a suitable vehicle for the gathering in of funds. However, any form of investment will only take place on the basis of the suitability of the terms gained in negotiations. Rangers as a club cannot continue in the current state of limbo with the threat of being run by the Lloyds Banking Group.

To move things on before the January transfer window we are formally inviting any potential credible investors to discuss their plans for the club with us. Rangers fans are by far the biggest financial investors in the club. We are determined that the club will continue to flourish and never again will it run the risk of falling into the hands of a bank. We call on fans to be patient but to unite behind sensible proposals we hope to recommend to them over the coming months.

The trust organised meetings with fans from Hamburg and Espanyol, who had pioneered members-run club models on the Continent, and enthusiastically pursued the novel solution.

All the while, the clock was ticking on the contracts of Walter Smith and his coaching staff. With three weeks to go before the deals expired, it was confirmed that Smith, Ally McCoist and Kenny McDowall would continue to work without fresh agreements in place. According to chief executive Martin Bain, the unorthodox administrative approach would guard against new owners inheriting a staff they did not want. Of course, it would also guard against new owners running scared from the substantial pay-offs that would be required to rid themselves of a management team they did not want.

Reading between the lines, it was fair to assume that the chances of a new owner materialising were rising. Was Murray finally going to free himself and pass the baton to a new man? The rumour mill was about to go into overdrive.

In March 2010, the news of interest from London-based property developer Andrew Ellis broke, with the club confirming that Murray had opened talks with the Englishman. Walter Smith, ever the voice of reason, cautiously welcomed the announcement, saying:

Everybody here has worked in this uncertain period for the club. It has not been easy for anybody. Everybody gets affected by the uncertainty and it would be nice if that's getting settled. But I think we've got a long way to go. There is a huge difference between someone declaring an interest in buying the club and actually doing it.

Ellis, for his part, went public with the proclamations that he would award Walter Smith a new contract if successful in his bid to take control at the club and would reward Murray for his cooperation with the tag of life president.

By June 2010, Ellis announced he was in 'advanced' negotiations to gain the controlling interest he craved. His consortium, named RFC, was reportedly being funded partially by finance from Dubai and Qatar. No timescale was set, but Ellis appeared supremely confident that he could carry through his intention and get his hands on a jewel in football's crown. The big question for every Rangers supporter was whether he had the finances to back up his assertion that Ibrox would soon be falling under his wing. Eventually, the answer came back as a negative and Ellis never went through with his stated intention of buying the club, at least not in his own right. He needed his ally Craig Whyte to make it happen.

When Smith led Rangers to the championship in May 2010, his reward was the promise of 'limited funds' to strengthen the team over the summer. The pledge came from Murray, at a time when his back was firmly against the wall.

With the HM Revenue and Customs investigation lingering to add to the woes, the situation was far from clear. It prompted Douglas Park, the Glaswegian businessman who had been credited as a Rangers suitor, to claim that nobody would buy the club with the tax probe hanging over it.

Murray hit back, stating:

> If Douglas, Dave King, Paul Murray or anyone else wants to buy the club, they all know what to do. Stop saying why you wouldn't buy it. What's the point continually trying to undermine Rangers when it's clear finances are improving? If you care about the club, would you endeavour to undermine it by making the kind of statements we've read from Douglas? One can only wonder why. Is it an attempt to weaken the club in the hope of getting it at a cheaper price? I don't know, but I do know Rangers are not in any danger because of their financial position. Rangers is a standalone company and there are no cross-guarantees tying them to the Murray Group's finances.

The tax case Park had referred to had first made it into the public domain in April 2010. Although confidentiality ensured details were scarce, it was reported that the action related to the use of offshore payments to employees. Initial estimates of the club's liability made for terrifying reading – £24 million was the first figure quoted in tax alone. With penalties and interest added on top, £50 million was another of the numbers floated. If true, these sums were potentially crippling – even if there was never any suggestion that the club had acted illegally.

A statement issued by Rangers in May 2010 said: 'This is an ongoing query raised by HMRC, which is part of a pending court case. On the basis of expert tax advice provided to Rangers, the club is robustly defending the matters raised.'

It was suggested that the greater part of the bill would land on the doorstep of Murray International Holdings rather than Rangers Football Club, although officials always maintained they had acted in good faith, regardless of who ultimately paid the price. As Rangers pointed out, HMRC never suggested illegal activity and, in another attempt at justification, it was highlighted that other businesses, including football clubs, used the same tax planning strategy.

Undoubtedly, the lingering fears about the level of outstanding tax made the club an unattractive proposition for potential owners. And, sure enough, within a month of issuing the statement vowing to fight the tax demands, Murray also announced that he had taken Rangers off the open market. Instead, the owner claimed to have a 'clear business plan' in place to move forward. It followed what were described as 'positive talks' with the club's bankers.

At the annual meeting in October 2010, takeover talk was still on everyone's lips. That included chairman Alastair Johnston, who told shareholders in Glasgow:

> All the expressions of interest identified to the club during this period have proved to be frivolous or have been aborted by Murray International Holdings' announcement it is no longer actively marketing its controlling stake in Rangers. Although this statement would not preclude any potential buyer pursuing a takeover, the general economic climate would temper our expectations of such an approach. In this context, supporters' anticipation about the benefit to the club of new ownership needs to be realistic.

One month after that meeting, the name Craig Whyte was mentioned fleetingly. It was widely welcomed by supporters, who were encouraged by what appeared to be firm interest from a man of means. The search for a new owner was about to take a huge leap forward and Johnston's time as chairman was sure to end if the deal could be clinched.

One of his final acts as the club's figurehead was to confirm what Walter Smith had stated so plainly all those months before – that the bank had been dictating policy when it came to squad restructuring.

Johnston, speaking as he revealed encouraging financial results that demonstrated a pre-tax profit of close to £12 million for the six months up to the end of 2010, stated:

> While we appreciate the support of the Lloyds Banking Group through the Bank of Scotland in extending our credit arrangement and recognising the progress that has been made in developing a template for collaboration, certain provisions imposed on the club continue to compromise, in our opinion, management's ability to conduct its role with maximum efficiency.

And there you had it: the man at the top concurring with exactly what Walter Smith had attempted to air in the first place. In the interim, the situation had not improved for the manager, who saw his hopes of bolstering an ageing squad dashed time after time but continued to produce winning teams on a shoestring budget.

He hoped for an end to the ownership debate and the wish was soon to be granted. Only the next chapter was not quite what he would have anticipated, with Whyte's arrival coinciding with the veteran manager's departure as he rode off into the sunset for a well-earned break.

When Smith returned to Ibrox in 2012, it was in a role he would not have expected when he strode out the previous year and threw the keys to the manager's office towards Ally McCoist. It was not in a director's position, an ambassadorial role or any other cosseted post. Instead, it was as one of the big guns wheeled out to spearhead the fightback in the wake of the shell-shock of administration.

Smith threw his weight behind the launch of the Rangers Fans Fighting Fund, a vehicle designed to allow supporters to contribute to the financial upkeep of their ailing club and protect the fabric of a proud institution.

Adminstrators had suggested there might not be enough money in the pot to see out the 2011–12 fixtures. The thought of that, of Rangers quitting midway through a campaign, caused horror among supporters across the globe and a rallying call was issued.

All the major supporters' groups came together, corralled by club men Sandy Jardine and Jim Hannah, the supporters' liaison chief, and came up with the RFFF. Money would be ring-fenced, distributed by a committee including Jardine and Smith as and when it was needed by the administrators.

Smith, who had reverted to his boyhood role as a fan when he left the payroll, dipping into his own pocket to buy a pair of Ibrox season tickets, knew better than most the human side of administration. Aside from his links to everyone at Ibrox, from the boot room to the ticket office and everyone in between, his son Neil, as part of the media team, was among those on the 'civilian' staff who had to watch and wait as the future of their employment was debated in a very public forum.

Nobody wanted to see any part of the Rangers family suffer, from the players who agreed to take pay cuts to protect the rank-and-file members of staff to the well-heeled fans who pledged individual donations running into six figures to get the fighting fund off the ground and the veteran players who turned out in the Legends match against AC Milan to boost the coffers.

In a time of great adversity, there was an incredible unity surrounding every facet of Ibrox life. With seats at home games snapped up and the stadium packed to capacity, even in the face of a trophy-less campaign, it was with a mix of defiance and sheer devotion that the Bears turned out week in and week out through to the bitter end of the season.

The RFFF was just an extension of that. Smith was bowled over by the early response to the idea and admitted: 'It has been an extremely difficult time for everyone associated with Rangers, but the supporters have shown unbelievable commitment to our club throughout the administration process and deserve great credit.'

For Jardine, himself a long-time employee of Rangers in a business capacity, the desire to come out fighting burned bright. Jardine said:

> The club has been inundated with messages of support from fans throughout the world and everyone associated with Rangers has shown their unwavering loyalty during these difficult times. Now, more than ever, we need their backing, and I know hundreds of thousands of supporters will do all they can for the club they love and make a donation to the campaign.

The plan for the fund had been born deep within Ibrox, but it was quickly adopted on the 'outside'. A closely controlled meeting of the main supporters' groups, devoid of media leaks, took place to float the idea and gauge opinion. It was embraced on the spot by leaders desperate to do their bit, although details did not emerge until the official launch several days later.

Jardine explained:

Jim Hannah and I came up with an idea, we ran it past the administrators – they were fine with it – and we looked to form a committee. In tandem with a lot of things the club is doing, we set about starting the Fighting Fund, whereby fans can donate any amount they like to the Rangers Supporters Assembly account.

We got all the supporters' club secretaries together to explain what we were doing and asked them to endorse it. Every one of them was fully behind it. At that meeting one chap came up and said he would pay £100,000, which is fantastic, so it shows you the level of interest and goodwill out there.

The North American and Australian supporters' groups were enlisted, as well as the massive contingent in Northern Ireland. Jardine also took it upon himself to sit down with the club's corporate supporters to encourage the business community to contribute, adding:

It's everyone within the Rangers family who is involved and hopefully we can get enough money to ensure that the club gets itself out of this predicament.

On a weekly basis we will meet with the administrators and drip-feed money into helping the running of the club. The one thing we don't want is liquidation and we hope that this initiative will go a long way to helping the club manage itself within its current problems. Then a new owner comes in and we can start to rebuild the club from there.

The mystery, complexity and intrigue of the Rangers finances in recent years had created a clamour to ensure the RFFF was far removed from those dark days. Instead, openness was promised by the fund's key-holders. Jardine stated:

Fans can rest assured that any money that comes in will be used to make sure that the club survives and pays its bills until a takeover is completed.

What we will do is meet with the administrators and decide how the money is spent and we will make sure it is spent properly. We want to be as honest as possible and as transparent as we can on how the money is spent.

If there is any money left over once a new owner comes in, then the money will be frozen and the committee will decide with Ally McCoist, depending on how much money is left, how it should be used. Will Ally want to use it to buy a player, do we want to invest it in Murray Park or perhaps on improvements at Ibrox?

Even the tone of the language was encouraging. It was not a case of 'if' a rescue deal could be done, more a question of 'when'. After a period of shock and distress, the Rangers family was ready to battle for a brighter future.

And so we land back where we started, with the conclusion that Ally McCoist had called it right with his prophetic declaration: 'We don't do walking away.'